SOURCES FOR SOCIAL AND ECONOMIC HISTORY

Readings in the Development of Economic Analysis 1776–1848

SOURCES FOR SOCIAL AND ECONOMIC HISTORY

FREE TRADE
Norman McCord
Reader in Modern & Mediaeval History
University of Newcastle upon Tyne

THE FACTORY SYSTEM   VOLUME I BIRTH AND GROWTH
J. T. Ward
Senior Lecturer in Economic History
University of Strathclyde

POOR LAW
Michael E. Rose
Lecturer in History, University of Manchester

READINGS IN THE DEVELOPMENT OF ECONOMIC ANALYSIS
R. D. C. Black
Professor of Economics, Queen's University of Belfast

SOURCES FOR SOCIAL AND ECONOMIC HISTORY

R. D. COLLISON BLACK

Professor of Economics
The Queen's University of Belfast

Readings in the Development of Economic Analysis 1776–1848

BARNES & NOBLE, Inc.

NEW YORK

PUBLISHERS & BOOKSELLERS SINCE 1873

COPYRIGHT NOTICE

© R. D. Collison Black 1971

First published in the United States, 1971
by Barnes & Noble, Inc.

ISBN 389–04434–2

Printed in Great Britain

Contents

Contents

Preface

Modern economics is more permeated and influenced by the ideas of past generations of economists than it is now fashionable to admit. Most students of the subject still take a course in the History of Economic Thought, but even those who do *not* inevitably find their reading and thinking interspersed with concepts which have a historical dimension—'classical monetary theory', 'rent in the Ricardian sense', 'Malthusian principles of population' and many others.

Many students who constantly deal with such ideas have never taken the trouble to investigate what the original authors actually said, and many are the misconceptions which result from the failure to do so. Yet it is hardly reasonable to expect the hard-pressed student of today to seek out the essential passages from a wide variety of early works, the majority of which are lengthy and not always readily accessible even in libraries. So this volume has a very simple purpose—to give the student of modern economics direct access to the passages in classical authors which are most significant for the development of economic theory, and to let the authors speak for themselves.

The term 'classical economists' is interpreted here in the sense of those who contributed fundamental ideas to orthodox political economy from Adam Smith in 1776 to John Stuart Mill in 1848. From their writings have been selected passages which contain these ideas. The criterion for selection has been their importance for the development of economic analysis purely; hence all the extensive and important writings of the classical economists on questions of economic policy are excluded.

It will be noticed at once that the extracts are of widely differing length. Needless to say, the length of a passage is no index of its importance or that of its author. The variation is due simply to the fact that some seminal ideas have been contained in a few pages, others are developed over a much greater length, and it would clearly be wrong to insist on fitting them to any sort of Procrustean bed. Similarly, the extracts are arranged in a strictly chronological order because any ordering by subjects would imply judgements about the significance of different topics and so conflict with the objective of interfering as little as possible between the original author and the reader.

However, some minimum of commentary seems necessary in order to place each extract in its proper context and perspective. Therefore, each reading is preceded by a brief biographical sketch of its author and a short commentary on the significance of the selected extract. An outline bibliography follows, designed to help the reader who wants to extend his knowledge of the work concerned and its author. In each case the most useful commentaries are listed, together with standard modern editions and fuller biographies of the author, where these are available.

R. D. COLLISON BLACK

Belfast
30 December 1970

I

ADAM SMITH

An Inquiry into the Nature and Causes of the Wealth of Nations 1776

Adam Smith, the generally acknowledged master of the English classical economists, was born at Kirkcaldy, Fifeshire, in 1723 and died at Edinburgh in 1790. Smith was an undergraduate at Glasgow from 1737 to 1740, and subsequently a Snell fellow at Balliol College, Oxford, until 1746. At Glasgow he studied under Francis Hutcheson; in 1751 Smith became Professor of Logic there and later in the year succeeded to the Chair of Moral Philosophy formerly held by Hutcheson.

Smith resigned his Glasgow chair in 1763 and from 1764 to 1766 travelled in Europe as tutor to the young Duke of Buccleuch; during this period he came into contact with many of the Physiocrats. A pension from the Duke of Buccleuch enabled Smith to devote the years from 1767 to 1776 mainly to the writing of the *Wealth of Nations* but from 1778 until his death he served as a Commissioner of Customs for Scotland.

An Inquiry into the Nature and Causes of the Wealth of Nations is one of the few economic classics to have enjoyed both an immediate success and a continuing respect, and to have proved significant in its implications for both theory and policy. From an analytical point of view, Smith's book provided the foundations for the classical theory of value and distribution, as well as a comprehensive account of the forces governing economic development. The selections given here cover the general plan of Smith's work on political economy, the essentials of his theory of value, and his treatment of capital accumulation, which modern authorities have recognised as particularly significant in relation to the development of labour surplus economies.

BIBLIOGRAPHY

A definitive edition of Smith's works is now in preparation for the Scottish Economic Society and it is intended to publish this in celebration of the bicentenary of the publication of the *Wealth of Nations*. At present, the standard edition of the *Wealth of Nations* is that by Edwin Cannan (2 volumes, 1904).

For commentaries on the *Wealth of Nations* and the main theories advanced in it, see J. M. Clark and others. *Adam Smith 1776–1926*, University of Chicago Press (1928); H. M. Robertson and W. L. Taylor. 'Adam Smith's approach to the Theory of Value', *Economic Journal*, Vol 67 (June 1957), 181–98; Hla Myint. *Theories of Welfare Economics* (London 1948); J. J. Spengler. 'Adam Smith's Theory of Economic Growth', *Southern Economic Journal*, Vol 25 (1959), 397–415, and Vol 26 (1959), 1–12; W. A. Lewis. 'Economic Development with Unlimited Supplies of Labour', *Manchester School*, Vol 22 (May 1954), 139–91; and V. W. Bladen. 'Adam Smith on Productive and Unproductive Labour: a Theory of Full Development', *Canadian Journal of Economics*, Vol 26 (November 1960), 625–30.

On the philosophical aspects of the *Wealth of Nations* and their relation to the rest of Smith's thought, see A. L. Macfie. *The Individual in Society* (London 1966); and H. J. Bittermann. 'Adam Smith's Empiricism and the Law of Nature', *Journal of Political Economy*, 48 (1940), 487–520, 703–34.

The standard *Life of Adam Smith* by John Rae (1895) has recently been reprinted with an excellent introduction and

guide by Jacob Viner (New York, Augustus M. Kelley, 1964).
More recent and detailed biographical material appears in
W. R. Scott. *Adam Smith as Student and Professor* (Glasgow 1937).

AN

INQUIRY

INTO THE

NATURE AND CAUSES

OF THE

WEALTH OF NATIONS.

INTRODUCTION AND PLAN OF THE WORK.

THE annual labour of every nation is the fund which originally
supplies it with all the necessaries and conveniences of life which
it annually consumes, and which consist always either in the
immediate produce of that labour, or in what is purchased with
that produce from other nations.

According therefore, as this produce, or what is purchased
with it, bears a greater or smaller proportion to the number of
those who are to consume it, the nation will be better or worse
supplied with all the necessaries and conveniences for which it
has occasion.

But this proportion must in every nation be regulated by
two different circumstances; first, by the skill, dexterity, and
judgment with which its labour is generally applied; and,
secondly, by the proportion between the number of those who
are employed in useful labour, and that of those who are not
so employed. Whatever be the soil, climate, or extent of territory
of any particular nation, the abundance of scantiness of its
annual supply must, in that particular situation, depend upon
those two circumstances.

The abundance or scantiness of this supply too seems to
depend more upon the former of those two circumstances than

upon the latter. Among the savage nations of hunters and fishers, every individual who is able to work, is more or less employed in useful labour, and endeavours to provide, as well as he can, the necessaries and conveniences of life, for himself, or such of his family or tribe as are either too old, or too young, or too infirm to go a hunting and fishing. Such nations, however, are so miserably poor, that from mere want, they are frequently reduced, or at least think themselves reduced, to the necessity sometimes of directly destroying, and sometimes of abandoning their infants, their old people, and those afflicted with lingering diseases, to perish with hunger, or to be devoured by wild beasts. Among civilized and thriving nations, on the contrary, though a great number of people do not labour at all, many of whom consume the produce of ten times, frequently of a hundred times more labour than the greater part of those who work; yet the produce of the whole labour of the society is so great, that all are often abundantly supplied, and a workman, even of the lowest and poorest order, if he is frugal and industrious, may enjoy a greater share of the necessaries and conveniences of life than it is possible for any savage to acquire.

The causes of this improvement in the productive powers of labour, and the order, according to which its produce is naturally distributed among the different ranks and conditions of men in the society, make the subject of the First Book of this Inquiry.

Whatever be the actual state of the skill, dexterity, and judgment with which labour is applied in any nation, the abundance or scantiness of its annual supply must depend, during the continuance of that state, upon the proportion between the number of those who are annually employed in useful labour, and that of those who are not so employed. The number of useful and productive labourers, it will hereafter appear, is every where in proportion to the quantity of capital stock which is employed in setting them to work, and to the particular way in which it is so employed. The Second Book, therefore, treats of the nature of capital stock, of the manner in which it is gradually accumulated, and of the different quantities of labour which it puts into motion, according to the different ways in which it is employed.

Nations tolerably well advanced as to skill, dexterity, and judgment, in the application of labour, have followed very different plans in the general conduct or direction of it; and those plans have not all been equally favourable to the greatness of its produce. The policy of some nations has given extraordinary encouragement to the industry of the country; that of others to the industry of towns. Scarce any nation has dealt equally and impartially with every sort of industry. Since the downfall of the Roman empire, the policy of Europe has been more favourable to arts, manufactures, and commerce, the industry of towns; than to agriculture, the industry of the country. The circumstances which seem to have introduced and established this policy are explained in the Third Book.

Though those different plans were, perhaps, first introduced by the private interests and prejudices of particular orders of men, without any regard to, or foresight of, their consequences upon the general welfare of the society; yet they have given occasion to very different theories of political economy; of which some magnify the importance of that industry which is carried on in towns, others of that which is carried on in the country. Those theories have had a considerable influence, not only upon the opinions of men of learning, but upon the public conduct of princes and sovereign states. I have endeavoured in the Fourth Book, to explain, as fully and distinctly as I can, those different theories, and the principal effects which they have produced in different ages and nations.

To explain in what has consisted the revenue of the great body of the people, or what has been the nature of those funds, which, in different ages and nations, have supplied their annual consumption, is the object of these Four first Books. The Fifth and last Book treats of the revenue of the sovereign, or commonwealth. In this Book I have endeavoured to show; first, what are the necessary expences of the sovereign, or common-wealth; which of those expences ought to be defrayed by the general contribution of the whole society; and which of them, by that of some particular part only, or of some particular members of it; secondly, what are the different methods in which the whole society may be made to contribute towards defraying the expenses incumbent on the whole society, and what are the principal advantages and inconveniences of each of those methods: and, thirdly and lastly, what are the reasons and causes which have induced almost all modern governments to mortgage some part of this revenue, or to contract debts, and what have been the effects of those debts upon the real wealth, the annual produce of the land and labour of the society.

Book I
PART OF CHAPTER IV

The word value, it is to be observed, has two different mean-ings, and sometimes expresses the utility of some particular object, and sometimes the power of purchasing other goods which the possession of that object conveys. The one may be called "value in use;" the other, "value in exchange." The things which have the greatest value in use have frequently little or no value in exchange; and, on the contrary, those which have the greatest value in exchange have frequently little or no value in use. Nothing is more useful than water: but it will purchase scarce anything; scarce anything can be had in exchange for it. A diamond, on the contrary, has scarce any value in use; but a very great quantity of other goods may frequently be had in exchange for it.

In order to investigate the principles which regulate the ex-changeable value of commodities, I shall endeavour to show,

First, what is the real measure of this exchangeable value; or, wherein consists the real price of all commodities.

Secondly, what are the different parts of which this real price is composed or made up.

And, lastly, what are the different circumstances which sometimes raise some or all of these different parts of price above, and sometimes sink them below their natural or ordinary rate; or, what are the causes which sometimes hinder the market price, that is, the actual price of commodities, from coinciding exactly with what may be called their natural price.

I shall endeavour to explain, as fully and distinctly as I can, those three subjects in the three following chapters, for which I must very earnestly entreat both the patience and attention of the reader: his patience in order to examine a detail which may perhaps in some places appear unnecessarily tedious; and his attention in order to understand what may, perhaps, after the fullest explication which I am capable of giving of it, appear still in some degree obscure. I am always willing to run some hazard of being tedious in order to be sure that I am perspicuous; and after taking the utmost pains that I can to be perspicuous, some obscurity may still appear to remain upon a subject in its own nature extremely abstracted.

CHAPTER V

OF THE REAL AND NOMINAL PRICE OF COMMODITIES, OR THEIR PRICE IN LABOUR, AND THEIR PRICE IN MONEY

EVERY man is rich or poor according to the degree in which he can afford to enjoy the necessaries, conveniences, and amusements of human life. But after the division of labour has once thoroughly taken place, it is but a very small part of these with which a man's own labour can supply him. The far greater part of them he must derive from the labour of other people, and he must be rich or poor according to the quantity of that labour which he can command, or which he can afford to purchase. The value of any commodity, therefore, to the person who possesses it, and who means not to use or consume it himself, but to exchange it for other commodities, is equal to

B

the quantity of labour which it enables him to purchase or command. Labour, therefore, is the real measure of the exchangeable value of all commodities.

The real price of everything, what everything really costs to the man who wants to acquire it, is the toil and trouble of acquiring it. What everything is really worth to the man who has acquired it, and who wants to dispose of it or exchange it for something else, is the toil and trouble which it can save to himself, and which it can impose upon other people. What is bought with money or with goods is purchased by labour as much as what we acquire by the toil of our own body. That money or those goods indeed save us this toil. They contain the value of a certain quantity of labour which we exchange for what is supposed at the time to contain the value of an equal quantity. Labour was the first price, the original purchase-money that was paid for all things. It was not by gold or by silver, but by labour, that all the wealth of the world was originally purchased; and its value, to those who possess it, and who want to exchange it for some new productions, is precisely equal to the quantity of labour which it can enable them to purchase or command.

Wealth, as Mr. Hobbes says, is power. But the person who either acquires, or succeeds to a great fortune, does not necessarily acquire or succeed to any political power, either civil or military. His fortune may, perhaps, afford him the means of acquiring both, but the mere possession of that fortune does not necessarily convey to him either. The power which that possession immediately and directly conveys to him, is the power of purchasing; a certain command over all the labour, or over all the produce of labour, which is then in the market. His fortune is greater or less, precisely in proportion to the extent of this power; or to the quantity either of other men's labour, or, what is the same thing, of the produce of other men's labour, which it enables him to purchase or command. The exchangeable value of everything must always be precisely equal to the extent of this power which it conveys to its owner.

But though labour be the real measure of the exchangeable value of all commodities, it is not that by which their value is commonly estimated. It is often difficult to ascertain the proportion between two different quantities of labour. The time spent in two different sorts of work will not always alone determine this proportion. The different degrees of hardship endured, and of ingenuity exercised, must likewise be taken into account. There may be more labour in an hour's hard work than in two hours' easy business; or in an hour's application to a trade which it cost ten years' labour to learn, than in a month's industry at an ordinary and obvious employment. But it is not easy to find any accurate measure either of hardship or ingenuity. In exchanging, indeed, the different productions of different sorts of labour for one another, some allowance is commonly made for both. It is adjusted, however, not by any accurate measure, but by the higgling and bargaining of the market, according to that sort of rough equality which, though not exact, is sufficient for carrying on the business of common life.

Every commodity, besides, is more frequently exchanged for, and thereby compared with, other commodities than with labour. It is more natural, therefore, to estimate its exchangeable value by the quantity of some other commodity than by that of the labour which it can purchase. The greater part of people, too, understand better what is meant by a quantity of a particular commodity than by a quantity of labour. The one is a plain palpable object; the other an abstract notion, which, though it can be made sufficiently intelligible, is not altogether so natural and obvious.

But when barter ceases, and money has become the common instrument of commerce, every particular commodity is more frequently exchanged for money than for any other commodity. The butcher seldom carries his beef or his mutton to the baker, or the brewer, in order to exchange them for bread or for beer; but he carries them to the market, where he exchanges them for money, and afterwards exchanges that money for bread and for beer. The quantity of money which he gets for them regulates, too, the quantity of bread and beer which he can afterwards purchase. It is more natural and obvious to him, therefore, to estimate their value by the quantity of money, the commodity for which he immediately exchanges them, than by that of bread and beer, the commodities for which he can exchange them only by the intervention of another commodity; and rather to say that his butcher's meat is worth threepence or fourpence a pound, than that it is worth three or four pounds of bread, or three or four quarts of small beer. Hence it comes to pass that the exchangeable value of every commodity is more frequently estimated by the quantity of money, than by the quantity either of labour or of any other commodity which can be had in exchange for it.

Gold and silver, however, like every other commodity, vary in their value, are sometimes cheaper and sometimes dearer, sometimes of easier and sometimes of more difficult purchase. The quantity of labour which any particular quantity of them can purchase or command, or the quantity of other goods which it will exchange for, depends always upon the fertility or barrenness of the mines which happen to be known about the time when such exchanges are made. The discovery of the abundant mines of America reduced, in the sixteenth century, the value of gold and silver in Europe to about a third of what it had been before. As it cost less labour to bring those metals from the mine to the market, so when they were brought thither they could purchase or command less labour; and this revolution in their value, though perhaps the greatest, is by no means the only one of which history gives some account. But as a measure of quantity, such as the natural foot, fathom, or handful, which is continually varying in its own quantity, can never be an accurate measure of the quantity of other things; so a commodity which is itself continually varying in its own value, can never be an accurate measure of the value of other commodities. Equal quantities of labour, at all times and places, may be said to be of equal value to the labourer. In his ordinary state of health, strength and spirits; in the ordinary degree of his skill and dexterity, he must always lay down the same portion of his ease, his liberty, and his happiness. The price which he pays must always be the same, whatever may be the quantity of goods which he receives in return for it. Of these, indeed, it may sometimes purchase a greater and sometimes a smaller quantity; but it is their value which varies, not that of the labour which purchases them. At all times and places that is dear which it is difficult to come at, or which it costs much labour to acquire; and that cheap which is to be had easily, or with very little labour. Labour alone, therefore, never varying in its own value, is alone the ultimate and real standard by which the value of all commodities can at all times and places be estimated and compared. It is their real price; money is their nominal price only.

But though equal quantities of labour are always of equal value to the labourer, yet to the person who employs him they appear sometimes to be of greater and sometimes of smaller value. He purchases them sometimes with a greater and sometimes with a smaller quantity of goods, and to him the price of labour seems to vary like that of all other things. It appears to him dear in the one case, and cheap in the other. In reality, however, it is the goods which are cheap in the one case, and dear in the other.

In this popular sense, therefore, labour, like commodities, may be said to have a real and a nominal price. Its real price may be said to consist in the quantity of the necessaries and conveniences of life which are given for it; its nominal price, in the quantity of money. The labourer is rich or poor, is well or ill rewarded, in proportion to the real, not to the nominal price of his labour.

The distinction between the real and the nominal price of commodities and labour is not a matter of mere speculation, but may sometimes be of considerable use in practice. The same real price is always of the same value; but on account of the variations in the value of gold and silver, the same nominal price is sometimes of very different values. When a landed estate, therefore, is sold with a reservation of a perpetual rent, if it is intended that this rent should always be of the same value, it is of importance to the family in whose favour it is reserved that it should not consist in a particular sum of money. Its value would in this case be liable to variations of two different kinds; first, to those which arise from the different quantities of gold and silver which are contained at different times in coin of the same denomination; and, secondly, to those which arise from the different values of equal quantities of gold and silver at different times.

Princes and sovereign states have frequently fancied that they had a temporary interest to diminish the quantity of pure metal contained in their coins; but they seldom have fancied that they had any to augment it. The quantity of metal contained in the coins, I believe of all nations, has, accordingly, been almost continually diminishing, and hardly ever augmenting. Such variations, therefore, tend almost always to diminish the value of a money rent.

The discovery of the mines of America diminished the value of gold and silver in Europe. This diminution, it is commonly supposed, though I apprehend without any certain proof, is still going on gradually, and is likely to continue to do so for a long time. Upon this supposition, therefore, such variations are more likely to diminish than to augment the value of a money rent, even though it should be stipulated to be paid, not in such a quantity of coined money of such a denomination (in so many pounds sterling, for example), but in so many ounces either of pure silver, or of silver of a certain standard.

The rents which have been reserved in corn have preserved their value much better than those which have been reserved in money, even where the denomination of the coin has not been altered. By the 18th of Elizabeth it was enacted, That a third of the rent of all college leases should be reserved in corn, to be paid, either in kind, or according to the current prices at the nearest public market. The money arising from this corn rent, though originally but a third of the whole, is in the present times, according to Doctor Blackstone, commonly near double of what arises from the other two-thirds. The old money rents of colleges must, according to this account, have sunk almost to a fourth part of their ancient value; or are worth little more than a fourth part of the corn which they were formerly worth. But since the reign of Philip and Mary the denomination of the English coin has undergone little or no alteration, and the same number of pounds, shillings and pence have contained very nearly the same quantity of pure silver. This degradation, therefore, in the value of the money rents of colleges, his arisen altogether from the degradation in the value of silver.

When the degradation in the value of silver is combined with the diminution of the quantity of it contained in the coin of the same denomination, the loss is frequently still greater. In Scotland, where the denomination of the coin has undergone much greater alterations than it ever did in England, and in France, where it has undergone still greater than it ever did in Scotland, some ancient rents, originally of considerable value, have in this manner been reduced almost to nothing.

Equal quantities of labour will at distant times be purchased more nearly with equal quantities of corn, the subsistence of the labourer, than with equal quantities of gold and silver, or perhaps of any other commodity. Equal quantities of corn, therefore, will, at distant times, be more nearly of the same real value, or enable the possessor to purchase or command more nearly the same quantity of the labour of other people. They will do this, I say, more nearly than equal quantities of almost any other commodity; for even equal quantities of corn will not do it exactly. The subsistence of the labourer, or the real price of labour, as I shall endeavour to show hereafter, is very different upon different occasions; more liberal in a society advancing to opulence than in one that is standing still; and in one that is standing still than in one that is going backwards. Every other commodity, however, will at any particular time purchase a greater or smaller quantity of labour in proportion to the quantity of subsistence which it can purchase at that time. A rent therefore reserved in corn is liable only to the variations in the quantity of labour which a certain quantity of corn can purchase. But a rent reserved in any other commodity is liable not only to the variations in the quantity of labour which any particular quantity of corn can purchase, but to the variations in the quantity of corn which can be purchased by any particular quantity of that commodity.

Though the real value of a corn rent, it is to be observed, however, varies much less from century to century than that of a money rent, it varies much more from year to year. The money price of labour, as I shall endeavour to show hereafter, does not fluctuate from year to year with the money price of corn, but seems to be everywhere accommodated, not to the temporary or occasional, but to the average or ordinary price of that necessary of life. The average or ordinary price of corn again is regulated, as I shall likewise endeavour to show here-after, by the value of silver, by the richness or barrenness of the mines which supply the market with that metal, or by the quantity of labour which must be employed, and consequently of corn which must be consumed, in order to bring any par-ticular quantity of silver from the mine to the market. But the value of silver, though it sometimes varies greatly from century to century, seldom varies much from year to year, but fre-quently continues the same, or very nearly the same, for half a century or a century together. The ordinary or average money price of corn, therefore, may, during so long a period, continue the same or very nearly the same too, and along with it the money price of labour, provided, at least, the society continues, in other respects, in the same or nearly in the same condition. In the meantime the temporary and occasional price of corn may frequently be double, one year, of what it had been the year before, or fluctuate, for example, from five and twenty to fifty shillings the quarter. But when corn is at the latter price, not only the nominal, but the real value of a corn rent will be double of what it is when at the former, or will command double the quantity either of labour or of the greater part of other commodities; the money price of labour, and along with it that of most other things, continuing the same during all these fluctuations.

Labour, therefore, it appears evidently, is the only universal, as well as the only accurate measure of value, or the only standard by which we can compare the values of different commodities at all times, and at all places. We cannot estimate, it is allowed, the real value of different commodities from century to century by the quantities of silver which were given for them. We cannot estimate it from year to year by the quantities of corn. By the quantities of labour we can, with the greatest accuracy, estimate it both from century to century and from year to year. From century to century, corn is a better measure than silver, because, from century to century, equal quantities of corn will command the same quantity of labour more nearly than equal quantities of silver. From year to year, on the contrary, silver is a better measure than corn, because equal quantities of it will more nearly command the same quantity of labour.

But though in establishing perpetual rents, or even in letting very long leases, it may be of use to distinguish between real and nominal price; it is of none in buying and selling, the more common and ordinary transactions of human life.

At the same time and place the real and the nominal price of all commodities are exactly in proportion to one another. The more or less money you get for any commodity, in the London market for example, the more or less labour it will at that time and place enable you to purchase or command. At the same time and place, therefore, money is the exact measure of the real exchangeable value of all commodities. It is so, however, at the same time and place only.

Though at distant places, there is no regular proportion between the real and the money price of commodities, yet the merchant who carries goods from the one to the other has nothing to consider but their money price, or the difference between the quantity of silver for which he buys them, and that for which he is likely to sell them. Half an ounce of silver at Canton in China may command a greater quantity both of labour and of the necessaries and conveniences of life than an ounce at London. A commodity, therefore, which sells for half an ounce of silver at Canton may there be really dearer, of more real importance to the man who possesses it there, than a commodity which sells for an ounce at London is to the man who possesses it at London. If a London merchant, however, can buy at Canton for half an ounce of silver, a commodity which he can afterwards sell at London for an ounce, he gains a hundred per cent. by the bargain, just as much as if an ounce of silver was at London exactly of the same value as at Canton. It is of no importance to him that half an ounce of silver at Canton would have given him the command of more labour and of a greater quantity of the necessaries and conveniences of life than an ounce can do at London. An ounce at London will always give him the command of double the quantity of all these which half an ounce could have done there, and this is precisely what he wants.

As it is the nominal or money price of goods, therefore, which finally determines the prudence or imprudence of all purchases and sales, and thereby regulates almost the whole business of common life in which price is concerned, we cannot wonder that it should have been so much more attended to than the real price.

In such a work as this, however, it may sometimes be of use to compare the different real values of a particular commodity at different times and places, or the different degrees of power over the labour of other people which it may, upon different occasions, have given to those who possessed it. We must in this case compare, not so much the different quantities of silver for which it was commonly sold, as the different quantities of labour which those different quantities of silver could have purchased. But the current prices of labour at distant times and places can scarce ever be known with any degree of exactness.

Those of corn, though they have in few places been regularly recorded, are in general better known and have been more frequently taken notice of by historians and other writers. We must generally, therefore, content ourselves with them, not as being always exactly in the same proportion as the current prices of labour, but as being the nearest approximation which can commonly be had to that proportion. I shall hereafter have occasion to make several comparisons of this kind.

In the progress of industry, commercial nations have found it convenient to coin several different metals into money; gold for larger payments, silver for purchases of moderate value, and copper, or some other coarse metal, for those of still smaller consideration. They have always, however, considered one of those metals as more peculiarly the measure of value than any of the other two; and this preference seems generally to have been given to the metal which they happened first to make use of as the instrument of commerce. Having once begun to use it as their standard, which they must have done when they had no other money, they have generally continued to do so even when the necessity was not the same.

The Romans are said to have had nothing but copper money till within five years before the first Punic war,[1] when they first began to coin silver. Copper, therefore, appears to have continued always the measure of value in that republic. At Rome all accounts appear to have been kept, and the value of all estates to have been computed either in *Asses* or in *Sestertii*. The *As* was always the denomination of a copper coin. The word *Sestertius* signifies two *Asses* and a half. Though the *Sestertius*, therefore, was originally a silver coin, its value was estimated in copper. At Rome, one who owed a great deal of money was said to have a great deal of other people's copper.

The northern nations who established themselves upon the ruins of the Roman empire, seem to have had silver money from the first beginning of their settlements, and not to have known either gold or copper coins for several ages thereafter.

[1] Pliny, lib. xxxiii. c. 3.

There were silver coins in England in the time of the Saxons; but there was little gold coined till the time of Edward III. nor any copper till that of James I. of Great Britain. In England, therefore, and for the same reason, I believe, in all other modern nations of Europe, all accounts are kept, and the value of all goods and of all estates is generally computed in silver: and when we mean to express the amount of a person's fortune, we seldom mention the number of guineas, but the number of pounds sterling which we suppose would be given for it.

Originally, in all countries, I believe, a legal tender of payment could be made only in the coin of that metal, which was peculiarly considered as the standard or measure of value. In England, gold was not considered as a legal tender for a long time after it was coined into money. The proportion between the values of gold and silver money was not fixed by any public law or proclamation; but was left to be settled by the market. If a debtor offered payment in gold, the creditor might either reject such payment altogether, or accept of it at such a valuation of the gold as he and his debtor could agree upon. Copper is not at present a legal tender except in the change of the smaller silver coins. In this state of things the distinction between the metal which was the standard, and that which was not the standard, was something more than a nominal distinction.

In process of time, and as people became gradually more familiar with the use of the different metals in coin, and consequently better acquainted with the proportion between their respective values, it has in most countries, I believe, been found convenient to ascertain this proportion, and to declare by a public law that a guinea, for example, of such a weight and fineness, should exchange for one-and-twenty shillings, or be a legal tender for a debt of that amount. In this state of things, and during the continuance of any one regulated proportion of this kind, the distinction between the metal which is the standard, and that which is not the standard, becomes little more than a nominal distinction.

In consequence of any change, however, in this regulated proportion, this distinction becomes, or at least seems to become, something more than nominal again. If the regulated value of a guinea, for example, was either reduced to twenty, or raised to two-and-twenty shillings, all accounts being kept and almost all obligations for debt being expressed in silver money, the greater part of payments could in either case be made with the same quantity of silver money as before; but would require very different quantities of gold money; a greater in the one case, and a smaller in the other. Silver would appear to be more invariable in its value than gold. Silver would appear to measure the value of gold, and gold would not appear to measure the value of silver. The value of gold would seem to depend upon the quantity of silver which it would exchange for; and the value of silver would not seem to depend upon the quantity of gold which it would exchange for. This difference, however, would be altogether owing to the custom of keeping accounts, and of expressing the amount of all great and small sums rather in silver than in gold money. One of Mr. Drummond's notes for five-and-twenty or fifty guineas would, after an alteration of this kind, be still payable with five-and-twenty or fifty guineas in the same manner as before. It would, after such an alteration, be payable with the same quantity of gold as before, but with very different quantities of silver. In the payment of such a note, gold would appear to be more invariable in its value than silver. Gold would appear to measure the value of silver, and silver would not appear to measure the value of gold. If the custom of keeping accounts, and of expressing promissory notes and other obligations for money in this manner, should ever become general, gold, and not silver, would be considered as the metal which was peculiarly the standard or measure of value.

In reality, during the continuance of any one regulated proportion between the respective values of the different metals in coin, the value of the most precious metal regulates the value of the whole coin. Twelve copper pence contain half a pound, avoirdupois, of copper, of not the best quality, which, before it is coined, is seldom worth sevenpence in silver. But as by the regulation twelve such pence are ordered to exchange for a shilling, they are in the market considered as worth a shilling, and a shilling can at any time be had for them. Even before the late reformation of the gold coin of Great Britain, the gold, that part of it at least which circulated in London and its neighbourhood, was in general less degraded below its standard weight than the greater part of the silver. One-and-twenty worn and defaced shillings, however, were considered as equivalent to a guinea, which perhaps, indeed, was worn and defaced too, but seldom so much so. The late regulations have brought the gold coin as near perhaps to its standard weight as it is possible to bring the current coin of any nation; and the order, to receive no gold at the public offices but by weight, is likely to preserve it so, as long as that order is enforced. The silver coin still continues in the same worn and degraded state as before the reformation of the gold coin. In the market, however, one-and-twenty shillings of this degraded silver coin are still considered as worth a guinea of this excellent gold coin.

The reformation of the gold coin has evidently raised the value of the silver coin which can be exchanged for it.

In the English mint a pound weight of gold is coined into forty-four guineas and a half, which, at one-and-twenty shillings the guinea, is equal to forty-six pounds fourteen shillings and sixpence. An ounce of such gold coin, therefore, is worth £3 17s. 10½d. in silver. In England no duty or seignorage is paid upon the coinage, and he who carries a pound weight or an ounce weight of standard gold bullion to the mint, gets back a pound weight or an ounce weight of gold in coin, without any deduction. Three pounds seventeen shillings and tenpence halfpenny an ounce, therefore, is said to be the mint price of gold in England, or the quantity of gold coin which the mint gives in return for standard gold bullion.

Before the reformation of the gold coin, the price of standard gold bullion in the market had for many years been upwards of £3 18s. sometimes £3 19s. and very frequently £4 an ounce; that sum, it is probable, in the worn and degraded gold coin, seldom containing more than an ounce of standard gold. Since the reformation of the gold coin, the market price of standard gold bullion seldom exceeds £3 17s. 7d. an ounce. Before the reformation of the gold coin, the market price was always more or less above the mint price. Since that reformation, the market price has been constantly below the mint price. But that market price is the same whether it is paid in gold or in silver coin. The late reformation of the gold coin, therefore, has raised not only the value of the gold coin, but likewise that of the silver coin in proportion to gold bullion, and probably, too, in proportion to all other commodities; through the price of the greater part of other commodities being influenced by so many other causes, the rise in the value either of gold or silver coin in proportion to them may not be so distinct and sensible.

In the English mint a pound weight of standard silver bullion is coined into sixty-two shillings, containing, in the same manner, a pound weight of standard silver. Five shillings and twopence an ounce, therefore, is said to be the mint price of silver in England, or the quantity of silver coin which the mint gives in return for standard silver bullion. Before the reformation of the gold coin, the market price of standard silver bullion was, upon different occasions, five shillings and fourpence, five shillings and fivepence, five shillings and sixpence, five shillings and sevenpence, and very often five shillings and eightpence an ounce. Five shillings and sevenpence, however, seems to have been the most common price. Since the reformation of the gold coin, the market price of standard silver bullion has fallen occasionally to five shillings and threepence, five shillings and fourpence, and five shillings and fivepence an ounce, which last price it has scarce ever exceeded. Though the market price of silver bullion has fallen considerably since the reformation of the gold coin, it has not fallen so low as the mint price.

In the proportion between the different metals in the English coin, as copper is rated very much above its real value, so silver is rated somewhat below it. In the market of Europe, in the French coin and in the Dutch coin, an ounce of fine gold exchanges for about fourteen ounces of fine silver. In the English coin, it exchanges for about fifteen ounces, that is, for more silver than it is worth according to the common estimation of Europe. But as the price of copper in bars is not, even in England, raised by the high price of copper in English coin, so the price of silver in bullion is not sunk by the low rate of silver in English coin. Silver in bullion still preserves its proper proportion to gold; for the same reason that copper in bars preserves its proper proportion to silver.

Upon the reformation of the silver coin in the reign of William III. the above price of silver bullion still continued to be somewhat above the mint price. Mr. Locke imputed this high price to the permission of exporting silver bullion, and to the prohibition of exporting silver coin. This permission of exporting, he said, rendered the demand for silver bullion greater than the demand for silver coin. But the number of people who want silver coin for the common uses of buying and selling at home, is surely much greater than that of those who want silver bullion either for the use of exportation or for any other use. There subsists at present a like permission of exporting gold bullion, and a like prohibition of exporting gold coin; and yet the price of gold bullion has fallen below the mint price. But in the English coin silver was then, in the same manner as now, underrated in proportion to gold, and the gold coin (which at that time too was not supposed to require any reformation) regulated then, as well as now, the real value of the whole coin. As the reformation of the silver coin did not then reduce the price of silver bullion to the mint price, it is not very probable that a like reformation will do so now.

Were the silver coin brought back as near to its standard weight as the gold, a guinea, it is probable, would, according to the present proportion, exchange for more silver in coin than it would purchase in bullion. The silver coin containing its full standard weight, there would in this case be a profit in melting it down, in order, first, to sell the bullion for gold coin, and afterwards to exchange this gold coin for silver coin to be melted down in the same manner. Some alteration in the present proportion seems to be the only method of preventing this inconveniency.

The inconveniency perhaps would be less if silver was rated in the coin as much above its proper proportion to gold as it is at present rated below it; provided it was at the same time enacted that silver should not be a legal tender for more than the change of a guinea, in the same manner as copper is not a legal tender for more than the change of a shilling. No creditor could in this case be cheated in consequence of the high valuation of silver in coin; as no creditor can at present be cheated in consequence of the high valuation of copper. The bankers only would suffer by this regulation. When a run comes upon them they sometimes endeavour to gain time by paying in sixpences, and they would be precluded by this regulation from this discreditable method of evading immediate payment. They would be obliged in consequence to keep at all times in their coffers a greater quantity of cash than at present; and though this might no doubt be a considerable inconveniency to them, it would at the same time be a considerable security to their creditors.

Three pounds seventeen shillings and tenpence halfpenny (the mint price of gold) certainly does not contain, even in our present excellent gold coin, more than an ounce of standard gold, and it may be thought, therefore, should not purchase more standard bullion. But gold in coin is more convenient than gold in bullion, and though, in England, the coinage is free, yet the gold which is carried in bullion to the mint can seldom be returned in coin to the owner till after a delay of several weeks. In the present hurry of the mint, it could not be returned till after a delay of several months. This delay is equivalent to a small duty, and renders gold in coin somewhat more valuable than an equal quantity of gold in bullion. If in the English coin silver was rated according to its proper propor-

C

tion to gold, the price of silver bullion would probably fall below the mint price even without any reformation of the silver coin; the value even of the present worn and defaced silver coin being regulated by the value of the excellent gold coin for which it can be changed.

A small seignorage or duty upon the coinage of both gold and silver would probably increase still more the superiority of those metals in coin above an equal quantity of either of them in bullion. The coinage would in this case increase the value of the metal coined in proportion to the extent of this small duty; for the same reason that the fashion increases the value of plate in proportion to the price of that fashion. The superiority of coin above bullion would prevent the melting down of the coin, and would discourage its exportation. If upon any public exigency it should become necessary to export the coin, the greater part of it would soon return again of its own accord. Abroad it could sell only for its weight in bullion. At home it would buy more than that weight. There would be a profit, therefore, in bringing it home again. In France a seignorage of about eight per cent. is imposed upon the coinage, and the French coin, when exported, is said to return home again of its own accord.

The occasional fluctuations in the market price of gold and silver bullion arise from the same causes as the like fluctuations in that of all other commodities. The frequent loss of those metals from various accidents by sea and by land, the continual waste of them in gilding and plating, in lace and embroidery, in the wear and tear of coin, and in that of plate; require, in all countries which possess no mines of their own, a continual importation, in order to repair this loss and this waste. The merchant importers, like all other merchants, we may believe, endeavour, as well as they can, to suit their occasional importations to what, they judge, is likely to be the immediate demand. With all their attention, however, they sometimes over-do the business, and sometimes under-do it. When they import more bullion than is wanted, rather than incur the risk and trouble of exporting it again, they are sometimes willing to sell a part of it for something less than the ordinary or average price. When, on the other hand, they import less than is wanted, they get something more than this price. But when, under all those occasional fluctuations, the market price either of gold or silver bullion continues for several years together steadily and constantly, either more or less above, or more or less below the mint price, we may be assured that this steady and constant, either superiority or inferiority of price, is the effect of something in the state of the coin, which, at that time, renders a certain quantity of coin either of more value or of less value than the precise quantity of bullion which it ought to contain. The constancy and steadiness of the effect supposes a proportionable constancy and steadiness in the cause.

The money of any particular country is, at any particular time and place, more or less an accurate measure of value according as the current coin is more or less exactly agreeable to its standard, or contains more or less exactly the precise quantity of pure gold or pure silver which it ought to contain. If in England, for example, forty-four guineas and a half contained exactly a pound weight of standard gold, or eleven ounces of fine gold and one ounce of alloy, the gold coin of England would be as accurate a measure of the actual value of goods at any particular time and place as the nature of the thing would admit. But if, by rubbing and wearing, forty-four guineas and a half generally contain less than a pound weight of standard gold; the diminution, however, being greater in some pieces than in others; the measure of value comes to be liable to the same sort of uncertainty to which all other weights and measures are commonly exposed. As it rarely happens that these are exactly agreeable to their standard, the merchant adjusts the price of his goods, as well as he can, not to what those weights and measures ought to be, but to what, upon an average, he finds by experience they actually are. In consequence of a like disorder in the coin, the price of goods comes in the same manner, to be adjusted, not to the quantity of pure gold or silver which the coin ought to contain, but to that which, upon an average, it is found by experience, it actually does contain.

By the money-price of goods, it is to be observed, I understand always the quantity of pure gold or silver for which they are sold, without any regard to the denomination of the coin. Six shillings and eightpence, for example, in the time of Edward I., I consider as the same money-price with a pound sterling in the present times; because it contained, as nearly as we can judge, the same quantity of pure silver.

CHAPTER VI

OF THE COMPONENT PARTS OF THE PRICE OF COMMODITIES

IN that early and rude state of society which precedes both the accumulation of stock and the appropriation of land, the proportion between the quantities of labour necessary for acquiring different objects seems to be the only circumstance which can afford any rule for exchanging them for one another. If among a nation of hunters, for example, it usually costs twice the labour to kill a beaver which it does to kill a deer, one beaver should naturally exchange for or be worth two deer. It is natural that what is usually the produce of two days' or two hours' labour, should be worth double of what is usually the produce of one day's or one hour's labour.

If the one species of labour should be more severe than the other, some allowance will naturally be made for this superior hardship; and the produce of one hour's labour in the one way may frequently exchange for that of two hours' labour in the other.

Or if the one species of labour requires an uncommon degree of dexterity and ingenuity, the esteem which men have for such talents will naturally give a value to their produce, superior to what would be due to the time employed about it. Such talents can seldom be acquired but in consequence of long application, and the superior value of their produce may frequently be no more than a reasonable compensation for the time and labour which must be spent in acquiring them. In the advanced state of society, allowances of this kind, for superior hardship and superior skill, are commonly made in the wages of labour; and something of the same kind must probably have taken place in its earliest and rudest period.

In this state of things, the whole produce of labour belongs to the labourer; and the quantity of labour commonly employed in acquiring or producing any commodity is the only circumstance which can regulate the quantity of labour which it ought commonly to purchase, command, or exchange for.

As soon as stock has accumulated in the hands of particular persons, some of them will naturally employ it in setting to work industrious people, whom they will supply with materials and subsistence, in order to make a profit by the sale of their work, or by what their labour adds to the value of the materials. In exchanging the complete manufacture either for money, for labour, or for other goods, over and above what may be sufficient to pay the price of the materials, and the wages of the workmen, something must be given for the profits of the undertaker of the work who hazards his stock in this adventure. The value which the workmen add to the materials, therefore, resolves itself in this case into two parts, of which the one pays their wages, the other the profits of their employer upon the whole stock of materials and wages which he advanced. He could have no interest to employ them, unless he expected from the sale of their work something more than what was sufficient to replace his stock to him; and he could have no interest to employ a great stock rather than a small one, unless his profits were to bear some proportion to the extent of his stock.

The profits of stock, it may perhaps be thought, are only a different name for the wages of a particular sort of labour, the labour of inspection and direction. They are, however, altogether different, are regulated by quite different principles, and bear no proportion to the quantity, the hardship, or the ingenuity of this supposed labour of inspection and direction. They are regulated altogether by the value of the stock employed, and are greater or smaller in proportion to the extent of this stock. Let us suppose, for example, that in some particular place, where the common annual profits of manufacturing stock are ten per cent., there are two different manufactures, in each of which twenty workmen are employed at the rate of fifteen pounds a year each, or at the expense of three hundred a year in each manufactory. Let us suppose, too, that the coarse materials annually wrought up in the one cost only seven hundred pounds, while the finer materials in the other cost seven thousand. The capital annually employed in the one will in this case amount only to one thousand pounds; whereas that employed in the other will amount to seven thousand three hundred pounds. At the rate of ten per cent., therefore, the undertaker of the one will expect a yearly profit of about one hundred pounds only; while that of the other will expect about seven hundred and thirty pounds. But though their profits are so very different, their labour of inspection and direction may be either altogether or very nearly the same. In many great works almost the whole labour of this kind is committed to some principal clerk. His wages properly express the value of this labour of inspection and direction. Though in settling them some regard is had commonly, not only to his labour and skill, but to the trust which is reposed in him, yet they never bear any regular proportion to the capital of which he oversees the management; and the owner of this capital, though he is thus discharged of almost all labour, still expects that his profits should bear a regular proportion to his capital. In the price of commodities, therefore, the profits of stock constitute a component part altogether different from the wages of labour, and regulated by quite different principles.

In this state of things, the whole produce of labour does not always belong to the labourer. He must in most cases share it with the owner of the stock which employs him. Neither is the quantity of labour commonly employed in acquiring or producing any commodity, the only circumstance which can regulate the quantity which it ought commonly to purchase, command, or exchange for. An additional quantity, it is evident, must be due for the profits of the stock which advanced the wages and furnished the materials of that labour.

As soon as the land of any country has all become private property, the landlords, like all other men, love to reap where they never sowed, and demand a rent even for its natural produce. The wood of the forest, the grass of the field, and all the natural fruits of the earth, which, when land was in common, cost the labourer only the trouble of gathering them, come, even to him, to have an additional price fixed upon them. He must then pay for the licence to gather them; and must give up to the landlord a portion of what his labour either collects or produces. This portion, or what comes to the same thing, the price of this portion, constitutes the rent of land, and in the price of the greater part of commodities makes a third component part.

The real value of all the different component parts of price, it must be observed, is measured by the quantity of labour which they can, each of them, purchase or command. Labour measures the value not only of that part of price which resolves itself into labour, but of that which resolves itself into rent, and of that which resolves itself into profit.

In every society the price of every commodity finally resolves itself into some one or other, or all of those three parts; and in every improved society, all the three enter more or less, as component parts, into the price of the far greater part of commodities.

In the price of corn, for example, one part pays the rent of the landlord, another pays the wages or maintenance of the labourers and labouring cattle employed in producing it, and the third pays the profit of the farmer. These three parts seem either immediately or ultimately to make up the whole price of corn. A fourth part, it may perhaps be thought, is necessary for replacing the stock of the farmer, or for compensating the wear and tear of his labouring cattle, and other instruments of husbandry. But it must be considered that the price of any instrument of husbandry, such as a labouring horse, is itself made up of the same three parts; the rent of the land upon which he is reared, the labour of tending and rearing him, and the profits of the farmer who advances both the rent of this land, and the wages of this labour. Though the price of the corn, therefore, may pay the price as well as the maintenance of the horse, the whole price still resolves itself either immediately or ultimately into the same three parts of rent, labour, and profit.

In the price of flour or meal, we must add to the price of the corn, the profits of the miller, and the wages of his servants; in the price of bread, the profits of the baker, and the wages of his servants; and in the price of both, the labour of transporting the corn from the house of the farmer to that of the miller, and from that of the miller to that of the baker, together with the profits of those who advance the wages of that labour.

The price of flax resolves itself into the same three parts as that of corn. In the price of linen we must add to this price the wages of the flax-dresser, of the spinner, of the weaver, of the bleacher, etc., together with the profits of their respective employers.

As any particular commodity comes to be more manufactured, that part of the price which resolves itself into wages and profit comes to be greater in proportion to that which resolves itself into rent. In the progress of the manufacture, not only the number of profits increase, but every subsequent profit is greater than the foregoing; because the capital from which it is derived must always be greater. The capital which employs the weavers, for example, must be greater than that which employs the spinners; because it not only replaces that capital with its profits, but pays, besides, the wages of the weavers; and the profits must always bear some proportion to the capital.

In the most improved societies, however, there are always a few commodities of which the price resolves itself into two parts only, the wages of labour, and the profits of stock; and a still smaller number, in which it consists altogether in the wages of labour. In the price of sea-fish, for example, one part pays the labour of the fishermen, and the other the profits of the capital employed in the fishery. Rent very seldom makes any part of it, though it does sometimes, as I shall show hereafter. It is otherwise, at least through the greater part of Europe, in river fisheries. A salmon fishery pays a rent, and rent, though it cannot well be called the rent of land, makes a part of the price of a salmon as well as wages and profit. In some parts of Scotland a few poor people make a trade of gathering, along the sea-shore, those little variegated stones commonly known by the name of Scotch Pebbles. The price which is paid to them by the stone-cutter is altogether the wages of their labour; neither rent nor profit make any part of it.

But the whole price of any commodity must still finally resolve itself into some one or other, or all of those three parts; as whatever part of it remains after paying the rent of the land, and the price of the whole labour employed in raising, manufacturing, and bringing it to market, must necessarily be profit to somebody.

As the price or exchangeable value of every particular commodity, taken separately, resolves itself into some one or other or all of those three parts; so that of all the commodities which compose the whole annual produce of the labour of every country, taken complexly, must resolve itself into the same three parts, and be parcelled out among different inhabitants of the country, either as the wages of their labour, the profits of their stock, or the rent of their land. The whole of what is annually either collected or produced by the labour of every society, or what comes to the same thing, the whole price of it, is in this manner originally distributed among some of its different members. Wages, profit, and rent, are the three original sources of all revenue as well as of all exchangeable value. All other revenue is ultimately derived from some one or other of these.

Whoever derives his revenue from a fund which is his own, must draw it either from his labour, from his stock, or from his land. The revenue derived from labour is called wages. That derived from stock, by the person who manages or employs it, is called profit. That derived from it by the person who does not employ it himself, but lends it to another, is called the interest or the use of money. It is the compensation which the borrower pays to the lender, for the profit which he has an opportunity of making by the use of the money. Part of that profit naturally belongs to the borrower, who runs the risk and takes the trouble of employing it; and part to the lender, who affords him the opportunity of making this profit. The interest of money is always a derivative revenue, which, if it is not paid from the profit which is made by the use of the money, must be paid from some other source of revenue, unless perhaps the borrower is a spendthrift, who contracts a second debt in order to pay the interest of the first. The revenue which proceeds altogether from land, is called rent, and belongs to the landlord. The revenue of the farmer is derived partly from his labour, and partly from his stock. To him, land is only the instrument which enables him to earn the wages of this labour, and to make the profits of this stock. All taxes, and all the revenue which is founded upon them, all salaries, pensions, and annuities of every kind, are ultimately derived from some one or other of those three original sources of revenue, and are paid either immediately or mediately from the wages of labour, the profits of stock, or the rent of land.

When those three different sorts of revenue belong to different persons, they are readily distinguished; but when they belong to the same they are sometimes confounded with one another, at least in common language.

A gentleman who farms a part of his own estate, after paying the expense of cultivation, should gain both the rent of the landlord and the profit of the farmer. He is apt to denominate, however, his whole gain, profit, and thus confounds rent with profit, at least in common language. The greater part of our

North American and West Indian planters are in this situation. They farm, the greater part of them, their own estates, and accordingly we seldom hear of the rent of a plantation, but frequently of its profit.

Common farmers seldom employ any overseer to direct the general operations of the farm. They generally, too, work a good deal with their own hands, as ploughmen, harrowers, etc. What remains of the crop after paying the rent, therefore, should not only replace to them their stock employed in cultivation, together with its ordinary profits, but pay them the wages which are due to them, both as labourers and overseers. Whatever remains, however, after paying the rent and keeping up the stock, is called profit. But wages evidently make a part of it. The farmer, by saving these wages, must necessarily gain them. Wages, therefore, are in this case confounded with profit.

An independent manufacturer, who has stock enough both to purchase materials, and to maintain himself till he can carry his work to market, should gain both the wages of a journeyman who works under a master, and the profit which that master makes by the sale of the journeyman's work. His whole gains, however, are commonly called profit, and wages are, in this case too, confounded with profit.

A gardener who cultivates his own garden with his own hands, unites in his own person the three different characters of landlord, farmer, and labourer. His produce, therefore, should pay him the rent of the first, the profit of the second, and the wages of the third. The whole, however, is commonly considered as the earnings of his labour. Both rent and profit are, in this case, confounded with wages.

As in a civilised country there are but few commodities of which the exchangeable value arises from labour only, rent and profit contributing largely to that of the far greater part of them, so the annual produce of its labour will always be sufficient to purchase or command a much greater quantity of labour than what was employed in raising, preparing, and bringing that produce to market. If the society were annually to employ all the labour which it can annually purchase, as the quantity of labour would increase greatly every year, so the produce of every succeeding year would be of vastly greater value than that of the foregoing. But there is no country in which the whole annual produce is employed in maintaining the industrious. The idle everywhere consume a great part of it; and according to the different proportions in which it is annually divided between those two different orders of people, its ordinary or average value must either annually increase, or diminish, or continue the same from one year to another.

CHAPTER VII

OF THE NATURAL AND MARKET PRICE OF COMMODITIES

THERE is in every society or neighbourhood an ordinary or average rate both of wages and profit in every different employment of labour and stock. This rate is naturally regulated, as I shall show hereafter, partly by the general circumstances of the society, their riches or poverty, their advancing, stationary, or declining condition; and partly by the particular nature of each employment.

There is likewise in every society or neighbourhood an ordinary or average rate of rent, which is regulated too, as I shall show hereafter, partly by the general circumstances of the society or neighbourhood in which the land is situated, and partly by the natural or improved fertility of the land.

These ordinary or average rates may be called the natural rates of wages, profit, and rent, at the time and place in which they commonly prevail.

When the price of any commodity is neither more nor less than what is sufficient to pay the rent of the land, the wages of the labour, and the profits of the stock employed in raising, preparing, and bringing it to market, according to their natural rates, the commodity is then sold for what may be called its natural price.

The commodity is then sold precisely for what it is worth, or for what it really costs the person who brings it to market; for though in common language what is called the prime cost of any commodity does not comprehend the profit of the person who is to sell it again, yet if he sell it at a price which does not allow him the ordinary rate of profit in his neighbourhood, he is evidently a loser by the trade; since by employing his stock in some other way he might have made that profit. His profit, besides, is his revenue, the proper fund of his subsistence. As, while he is preparing and bringing the goods to market, he advances to his workmen their wages, or their subsistence; so he advances to himself, in the same manner, his own subsistence, which is generally suitable to the profit which he may reasonably expect from the sale of his goods. Unless they yield him this profit, therefore, they do not repay him what they may very properly be said to have really cost him.

Though the price, therefore, which leaves him this profit is not always the lowest at which a dealer may sometimes sell his goods, it is the lowest at which he is likely to sell them for any considerable time; at least where there is perfect liberty, or where he may change his trade as often as he pleases.

The actual price at which any commodity is commonly sold is called its market price. It may either be above, or below, or exactly the same with its natural price.

The market price of every particular commodity is regulated by the proportion between the quantity which is actually brought to market, and the demand of those who are willing to pay the natural price of the commodity, or the whole value of the rent, labour, and profit, which must be paid in order to bring it thither. Such people may be called the effectual demanders, and their demand the effectual demand; since it may be sufficient to effectuate the bringing of the commodity to market. It is different from the absolute demand. A very poor man may be said in some sense to have a demand for a coach and six; he might like to have it; but his demand is not an effectual demand, as the commodity can never be brought to market in order to satisfy it.

When the quantity of any commodity which is brought to market falls short of the effectual demand, all those who are willing to pay the whole value of the rent, wages, and profit, which must be paid in order to bring it thither, cannot be supplied with the quantity which they want. Rather than want it altogether, some of them will be willing to give more. A competition will immediately begin among them, and the market price will rise more or less above the natural price, according as either the greatness of the deficiency, or the wealth and wanton luxury of the competitors, happen to animate more or less the eagerness of the competition. Among competitors of equal wealth and luxury the same deficiency will generally occasion a more or less eager competition, according as the acquisition of the commodity happens to be of more or less importance to them. Hence the exorbitant price of the necessaries of life during the blockade of a town or in a famine.

When the quantity brought to market exceeds the effectual demand, it cannot be all sold to those who are willing to pay the whole value of the rent, wages, and profit, which must be paid in order to bring it thither. Some part must be sold to those who are willing to pay less, and the low price which they give for it must reduce the price of the whole. The market price will sink more or less below the natural price, according as the greatness of the excess increases more or less the competition of the sellers, or according as it happens to be more or less important to them to get immediately rid of the commodity. The same excess in the importation of perishable, will occasion a much greater competition than in that of durable commodities; in the importation of oranges, for example, than in that of old iron.

When the quantity brought to market is just sufficient to supply the effectual demand, and no more, the market price naturally comes to be either exactly, or as nearly as can be judged of, the same with the natural price. The whole quantity upon hand can be disposed of for this price, and cannot be disposed of for more. The competition of the different dealers obliges them all to accept of this price, but does not oblige them to accept of less.

The quantity of every commodity brought to market naturally suits itself to the effectual demand. It is the interest of all those who employ their land, labour, or stock, in bringing any commodity to market, that the quantity never should exceed the effectual demand; and it is the interest of all other people that it never should fall short of that demand.

If at any time it exceeds the effectual demand, some of the component parts of its price must be paid below their natural rate. If it is rent, the interest of the landlords will immediately prompt them to withdraw a part of their land; and if it is wages or profit, the interest of the labourers in the one case, and of their employers in the other, will prompt them to withdraw a part of their labour or stock from this employment. The quantity brought to market will soon be no more than sufficient to supply the effectual demand. All the different parts of its price will rise to their natural rate, and the whole price to its natural price.

If, on the contrary, the quantity brought to market should at any time fall short of the effectual demand, some of the component parts of its price must rise above their natural rate. If it is rent, the interest of all other landlords will naturally prompt them to prepare more land for the raising of this commodity; if it is wages or profit, the interest of all other labourers and dealers will soon prompt them to employ more labour and stock in preparing and bringing it to market. The quantity brought thither will soon be sufficient to supply the effectual demand. All the different parts of its price will soon sink to their natural rate, and the whole price to its natural price.

The natural price, therefore, is, as it were, the central price, to which the prices of all commodities are continually gravitating. Different accidents may sometimes keep them suspended a good deal above it, and sometimes force them down even some-

what below it. But whatever may be the obstacles which hinder
them from settling in this centre of repose and continuance,
they are constantly tending towards it.

The whole quantity of industry annually employed in order
to bring any commodity to market naturally suits itself in this
manner to the effectual demand. It naturally aims at bringing
always that precise quantity thither which may be sufficient to
supply, and no more than supply, that demand.

But in some employments the same quantity of industry will
in different years produce very different quantities of commodities; while in others it will produce always the same, or
very nearly the same. The same number of labourers in husbandry will, in different years, produce very different quantities
of corn, wine, oil, hops, etc. But the same number of spinners
and weavers will every year produce the same or very nearly
the same quantity of linen and woollen cloth. It is only the
average produce of the one species of industry which can be
suited in any respect to the effectual demand; and as its actual
produce is frequently much greater and frequently much less
than its average produce, the quantity of the commodities
brought to market will sometimes exceed a good deal, and sometimes fall short a good deal, of the effectual demand. Even
though that demand therefore should continue always the same,
their market price will be liable to great fluctuations, will sometimes fall a good deal below, and sometimes rise a good deal
above their natural price. In the other species of industry, the
produce of equal quantities of labour being always the same, or
very nearly the same, it can be more exactly suited to the
effectual demand. While that demand continues the same,
therefore, the market price of the commodities is likely to do
so too, and to be either altogether, or as nearly as can be judged
of, the same with the natural price. That the price of linen
and woollen cloth is liable neither to such frequent nor to such
great variations as the price of corn, every man's experience
will inform him. The price of the one species of commodities
varies only with the variations in the demand: that of the

other varies, not only with the variations in the demand, but with the much greater and more frequent variations in the quantity of what is brought to market in order to supply that demand.

The occasional and temporary fluctuations in the market price of any commodity fall chiefly upon those parts of its price which resolve themselves into wages and profit. That part which resolves itself into rent is less affected by them. A rent certain in money is not in the least affected by them either in its rate or in its value. A rent which consists either in a certain proportion or in a certain quantity of the rude produce, is no doubt affected in its yearly value by all the occasional and temporary fluctuations in the market price of that rude produce; but it is seldom affected by them in its yearly rate. In settling the terms of the lease, the landlord and farmer endeavour, according to their best judgment, to adjust that rate, not to the temporary and occasional, but to the average and ordinary price of the produce.

Such fluctuations affect both the value and the rate either of wages or of profit, according as the market happens to be either over-stocked or under-stocked with commodities or with labour; with work done, or with work to be done. A public mourning raises the price of black cloth (with which the market is almost always under-stocked upon such occasions), and augments the profits of the merchants who possess any considerable quantity of it. It has no effect upon the wages of the weavers. The market is under-stocked with commodities, not with labour; with work done, not with work to be done. It raises the wages of journeymen tailors. The market is here under-stocked with labour. There is an effectual demand for more labour, for more work to be done than can be had. It sinks the price of coloured silks and cloths, and thereby reduces the profits of the merchants who have any considerable quantity of them upon hand. It sinks, too, the wages of the workmen employed in preparing such commodities, for which all demand is stopped for six months, perhaps for a twelvemonth. The

D

market is here over-stocked both with commodities and with labour.

But though the market price of every particular commodity is in this manner continually gravitating, if one may say so, towards the natural price, yet sometimes particular accidents, sometimes natural causes, and sometimes particular regulations of police, may, in many commodities, keep up the market price, for a long time together, a good deal above the natural price.

When by an increase in the effectual demand, the market price of some particular commodity happens to rise a good deal above the natural price, those who employ their stocks in supplying that market are generally careful to conceal this change. If it was commonly known, their great profit would tempt so many new rivals to employ their stocks in the same way that, the effectual demand being fully supplied, the market price would soon be reduced to the natural price, and perhaps for some time even below it. If the market is at a great distance from the residence of those who supply it, they may sometimes be able to keep the secret for several years together, and may so long enjoy their extraordinary profits without any new rivals. Secrets of this kind, however, it must be acknowledged, can seldom be long kept; and the extraordinary profit can last very little longer than they are kept.

Secrets in manufactures are capable of being longer kept than secrets in trade. A dyer who has found the means of producing a particular colour with materials which cost only half the price of those commonly made use of, may, with good management, enjoy the advantage of his discovery as long as he lives, and even leave it as a legacy to his posterity. His extraordinary gains arise from the high price which is paid for his private labour. They properly consist in the high wages of that labour. But as they are repeated upon every part of his stock, and as their whole amount bears, upon that account, a regular proportion to it, they are commonly considered as extraordinary profits of stock.

Such enhancements of the market price are evidently the

effects of particular accidents, of which, however, the operation may sometimes last for many years together.

Some natural productions require such a singularity of soil and situation that all the land in a great country, which is fit for producing them, may not be sufficient to supply the effectual demand. The whole quantity brought to market, therefore, may be disposed of to those who are willing to give more than what is sufficient to pay the rent of the land which produced them, together with the wages of the labour, and the profits of the stock which were employed in preparing and bringing them to market, according to their natural rates. Such commodities may continue for whole centuries together to be sold at this high price; and that part of it which resolves itself into the rent of land is in this case the part which is generally paid above its natural rate. The rent of the land which affords such singular and esteemed productions, like the rent of some vineyards in France of a peculiarly happy soil and situation, bears no regular proportion to the rent of other equally fertile and equally well-cultivated land in its neighbourhood. The wages of the labour and the profits of the stock employed in bringing such commodities to market, on the contrary, are seldom out of their natural proportion to those of the other employments of labour and stock in their neighbourhood.

Such enhancements of the market price are evidently the effect of natural causes which may hinder the effectual demand from ever being fully supplied, and which may continue, therefore, to operate for ever.

A monopoly granted either to an individual or to a trading company has the same effect as a secret in trade or manufactures. The monopolists, by keeping the market constantly understocked, by never fully supplying the effectual demand, sell their commodities much above the natural price, and raise their emoluments, whether they consist in wages or profit, greatly above their natural rate.

The price of monopoly is upon every occasion the highest which can be got. The natural price, or the price of free competition, on the contrary, is the lowest which can be taken, not upon every occasion, indeed, but for any considerable time together. The one is upon every occasion the highest which can be squeezed out of the buyers, or which, it is supposed, they will consent to give: the other is the lowest which the sellers can commonly afford to take, and at the same time continue their business.

The exclusive privileges of corporations, statutes of apprenticeship, and all those laws which restrain, in particular employments, the competition to a smaller number than might otherwise go into them, have the same tendency, though in a less degree. They are a sort of enlarged monopolies, and may frequently, for ages together, and in whole classes of employments, keep up the market price of particular commodities above the natural price, and maintain both the wages of the labour and the profits of the stock employed about them somewhat above their natural rate.

Such enhancements of the market price may last as long as the regulations of police which give occasion to them.

The market price of any particular commodity, though it may continue long above, can seldom continue long below its natural price. Whatever part of it was paid below the natural rate, the persons whose interest it affected would immediately feel the loss, and would immediately withdraw either so much land, or so much labour, or so much stock, from being employed about it, that the quantity brought to market would soon be no more than sufficient to supply the effectual demand. Its market price, therefore, would soon rise to the natural price. This at least would be the case where there was perfect liberty.

The same statutes of apprenticeship and other corporation laws indeed, which, when a manufacture is in prosperity, enable the workman to raise his wages a good deal above their natural rate, sometimes oblige him, when it decays, to let them down a good deal below it. As in the one case they exclude many people from his employment, so in the other they exclude him from many employments. The effect of such regulations, however, is not near so durable in sinking the workman's wages below, as in raising them above their natural rate. Their operation in the one way may endure for many centuries, but in the other it can last no longer than the lives of some of the workmen who were bred to the business in the time of its prosperity. When they are gone, the number of those who are afterwards educated to the trade will naturally suit itself to the effectual demand. The police must be as violent as that of Indostan or ancient Egypt (where every man was bound by a principle of religion to follow the occupation of his father, and was supposed to commit the most horrid sacrilege if he changed it for another), which can in any particular employment, and for several generations together, sink either the wages of labour or the profits of stock below their natural rate.

This is all that I think necessary to be observed at present concerning the deviations, whether occasional or permanent, of the market price of commodities from the natural price.

The natural price itself varies with the natural rate of each of its component parts, of wages, profit, and rent; and in every society this rate varies according to their circumstances, according to their riches or poverty, their advancing, stationary, or declining condition. I shall, in the four following chapters, endeavour to explain, as fully and distinctly as I can, the causes of those different variations.

First, I shall endeavour to explain what are the circumstances which naturally determine the rate of wages, and in what manner those circumstances are affected by the riches or poverty, by the advancing, stationary, or declining state of the society.

Secondly, I shall endeavour to show what are the circumstances which naturally determine the rate of profit, and in what manner, too, those circumstances are affected by the like variations in the state of the society.

Though pecuniary wages and profit are very different in the different employments of labour and stock; yet a certain proportion seems commonly to take place between both the pecuniary wages in all the different employments of labour, and the pecuniary profits in all the different employments of stock. This proportion, it will appear hereafter, depends partly upon the nature of the different employments, and partly upon the different laws and policy of the society in which they are carried on. But though in many respects dependent upon the laws and policy, this proportion seems to be little affected by the riches or poverty of that society; by its advancing, stationary, or declining condition; but to remain the same or very nearly the same in all those different states. I shall, in the third place, endeavour to explain all the different circumstances which regulate this proportion.

In the fourth and last place, I shall endeavour to show what are the circumstances which regulate the rent of land, and which either raise or lower the real price of all the different substances which it produces.

Book II

CHAPTER III

OF THE ACCUMULATION OF CAPITAL, OR OF PRODUCTIVE
AND UNPRODUCTIVE LABOUR

THERE is one sort of labour which adds to the value of the subject upon which it is bestowed: there is another which has no such effect. The former, as it produces a value, may be called productive; the latter, unproductive[1] labour. Thus the labour of a manufacturer adds, generally, to the value of the materials which he works upon, that of his own maintenance, and of his master's profit. The labour of a menial servant, on the contrary, adds to the value of nothing. Though the manufacturer has his wages advanced to him by his master, he, in reality, costs him no expense, the value of those wages being

---

[1] Some French authors of great learning and ingenuity have used those words in a different sense. In the last chapter of the fourth book I shall endeavour to show that their sense is an improper one.

generally restored, together with a profit, in the improved value of the subject upon which his labour is bestowed. But the maintenance of a menial servant never is restored. A man grows rich by employing a multitude of manufacturers: he grows poor by maintaining a multitude of menial servants. The labour of the latter, however, has its value, and deserves its reward as well as that of the former. But the labour of the manufacturer fixes and realises itself in some particular subject or vendible commodity, which lasts for some time at least after that labour is past. It is, as it were, a certain quantity of labour stocked and stored up to be employed, if necessary, upon some other occasion. That subject, or what is the same thing, the price of that subject, can afterwards, if necessary, put into motion a quantity of labour equal to that which had originally produced it. The labour of the menial servant, on the contrary, does not fix or realise itself in any particular subject or vendible commodity. His services generally perish in the very instant of their performance, and seldom leave any trace or value behind them for which an equal quantity of service could afterwards be procured.

The labour of some of the most respectable orders in the society is, like that of menial servants, unproductive of any value, and does not fix or realise itself in any permanent subject, or vendible commodity, which endures after that labour is past, and for which an equal quantity of labour could afterwards be procured. The sovereign, for example, with all the officers both of justice and war who serve under him, the whole army and navy, are unproductive labourers. They are the servants of the public, and are maintained by a part of the annual produce of the industry of other people. Their service, how honourable, how useful, or how necessary soever, produces nothing for which an equal quantity of service can afterwards be procured. The protection, security, and defence of the commonwealth, the effect of their labour this year will not purchase its protection, security, and defence for the year to come. In the same class must be ranked, some both of the gravest and most important, and some of the most frivolous professions: churchmen, lawyers, physicians, men of letters of all kinds; players, buffoons, musicians, opera-singers, opera-dancers, etc. The labour of the meanest of these has a certain value, regulated by the very same principles which regulate that of every other sort of labour; and that of the noblest and most useful, produces nothing which could afterwards purchase or procure an equal quantity of labour. Like the declamation of the actor, the harangue of the orator, or the tune of the musician, the work of all of them perishes in the very instant of its production.

Both productive and unproductive labourers, and those who do not labour at all, are all equally maintained by the annual produce of the land and labour of the country. This produce, how great soever, can never be infinite, but must have certain limits. According, therefore, as a smaller or greater proportion of it is in any one year employed in maintaining unproductive hands, the more in the one case and the less in the other will remain for the productive, and the next year's produce will be greater or smaller accordingly; the whole annual produce, if we except the spontaneous productions of the earth, being the effect of productive labour.

Though the whole annual produce of the land and labour of every country is, no doubt, ultimately destined for supplying the consumption of its inhabitants, and for procuring a revenue to them, yet when it first comes either from the ground, or from the hands of the productive labourers, it naturally divides itself into two parts. One of them, and frequently the largest, is, in the first place, destined for replacing a capital, or for renewing the provisions, materials, and finished work, which had been withdrawn from a capital; the other for constituting a revenue either to the owner of this capital, as the profit of his stock, or to some other person, as the rent of his land. Thus, of the produce of land, one part replaces the capital of the farmer; the other pays his profit and the rent of the landlord; and thus constitutes a revenue both to the owner of this capital, as the profits of his stock; and to some other person, as the rent of his land. Of the produce of a great manufactory, in the same manner, one part, and that always the largest, replaces the capital of the undertaker of the work; the other pays his profit, and thus constitutes a revenue to the owner of this capital.

That part of the annual produce of the land and labour of any country which replaces a capital never is immediately employed to maintain any but productive hands. It pays the wages of productive labour only. That which is immediately destined for constituting a revenue, either as profit or as rent, may maintain indifferently either productive or unproductive hands.

Whatever part of his stock a man employs as a capital, he always expects it to be replaced to him with a profit. He employs it, therefore, in maintaining productive hands only; and after having served in the function of a capital to him, it constitutes a revenue to them. Whenever he employs any part of it in maintaining unproductive hands of any kind, that part is, from that moment, withdrawn from his capital, and placed in his stock reserved for immediate consumption.

Unproductive labourers, and those who do not labour at all, are all maintained by revenue; either, first, by that part of the annual produce which is originally destined for constituting a revenue to some particular persons, either as the rent of land or as the profits of stock; or, secondly, by that part which, though originally destined for replacing a capital and for maintaining productive labourers only, yet when it comes into their hands whatever part of it is over and above their necessary subsistence may be employed in maintaining indifferently either productive or unproductive hands. Thus, not only the great landlord or the rich merchant, but even the common workman, if his wages are considerable, may maintain a menial servant; or he may sometimes go to a play or a puppet-show, and so contribute his share towards maintaining one set of unproductive labourers, or he may pay some taxes, and thus help to maintain another set, more honourable and useful, indeed, but equally unproduc-

tive. No part of the annual produce, however, which had been
originally destined to replace a capital, is ever directed towards
maintaining unproductive hands till after it has put into motion
its full complement of productive labour, or all that it could
put into motion in the way in which it was employed. The
workman must have earned his wages by work done before he
can employ any part of them in this manner. That part, too, is
generally but a small one. It is his spare revenue only, of which
productive labourers have seldom a great deal. They generally
have some, however; and in the payment of taxes the greatness
of their number may compensate, in some measure, the small-
ness of their contribution. The rent of land and the profits
of stock are everywhere, therefore, the principal sources from
which unproductive hands derive their subsistence. These are
the two sorts of revenue of which the owners have generally
most to spare. They might both maintain indifferently either
productive or unproductive hands. They seem, however, to
have some predilection for the latter. The expense of a great
lord feeds generally more idle than industrious people. The
rich merchant, though with his capital he maintains industrious
people only, yet by his expense, that is, by the employment of
his revenue, he feeds commonly the very same sort as the great
lord.

The proportion, therefore, between the productive and unproductive hands, depends very much in every country upon
the proportion between that part of the annual produce, which,
as soon as it comes either from the ground or from the hands of
the productive labourers, is destined for replacing a capital, and
that which is destined for constituting a revenue, either as rent
or as profit. This proportion is very different in rich from what
it is in poor countries.

Thus, at present, in the opulent countries of Europe, a very
large, frequently the largest portion of the produce of the land
is destined for replacing the capital of the rich and independent
farmer; the other for paying his profits and the rent of the landlord. But anciently, during the prevalency of the feudal govern-

ment, a very small portion of the produce was sufficient to replace the capital employed in cultivation. It consisted commonly in a few wretched cattle, maintained altogether by the spontaneous produce of uncultivated land, and which might, therefore, be considered as a part of that spontaneous produce. It generally, too, belonged to the landlord, and was by him advanced to the occupiers of the land. All the rest of the produce properly belonged to him too, either as rent for his land, or as profit upon this paltry capital. The occupiers of land were generally bondmen, whose persons and effects were equally his property. Those who were not bondmen were tenants at will, and though the rent which they paid was often nominally little more than a quit-rent, it really amounted to the whole produce of the land. Their lord could at all times command their labour in peace and their service in war. Though they lived at a distance from his house, they were equally dependent upon him as his retainers who lived in it. But the whole produce of the land undoubtedly belongs to him who can dispose of the labour and service of all those whom it maintains. In the present state of Europe, the share of the landlord seldom exceeds a third, sometimes not a fourth part of the whole produce of the land. The rent of land, however, in all the improved parts of the country, has been tripled and quadrupled since those ancient times; and this third or fourth part of the annual produce is, it seems, three or four times greater than the whole had been before. In the progress of improvement, rent, though it increases in proportion to the extent, diminishes in proportion to the produce of the land.

In the opulent countries of Europe, great capitals are at present employed in trade and manufactures. In the ancient state, the little trade that was stirring, and the few homely and coarse manufactures that were carried on, required but very small capitals. These, however, must have yielded very large profits. The rate of interest was nowhere less than ten per cent., and their profits must have been sufficient to afford this great interest. At present the rate of interest, in the improved parts of Europe, is nowhere higher than six per cent., and in some of the most improved it is so low as four, three, and two per cent. Though that part of the revenue of the inhabitants which is derived from the profits of stock is always much greater in rich than in poor countries, it is because the stock is much greater: in proportion to the stock the profits are generally much less.

That part of the annual produce, therefore, which, as soon as it comes either from the ground or from the hands of the productive labourers, is destined for replacing a capital, is not only much greater in rich than in poor countries, but bears a much greater proportion to that which is immediately destined for constituting a revenue either as rent or as profit. The funds destined for the maintenance of productive labour are not only much greater in the former than in the latter, but bear a much greater proportion to those which, though they may be employed to maintain either productive or unproductive hands, have generally a predilection for the latter.

The proportion between those different funds necessarily determines in every country the general character of the inhabitants as to industry or idleness. We are more industrious than our forefathers; because in the present times the funds destined for the maintenance of industry are much greater in proportion to those which are likely to be employed in the maintenance of idleness than they were two or three centuries ago. Our ancestors were idle for want of a sufficient encouragement to industry. It is better, says the proverb, to play for nothing than to work for nothing. In mercantile and manufacturing towns, where the inferior ranks of people are chiefly maintained by the employment of capital, they are in general industrious, sober, and thriving; as in many English, and in most Dutch towns. In those towns which are principally supported by the constant or occasional residence of a court, and in which the inferior ranks of people are chiefly maintained by the spending of revenue, they are in general idle, dissolute, and poor; as at Rome, Versailles, Compiegne, and Fontainebleau. If you except Rouen and Bordeaux, there is little trade or industry in any of the parliament towns of France; and the inferior ranks of people, being chiefly maintained by the expense of the members of the courts of justice, and of those who come to plead before them, are in general idle and poor. The great trade of Rouen and Bordeaux seems to be altogether the effect of their situation. Rouen is necessarily the entrepôt of almost all the goods which are brought either from foreign countries, or from the maritime provinces of France, for the consumption of the great city of Paris. Bordeaux is in the same manner the entrepôt of the wines which grow upon the banks of the Garonne, and of the rivers which run into it, one of the richest wine countries in the world, and which seems to produce the wine fittest for exportation, or best suited to the taste of foreign nations. Such advantageous situations necessarily attract a great capital by the great employment which they afford it; and the employment of this capital is the cause of the industry of those two cities. In the other parliament towns of France, very little more capital seems to be employed than what is necessary for supplying their own consumption; that is, little more than the smallest capital which can be employed in them. Of those three cities, Paris is by far the most industrious; but Paris itself is the principal market of all the manufactures established at Paris, and its own consumption is the principal object of all the trade which it carries on. London, Lisbon, and Copenhagen, are, perhaps, the only three cities in Europe which are both the constant residence of a court, and can at the same time be considered as trading cities, or as cities which trade not only for their own consumption, but for that of other cities and countries. The situation of all the three is extremely advantageous, and naturally fits them to be the entrepôts of a great part of the goods destined for the consumption of distant places. In a city where a great revenue is spent, to employ with advantage a capital for any other purpose than for supplying the consumption of that city is probably more difficult than in one in which the inferior ranks of people have no other maintenance but what they derive from the employment of such a capital. The idleness of the greater part of the people who are maintained by the expense of revenue corrupts, it is probable, the industry of those who ought to be maintained by the employment of capital, and renders it less advantageous to employ a capital there than in other places. There was little trade or industry in Edinburgh before the union. When the Scotch parliament was no longer to be assembled in it, when it ceased to be the necessary residence of the principal nobility and gentry of Scotland, it became a city of some trade and industry. It still continues, however, to be the residence of the principal courts of justice in Scotland, of the boards of customs and excise, etc. A considerable revenue, therefore, still continues to be spent in it. In trade and industry it is much inferior to Glasgow, of which the inhabitants are chiefly maintained by the employment of capital. The inhabitants of a large village, it has sometimes been observed, after having made considerable progress in manufactures, have become idle and poor in consequence of a great lord having taken up his residence in their neighbourhood.

The proportion between capital and revenue, therefore, seems everywhere to regulate the proportion between industry and idleness. Wherever capital predominates, industry prevails: wherever revenue, idleness. Every increase or diminution of capital, therefore, naturally tends to increase or diminish the real quantity of industry, the number of productive hands, and consequently the exchangeable value of the annual produce of the land and labour of the country, the real wealth and revenue of all its inhabitants.

Capitals are increased by parsimony, and diminished by prodigality and misconduct.

Whatever a person saves from his revenue he adds to his capital, and either employs it himself in maintaining an additional number of productive hands, or enables some other person to do so, by lending it to him for an interest, that is, for a share of the profits. As the capital of an individual can be increased only by what he saves from his annual revenue or his annual gains, so the capital of a society, which is the same with that of all the individuals who compose it, can be increased only in the same manner.

Parsimony, and not industry, is the immediate cause of the increase of capital. Industry, indeed, provides the subject which parsimony accumulates. But whatever industry might acquire, if parsimony did not save and store up, the capital would never be the greater.

Parsimony, by increasing the fund which is destined for the maintenance of productive hands, tends to increase the number of those hands whose labour adds to the value of the subject upon which it is bestowed. It tends, therefore, to increase the exchangeable value of the annual produce of the land and labour of the country. It puts into motion an additional quantity of industry, which gives an additional value to the annual produce.

What is annually saved is as regularly consumed as what is annually spent, and nearly in the same time too; but it is consumed by a different set of people. That portion of his revenue which a rich man annually spends is in most cases consumed by idle guests and menial servants, who leave nothing behind them in return for their consumption. That portion which he annually saves, as for the sake of the profit it is immediately employed as a capital, is consumed in the same manner, and nearly in the same time too, but by a different set of people, by labourers, manufacturers, and artificers, who re-produce with a profit the value of their annual consumption. His revenue, we shall suppose, is paid him in money. Had he spent the whole, the food, clothing, and lodging, which the whole could have purchased, would have been distributed among the former set of people. By saving a part of it, as that part is for the sake of the profit immediately employed as a capital either by himself or by some other person, the food, clothing, and lodging, which may be purchased with it, are necessarily reserved for the latter. The consumption is the same, but the consumers are different.

By what a frugal man annually saves, he not only affords maintenance to an additional number of productive hands, for that or the ensuing year, but, like the founder of a public work-house, he establishes as it were a perpetual fund for the main-tenance of an equal number in all times to come. The perpetual allotment and destination of this fund, indeed, is not always guarded by any positive law, by any trust-right or deed of mortmain. It is always guarded, however, by a very powerful principle, the plain and evident interest of every individual to whom any share of it shall ever belong. No part of it can ever afterwards be employed to maintain any but productive hands without an evident loss to the person who thus perverts it from its proper destination.

The prodigal perverts it in this manner. By not confining his expense within his income, he encroaches upon his capital. Like him who perverts the revenues of some pious foundation to profane purposes, he pays the wages of idleness with those funds which the frugality of his forefathers had, as it were, con-secrated to the maintenance of industry. By diminishing the funds destined for the employment of productive labour, he necessarily diminishes, so far as it depends upon him, the quantity of that labour which adds a value to the subject upon which it is bestowed, and, consequently, the value of the annual produce of the land and labour of the whole country, the real wealth and revenue of its inhabitants. If the prodigality of some was not compensated by the frugality of others, the conduct of every prodigal, by feeding the idle with the bread of the industrious, tends not only to beggar himself, but to impoverish his country.

Though the expense of the prodigal should be altogether in home-made, and no part of it in foreign commodities, its effect upon the productive funds of the society would still be the same. Every year there would still be a certain quantity of food and clothing, which ought to have maintained productive, em-ployed in maintaining unproductive hands. Every year, there-fore, there would still be some diminution in what would otherwise have been the value of the annual produce of the land and labour of the country.

This expense, it may be said indeed, not being in foreign goods, and not occasioning any exportation of gold and silver, the same quantity of money would remain in the country as before. But if the quantity of food and clothing, which were thus consumed by unproductive, had been distributed among productive hands, they would have reproduced, together with a profit, the full value of their consumption. The same quantity of money would in this case equally have remained in the country, and there would besides have been a reproduction of an equal value of consumable goods. There would have been two values instead of one.

The same quantity of money, besides, cannot long remain in any country in which the value of the annual produce diminishes. The sole use of money is to circulate consumable goods. By means of it, provisions, materials, and finished work, are bought and sold, and distributed to their proper consumers. The quantity of money, therefore, which can be annually employed in any country must be determined by the value of the consumable goods annually circulated within it. These must consist either in the immediate produce of the land and labour of the country itself, or in something which had been purchased with some part of that produce. Their value, therefore, must diminish as the value of that produce diminishes, and along with it the quantity of money which can be employed in circulating them. But the money which by this annual diminution of produce is annually thrown out of domestic circulation will not be allowed to lie idle. The interest of whoever possesses it requires that it should be employed. But having no employment at home, it will, in spite of all laws and prohibitions, be sent abroad, and employed in purchasing consumable goods which may be of some use at home. Its annual exportation will in this matter continue for some time to add something to the annual consumption of the country beyond the value of its own annual produce. What in the days of its

E

prosperity had been saved from that annual produce, and employed in purchasing gold and silver, will contribute for some little time to support its consumption in adversity. The exportation of gold and silver is, in this case, not the cause, but the effect of its declension, and may even, for some little time, alleviate the misery of that declension.

The quantity of money, on the contrary, must in every country naturally increase as the value of the annual produce increases. The value of the consumable goods annually circulated within the society being greater will require a greater quantity of money to circulate them. A part of the increased produce, therefore, will naturally be employed in purchasing, wherever it is to be had, the additional quantity of gold and silver necessary for circulating the rest. The increase of those metals will in this case be the effect, not the cause, of the public prosperity. Gold and silver are purchased everywhere in the same manner. The food, clothing, and lodging, the revenue and maintenance of all those whose labour or stock is employed in bringing them from the mine to the market, is the price paid for them in Peru as well as in England. The country which has this price to pay will never be long without the quantity of those metals which it has occasion for; and no country will ever long retain a quantity which it has no occasion for.

Whatever, therefore, we may imagine the real wealth and revenue of a country to consist in, whether in the value of the annual produce of its land and labour, as plain reason seems to dictate; or in the quantity of the precious metals which circulate within it, as vulgar prejudices suppose; in either view of the matter, every prodigal appears to be a public enemy, and every frugal man a public benefactor.

The effects of misconduct are often the same as those of prodigality. Every injudicious and unsuccessful project in agriculture, mines, fisheries, trade, or manufactures, tends in the same manner to diminish the funds destined for the maintenance of productive labour. In every such project, though the capital is consumed by productive hands only, yet, as by the injudicious manner in which they are employed they do not reproduce the full value of their consumption, there must always be some diminution in what would otherwise have been the productive funds of the society.

It can seldom happen, indeed, that the circumstances of a great nation can be much affected either by the prodigality or misconduct of individuals; the profusion or imprudence of some being always more than compensated by the frugality and good conduct of others.

With regard to profusion, the principle which prompts to expense is the passion for present enjoyment; which, though sometimes violent and very difficult to be restrained, is in general only momentary and occasional. But the principle which prompts to save is the desire of bettering our condition, a desire which, though generally calm and dispassionate, comes with us from the womb, and never leaves us till we go into the grave. In the whole interval which separates those two moments, there is scarce perhaps a single instant in which any man is so perfectly and completely satisfied with his situation as to be without any wish of alteration or improvement of any kind. An augmentation of fortune is the means by which the greater part of men propose and wish to better their condition. It is the means the most vulgar and the most obvious; and the most likely way of augmenting their fortune is to save and accumulate some part of what they acquire, either regularly and annually, or upon some extraordinary occasions. Though the principle of expense, therefore, prevails in almost all men upon some occasions, and in some men upon almost all occasions, yet in the greater part of men, taking the whole course of their life at an average, the principle of frugality seems not only to predominate, but to predominate very greatly.

With regard to misconduct, the number of prudent and successful undertakings is everywhere much greater than that of injudicious and unsuccessful ones. After all our complaints of the frequency of bankruptcies, the unhappy men who fall into this misfortune make but a very small part of the whole number engaged in trade, and all other sorts of business; not much more perhaps than one in a thousand. Bankruptcy is perhaps the greatest and most humiliating calamity which can befall an innocent man. The greater part of men, therefore, are sufficiently careful to avoid it. Some, indeed, do not avoid it; as some do not avoid the gallows.

Great nations are never impoverished by private, though they sometimes are by public prodigality and misconduct. The whole, or almost the whole public revenue, is in most countries employed in maintaining unproductive hands. Such are the people who compose a numerous and splendid court, a great ecclesiastical establishment, great fleets and armies, who in time of peace produce nothing, and in time of war acquire nothing which can compensate the expense of maintaining them, even while the war lasts. Such people, as they themselves produce nothing, are all maintained by the produce of other men's labour. When multiplied, therefore, to an unnecessary number, they may in a particular year consume so great a share of this produce, as not to leave a sufficiency for maintaining the productive labourers, who should reproduce it next year. The next year's produce, therefore, will be less than that of the foregoing, and if the same disorder should continue, that of the third year will be still less than that of the second. Those unproductive hands, who should be maintained by a part only of the spare revenue of the people, may consume so great a share of their whole revenue, and thereby oblige so great a number to encroach upon their capitals, upon the funds destined for the maintenance of productive labour, that all the frugality and good conduct of individuals may not be able to compensate the waste and degradation of produce occasioned by this violent and forced encroachment.

This frugality and good conduct, however, is upon most occasions, it appears from experience, sufficient to compensate, not only the private prodigality and misconduct of individuals, but the public extravagance of government. The uniform, constant, and uninterrupted effort of every man to better his condition, the principle from which public and national, as well as private opulence is originally derived, is frequently powerful enough to maintain the natural progress of things toward improvement, in spite both of the extravagance of government and of the greatest errors of administration. Like the unknown principle of animal life, it frequently restores health and vigour to the constitution, in spite, not only of the disease, but of the absurd prescriptions of the doctor.

The annual produce of the land and labour of any nation can be increased in its value by no other means but by increasing either the number of its productive labourers, or the productive powers of those labourers who had before been employed. The number of its productive labourers, it is evident, can never be much increased, but in consequence of an increase of capital, or of the funds destined for maintaining them. The productive powers of the same number of labourers cannot be increased, but in consequence either of some addition and improvement to those machines and instruments which facilitate and abridge labour; or of a more proper division and distribution of employment. In either case an additional capital is almost always required. It is by means of an additional capital only that the undertaker of any work can either provide his workmen with better machinery or make a more proper distribution of employment among them. When the work to be done consists of a number of parts, to keep every man constantly employed in one way requires a much greater capital than where every man is occasionally employed in every different part of the work. When we compare, therefore, the state of a nation at two different periods, and find, that the annual produce of its land and labour is evidently greater at the latter than at the former, that its lands are better cultivated, its manufactures more numerous and more flourishing, and its trade more extensive, we may be assured that its capital must have increased during the interval between those two periods, and that more must have been added to it by the good conduct of some than had been taken from it either by the private misconduct of others or by the public extravagance of government. But we shall find this to have been the case of almost all nations, in all tolerably quiet and peaceable times, even of those who have not enjoyed the most prudent and parsimonious governments. To form a right judgment of it, indeed, we must compare the state of the country at periods somewhat distant from one another. The progress is frequently so gradual that, at near periods, the improvement is not only not sensible, but from the declension either of certain branches of industry, or of certain districts of the country, things which sometimes happen though the country in general be in great prosperity, there frequently arises a suspicion that the riches and industry of the whole are decaying.

The annual produce of the land and labour of England, for example, is certainly much greater than it was, a little more than a century ago, at the restoration of Charles II. Though, at present, few people, I believe, doubt of this, yet during this period, five years have seldom passed away in which some book or pamphlet has not been published, written, too, with such abilities as to gain some authority with the public, and pretending to demonstrate that the wealth of the nation was fast declining, that the country was depopulated, agriculture neglected, manufactures decaying, and trade undone. Nor have these publications been all party pamphlets, the wretched off-spring of falsehood and venality. Many of them have been written by very candid and very intelligent people, who wrote nothing but what they believed, and for no other reason but because they believed it.

The annual produce of the land and labour of England, again, was certainly much greater at the restoration, than we can suppose it to have been about an hundred years before, at the accession of Elizabeth. At this period, too, we have all reason to believe, the country was much more advanced in improvement than it had been about a century before, towards the close of the dissensions between the houses of York and Lancaster. Even then it was, probably, in a better condition than it had been at the Norman conquest, and at the Norman conquest than during the confusion of the Saxon Heptarchy. Even at this early period, it was certainly a more improved country than at the invasion of Julius Cæsar, when its inhabitants were nearly in the same state with the savages in North America.

In each of those periods, however, there was not only much private and public profusion, many expensive and unnecessary wars, great perversion of the annual produce from maintaining productive to maintain unproductive hands; but sometimes, in the confusion of civil discord, such absolute waste and destruction of stock, as might be supposed, not only to retard, as it certainly did, the natural accumulation of riches, but to have left the country, at the end of the period, poorer than at the beginning. Thus, in the happiest and most fortunate period of them all, that which has passed since the restoration, how many disorders and misfortunes have occurred, which, could they have been foreseen, not only the impoverishment, but the total ruin of the country would have been expected from them? The fire and the plague of London, the two Dutch wars, the disorders of the revolution, the war in Ireland, the four expensive French wars of 1688, 1702, 1742, and 1756, together with the two rebellions of 1715 and 1745. In the course of the four French wars, the nation has contracted more than a hundred and forty-five millions of debt, over and above all the other extraordinary annual expense which they occasioned, so that the whole cannot be computed at less than two hundred millions. So great a share of the annual produce of the land and labour of the country has, since the revolution, been employed upon different occasions in maintaining an extraordinary number of unproductive hands. But had not those wars given this particular direction to so large a capital, the greater part of it would naturally have been employed in maintaining productive hands, whose labour would have replaced, with a profit, the whole value of their consumption. The value of the annual produce of the land and labour of the country would have been considerably increased by it every year, and every year's increase would have augmented still more that of the following year. More houses would have been built, more lands would have been improved, and those which had been improved before would have been better cultivated, more manufactures would have been established, and those which had been established before would have been more extended; and to what height the real wealth and revenue of the country might, by this time, have been raised, it is not perhaps very easy even to imagine.

But though the profusion of government must, undoubtedly, have retarded the natural progress of England towards wealth and improvement, it has not been able to stop it. The annual produce of its land and labour is, undoubtedly, much greater at present than it was either at the restoration or at the revolution. The capital, therefore, annually employed in cultivating this land, and in maintaining this labour, must likewise be much greater. In the midst of all the exactions of government, this capital has been silently and gradually accumulated by the private frugality and good conduct of individuals, by their universal, continual, and uninterrupted effort to better their own condition. It is this effort, protected by law and allowed by liberty to exert itself in the manner that is most advantageous, which has maintained the progress of England towards opulence and improvement in almost all former times, and which, it is to be hoped, will do so in all future times. England, however, as it has never been blessed with a very parsimonious government, so parsimony has at no time been the characteristical virtue of its inhabitants. It is the highest impertinence and presumption, therefore, in kings and ministers, to pretend to watch over the economy of private people, and to restrain their expense, either by sumptuary laws, or by prohibiting the importation of foreign luxuries. They are themselves always, and without any exception, the greatest spendthrifts in the society. Let them look well after their own expense, and they may safely trust private people with theirs. If their own extravagance does not ruin the state, that of their subjects never will.

As frugality increases and prodigality diminishes the public capital, so the conduct of those whose expense just equals their revenue, without either accumulating or encroaching, neither increases nor diminishes it. Some modes of expense, however, seem to contribute more to the growth of public opulence than others.

The revenue of an individual may be spent either in things which are consumed immediately, and in which one day's expense can neither alleviate nor support that of another, or it may be spent in things more durable, which can therefore be accumulated, and in which every day's expense may, as he chooses, either alleviate or support and heighten the effect of that of the following day. A man of fortune, for example, may either spend his revenue in a profuse and sumptuous table, and in maintaining a great number of menial servants, and a multitude of dogs and horses; or contenting himself with a frugal table and few attendants, he may lay out the greater part of it in adorning his house or his country villa, in useful or ornamental buildings, in useful or ornamental furniture, in collecting books, statues, pictures; or in things more frivolous, jewels, baubles, ingenious trinkets of different kinds; or, what is most trifling of all, in amassing a great wardrobe of fine clothes, like the favourite and minister of a great prince who died a few years ago. Were two men of equal fortune to spend their revenue, the one chiefly in the one way, the other in the other, the magnificence of the person whose expense had been chiefly in durable commodities, would be continually increasing, every day's expense contributing something to support and heighten the effect of that of the following day: that of the other, on the contrary, would be no greater at the end of the period than at the beginning. The former, too, would, at the end of the period, be the richer man of the two. He would have a stock of goods of some kind or other, which, though it might not be worth all that it cost, would always be worth something. No trace or vestige of the expense of the latter would remain, and the effects of ten or twenty years profusion would be as completely annihilated as if they had never existed.

As the one mode of expense is more favourable than the other to the opulence of an individual, so is it likewise to that of a nation. The houses, the furniture, the clothing of the rich, in a little time, become useful to the inferior and middling ranks of people. They are able to purchase them when their superiors grow weary of them, and the general accommodation of the whole people is thus gradually improved, when this mode of expense becomes universal among men of fortune. In countries which have long been rich, you will frequently find the inferior ranks of people in possession both of houses and furniture perfectly good and entire, but of which neither the one could have been built, nor the other have been made for their use. What was formerly a seat of the family of Seymour is now an inn upon the Bath road. The marriage-bed of James the First of Great Britain, which his queen brought with her from Denmark as a present fit for a sovereign to make a sovereign, was, a few years ago, the ornament of an alehouse at Dunfermline. In some ancient cities, which either have been long stationary, or have gone somewhat to decay, you will sometimes scarce find a single house which could have been built for its present inhabitants. If you go into those houses too, you will frequently find many excellent, though antiquated pieces of furniture, which are still very fit for use, and which could as little have been made for them. Noble palaces, magnificent villas, great collections of books, statues, pictures, and other curiosities, are frequently both an ornament and an honour, not only to the neighbourhood, but to the whole country to which they belong. Versailles is an ornament and an honour to France, Stowe and Wilton to England. Italy still continues to command some sort of veneration by the number of monuments of this kind which it possesses, though the wealth which produced them has decayed, and though the genius which planned them seems to be extinguished, perhaps from not having the same employment.

The expense too, which is laid out in durable commodities, is favourable, not only to accumulation, but to frugality. If a person should at any time exceed in it, he can easily reform without exposing himself to the censure of the public. To reduce very much the number of his servants, to reform his table from great profusion to great frugality, to lay down his equipage after he has once set it up, are changes which cannot escape the observation of his neighbours, and which are supposed to imply some acknowledgment of preceding bad conduct. Few, therefore, of those who have once been so unfortunate as to launch out too far into this sort of expense, have afterwards the courage to reform, till ruin and bankruptcy oblige them. But if a person has, at any time, been at too great an expense in building, in furniture, in books or pictures, no imprudence can be inferred from his changing his conduct. These are things in which further expense is frequently rendered unnecessary by former expense; and when a person stops short, he appears to do so, not because he has exceeded his fortune, but because he has satisfied his fancy.

The expense, besides, that is laid out in durable commodities gives maintenance, commonly, to a greater number of people than that which is employed in the most profuse hospitality. Of two or three hundredweight of provisions, which may sometimes be served up at a great festival, one-half, perhaps, is thrown to the dunghill, and there is always a great deal wasted and abused. But if the expense of this entertainment had been employed in setting to work masons, carpenters, upholsterers, mechanics, etc., a quantity of provisions, of equal value, would have been distributed among a still greater number of people who would have bought them in pennyworths and pound weights, and not have lost or thrown away a single ounce of them. In the one way, besides, this expense maintains productive, in the other unproductive hands. In the one way, therefore, it increases, in the other, it does not increase, the exchangeable value of the annual produce of the land and labour of the country.

I would not, however, by all this be understood to mean that the one species of expense always betokens a more liberal or generous spirit than the other. When a man of fortune spends his revenue chiefly in hospitality, he shares the greater part of it with his friends and companions; but when he employs it in purchasing such durable commodities, he often spends the whole upon his own person, and gives nothing to anybody without an equivalent. The latter species of expense, therefore, especially when directed towards frivolous objects, the little ornaments of dress and furniture, jewels, trinkets, gewgaws, frequently indicates, not only a trifling, but a base and selfish disposition. All that I mean is, that the one sort of expense, as it always occasions some accumulation of valuable commodities, as it is more favourable to private frugality, and, consequently, to the increase of the public capital, and as it maintains productive, rather than unproductive hands, conduces more than the other to the growth of public opulence.

II

THOMAS ROBERT MALTHUS

An Essay on the Principle of Population 1798

Thomas Robert Malthus was born near Dorking in 1766 and died at Claverton, near Bath, in 1835. His personal life was as tranquil as his writings were controversial. Keynes claimed Malthus as 'the first of the Cambridge economists'—he went up to Jesus College in 1784, and gained a fellowship there in 1793, which he held until his marriage in 1804. In this period he also held an Anglican curacy at Albury, succeeding to a Lincolnshire living in 1803; but in 1804 he became the holder of the earliest chair of political economy to be established in England. This, the Professorship of Modern History and Political Economy at the East India College at Haileybury, he held until his death.

In relation to classical political economy, Malthus was both a fundamental contributor and a fundamental critic. His theory of population, which was to become one of the cornerstones of the classical edifice, was first presented in 1798 in his *Essay on the Principle of Population, as it affects the future improvement of Society: with remarks on the speculations of Mr. Godwin, M. Condorcet and other writers*. In this first edition Malthus presented his thesis 'that the power of population is indefinitely greater than the power in the earth to produce subsistence for man', without the voluminous mass of supporting evidence or the qualifying allowance for 'prudential checks' which came to occupy so much space in the second edition of 1803 and later editions. In the chapters here reprinted from the 1798 edition the 'Malthusian doctrine', which has never since ceased to give rise to discussion and controversy, is presented in all its original stark clarity.

BIBLIOGRAPHY

The literature on Malthus's theory of population is vast in both quantity and range: the most complete listing of it is that in Keitaro Amano. *Bibliography of the Classical Economics, Part II, Malthus* (Science Council of Japan, Tokyo, 1961).

Among recent commentaries, some of the must useful are G. F. McCleary. *The Malthusian Population Theory* (London 1953); K. Smith. *The Malthusian Controversy* (London 1951); and J. Stassart. *Malthus et le Population* (Liége 1957).

In a somewhat different category is D. V. Glass. *Introduction to Malthus* (London 1953), which combines essays on 'The Historical Context of the Essay on Population' by H. L. Beales, 'Malthus and the Limitation of Population Growth' by D. V. Glass, and 'Malthus in the Twentieth Century' by A. T. Peacock, with reprints of two short works of Malthus and a bibliography of British writings on the population question from 1793 to 1880.

In view of the well known opposition of Marx and Marxists to the Malthusian theory of population, special interest attaches to R. L. Meek's book of selections, *Marx and Engels on Malthus* (London 1953).

By far the best biographical sketch of Malthus is Keynes's elegant essay 'Robert Malthus 1766–1835, the First of the Cambridge Economists', *Essays in Biography* (1951 ed), 81–124. A fuller treatment by a contemporary is contained in the biography which his friend Bishop Otter prefaced to the second edition of Malthus's *Principles of Political Economy*, published in 1836.

AN

ESSAY

ON THE

PRINCIPLE OF POPULATION.

CHAPTER I.

Question stated.—Little prospect of a determination of it, from the enmity of the opposing parties.—The principal argument against the perfectibility of man and of society has never been fairly answered.—Nature of the difficulty arising from population.—Outline of the principal argument of the essay.

THE great and unlooked for discoveries that have taken place of late years in natural philosophy; the increasing diffusion of general knowledge from the extension of the art of printing; the ardent and unshackled spirit of inquiry that prevails throughout the lettered, and even unlettered world; the new and extraordinary lights that have been thrown on political subjects, which dazzle, and astonish the understanding; and particularly that tremendous phenomenon in the political horizon the French revolution, which, like a blazing comet, seems destined either to inspire with fresh life and vigour, or to scorch up and destroy the shrinking inhabitants of the earth, have all concurred to lead many able men into the opinion, that we were touching on a period big with the most important changes, changes that would in some measure be decisive of the future fate of mankind.

It has been said, that the great question is now at issue, whether man shall henceforth start forwards with accelerated velocity towards illimitable, and hitherto unconceived improvement; or be condemned to a perpetual oscillation between happiness and misery, and after every effort remain still at an immeasurable distance from the wished-for goal.

Yet, anxiously as every friend of mankind must look forwards to the termination of this painful suspense; and, eagerly as the inquiring mind would hail every ray of light that might assist its view into futurity, it is much to be lamented, that the writers on each side of this momentous question still keep far aloof from each other. Their mutual arguments do not meet with a candid examination. The question is not brought to rest on fewer points; and even in theory scarcely seems to be approaching to a decision.

The advocate for the present order of things, is apt to treat the sect of speculative philosophers, either as a set of artful and designing knaves, who preach up ardent benevolence, and draw captivating pictures of a happier state of society, only the better to enable them to destroy the present establishments, and to forward their own deep-laid schemes of ambition: or, as wild and mad-headed enthusiasts, whose silly speculations, and absurd paradoxes, are not worthy the attention of any reasonable man.

The advocate for the perfectibility of man, and of society, retorts on the defender of establishments a more than equal contempt. He brands him as the slave of the most miserable, and narrow prejudices; or, as the defender of the abuses of civil society, only because he profits by them. He paints him either as a character who prostitutes his understanding to his interest; or as one whose powers of mind are not of a size to grasp any thing great and noble; who cannot see above five yards before him; and who must therefore be utterly unable to take in the views of the enlightened benefactor of mankind.

In this unamicable contest, the cause of truth cannot but suffer. The really good arguments on each side of the question are not allowed to have their proper weight. Each pursues his own theory, little solicitous to correct, or improve it, by an attention to what is advanced by his opponents.

The friend of the present order of things condemns all political speculations in the gross. He will not even condescend to examine the grounds from which the perfectibility of society is inferred. Much less will he give himself the trouble in a fair and candid manner to attempt an exposition of their fallacy.

The speculative philosopher equally offends against the cause of truth. With eyes fixed on a happier state of society, the blessings of which he paints in the most captivating colours, he allows himself to indulge in the most bitter invectives against every present establishment, without applying his talents to consider the best and safest means of removing abuses, and without seeming to be aware of the tremendous obstacles that threaten, even in theory, to oppose the progress of man towards perfection.

It is an acknowledged truth in philosophy, that a just theory will always be confirmed by experiment. Yet so much friction, and so many minute circumstances occur in practice, which it is next to impossible for the most enlarged and penetrating mind to foresee, that on few subjects can any theory be pronounced just, that has not stood the test of experience. But an untried theory cannot fairly be advanced as probable, much less as just, till all the arguments against it, have been maturely weighed, and clearly and consistently refuted.

I have read some of the speculations on the perfectibility of man and of society, with great pleasure. I have been warmed and delighted with the enchanting picture which they hold forth. I ardently wish for such happy improvements. But I see great, and, to my understanding, unconquerable difficulties in the way to them. These difficulties it is my present purpose to state; declaring, at the same time, that so far from exulting in them, as a cause of triumph over the friends of innovation, nothing would give me greater pleasure than to see them completely removed.

The most important argument that I shall adduce is certainly not new. The principles on which it depends have been explained in part by Hume, and more at large by Dr. Adam Smith. It has been advanced and applied to the present subject, though not with its proper weight, or in the most forcible point of view, by Mr. Wallace: and it may probably have been stated by many writers that I have never met with. I should certainly therefore not think of advancing it again, though I mean to

F

place it in a point of view in some degree different from any that I have hitherto seen, if it had ever been fairly and satisfactorily answered.

The cause of this neglect on the part of the advocates for the perfectibility of mankind, is not easily accounted for. I cannot doubt the talents of such men as Godwin and Condorcet. I am unwilling to doubt their candour. To my understanding, and probably to that of most others, the difficulty appears insurmountable. Yet these men of acknowledged ability and penetration, scarcely deign to notice it, and hold on their course in such speculations, with unabated ardour, and undiminished confidence. I have certainly no right to say that they purposely shut their eyes to such arguments. I ought rather to doubt the validity of them, when neglected by such men, however forcibly their truth may strike my own mind. Yet in this respect it must be acknowledged that we are all of us too prone to err. If I saw a glass of wine repeatedly presented to a man, and he took no notice of it, I should be apt to think that he was blind or uncivil. A juster philosophy might teach me rather to think that my eyes deceived me, and that the offer was not really what I conceived it to be.

In entering upon the argument I must premise that I put out of the question, at present, all mere conjectures; that is, all suppositions, the probable realization of which cannot be inferred upon any just philosophical grounds. A writer may tell me that he thinks man will ultimately become an ostrich. I cannot properly contradict him. But before he can expect to bring any reasonable person over to his opinion, he ought to shew, that the necks of mankind have been gradually elongating; that the lips have grown harder, and more prominent; that the legs and feet are daily altering their shape; and that the hair is beginning to change into stubs of feathers. And till the probability of so wonderful a conversion can be shewn, it is surely lost time and lost eloquence to expatiate on the happiness of man in such a state; to describe his powers, both of running and flying; to paint him in a condition where all narrow luxuries would be condemned; where he would be employed only in collecting the necessaries of life; and where, consequently, each man's share of labour would be light, and his portion of leisure ample.

I think I may fairly make two postulata.

First, That food is necessary to the existence of man.

Secondly, That the passion between the sexes is necessary, and will remain nearly in its present state.

These two laws ever since we have had any knowledge of mankind, appear to have been fixed laws of our nature; and, as we have not hitherto seen any alteration in them, we have no right to conclude that they will ever cease to be what they now are, without an immediate act of power in that Being who first arranged the system of the universe; and for the advantage of his creatures, still executes, according to fixed laws, all its various operations.

I do not know that any writer has supposed that on this earth man will ultimately be able to live without food. But Mr. Godwin has conjectured that the passion between the sexes may in time be extinguished. As, however, he calls this part of his work, a deviation into the land of conjecture, I will not dwell longer upon it at present, than to say, that the best arguments for the perfectibility of man, are drawn from a contemplation of the great progress that he has already made from the savage state, and the difficulty of saying where he is to stop. But towards the extinction of the passion between the sexes, no progress whatever has hitherto been made. It appears to exist in as much force at present as it did two thousand, or four thousand years ago. There are individual exceptions now as there always have been. But, as these exceptions do not appear to increase in number, it would surely be a very unphilosophical mode of arguing, to infer merely from the existence of an exception, that the exception would, in time, become the rule, and the rule the exception.

Assuming then, my postulata as granted, I say, that the power of population is indefinitely greater than the power in the earth to produce subsistence for man.

Population, when unchecked, increases in a geometrical ratio. Subsistence increases only in an arithmetical ratio. A slight acquaintance with numbers will shew the immensity of the first power in comparison of the second.

By that law of our nature which makes food necessary to the life of man, the effects of these two unequal powers must be kept equal.

This implies a strong and constantly operating check on population from the difficulty of subsistence. This difficulty must fall some where; and must necessarily be severely felt by a large portion of mankind.

Through the animal and vegetable kingdoms, nature has scattered the seeds of life abroad with the most profuse and liberal hand. She has been comparatively sparing in the room, and the nourishment necessary to rear them. The germs of existence contained in this spot of earth, with ample food, and ample room to expand in, would fill millions of worlds in the course of a few thousand years. Necessity, that imperious all pervading law of nature, restrains them within the prescribed bounds. The race of plants, and the race of animals shrink under this great restrictive law. And the race of man cannot, by any efforts of reason, escape from it. Among plants and animals its effects are waste of seed, sickness, and premature death. Among mankind, misery and vice. The former, misery, is an absolutely necessary consequence of it. Vice is a highly probable consequence, and we therefore see it abundantly prevail; but it ought not, perhaps, to be called an absolutely necessary consequence. The ordeal of virtue is to resist all temptation to evil.

This natural inequality of the two powers of population, and of production in the earth, and that great law of our nature which must constantly keep their effects equal, form the great difficulty that to me appears insurmountable in the way to the perfectibility of society. All other arguments are of slight and subordinate consideration in comparison of this. I see no way by which man can escape from the weight of this law which pervades all animated nature. No fancied equality, no agrarian regulations in their utmost extent, could remove the pressure of it even for a single century. And it appears, therefore, to be decisive against the possible existence of a society, all the members of which, should live in ease, happiness, and comparative leisure; and feel no anxiety about providing the means of subsistence for themselves and families.

Consequently, if the premises are just, the argument is conclusive against the perfectibility of the mass of mankind.

I have thus sketched the general outline of the argument; but I will examine it more particularly; and I think it will be found that experience, the true source and foundation of all knowledge, invariably confirms its truth.

CHAP. II.

The different ratios in which population and food increase.—The necessary effects of these different ratios of increase.—Oscillation produced by them in the condition of the lower classes of society.—Reasons why this oscillation has not been so much observed as might be expected.—Three propositions on which the general argument of the essay depends.—The different states in which mankind have been known to exist proposed to be examined with reference to these three propositions.

I SAID that population, when unchecked, increased in a geometrical ratio; and subsistence for man in an arithmetical ratio.

Let us examine whether this position be just.

I think it will be allowed, that no state has hitherto existed (at least that we have any account of) where the manners were so pure and simple, and the means of subsistence so abundant, that no check whatever has existed to early marriages; among the lower classes, from a fear of not providing well for their families; or among the higher classes, from a fear of lowering their condition in life. Consequently in no state that we have yet known, has the power of population been left to exert itself with perfect freedom.

Whether the law of marriage be instituted, or not, the dictate of nature and virtue, seems to be an early attachment to one woman. Supposing a liberty of changing in the case of an unfortunate choice, this liberty would not affect population till it arose to a height greatly vicious; and we are now supposing the existence of a society where vice is scarcely known.

In a state therefore of great equality and virtue, where pure and simple manners prevailed, and where the means of subsistence were so abundant, that no part of the society could have any fears about providing amply for a family, the power of population being left to exert itself unchecked, the increase of the human species would evidently be much greater than any increase that has been hitherto known.

In the United States of America, where the means of subsistence have been more ample, the manners of the people more pure, and consequently the checks to early marriages fewer, than in any of the modern states of Europe, the population has been found to double itself in twenty-five years.

This ratio of increase, though short of the utmost power of population, yet as the result of actual experience, we will take as our rule; and say,

That population, when unchecked, goes on doubling itself every twenty-five years, or increases in a geometrical ratio.

Let us now take any spot of earth, this Island for instance, and see in what ratio the subsistence it affords can be supposed to increase. We will begin with it under its present state of cultivation.

If I allow that by the best possible policy, by breaking up more land, and by great encouragements to agriculture, the produce of this Island may be doubled in the first twenty-five years, I think it will be allowing as much as any person can well demand.

In the next twenty-five years, it is impossible to suppose that the produce could be quadrupled. It would be contrary to all our knowledge of the qualities of land. The very utmost that we can conceive, is, that the increase in the second twenty-five years might equal the present produce. Let us then take this for our rule, though certainly far beyond the truth; and allow that by great exertion, the whole produce of the Island might be increased every twenty-five years, by a quantity of subsistence equal to what it at present produces. The most enthusiastic speculator cannot suppose a greater increase than this. In a few centuries it would make every acre of land in the Island like a garden.

Yet this ratio of increase is evidently arithmetical.

It may be fairly said, therefore, that the means of subsistence increase in an arithmetical ratio.

Let us now bring the effects of these two ratios together.

The population of the Island is computed to be about seven millions; and we will suppose the present produce equal to the support of such a number. In the first twenty-five years the population would be fourteen millions; and the food being also doubled, the means of subsistence would be equal to this increase. In the next twenty-five years the population would be twenty-eight millions; and the means of subsistence only equal to the support of twenty-one millions. In the next period, the population would be fifty-six millions, and the means of subsistence just sufficient for half that number. And at the conclusion of the first century, the population would be one hundred and twelve millions, and the means of subsistence only equal to the support of thirty-five millions; which would leave a population of seventy-seven millions totally unprovided for.

A great emigration necessarily implies unhappiness of some kind or other in the country that is deserted. For few persons will leave their families, connections, friends, and native land, to seek a settlement in untried foreign climes, without some strong subsisting causes of uneasiness where they are, or the hope of some great advantages in the place to which they are going.

But to make the argument more general, and less interrupted by the partial views of emigration, let us take the whole earth, instead of one spot, and suppose that the restraints to population were universally removed. If the subsistence for man that the earth affords was to be increased every twenty-five years by a quantity equal to what the whole world at present produces; this would allow the power of production in the earth to be absolutely unlimited, and its ratio of increase much greater than we can conceive that any possible exertions of mankind could make it.

Taking the population of the world at any number, a thousand millions, for instance, the human species would increase in the ratio of—1, 2, 4, 8, 16, 32, 64, 128, 256, 512, &c. and subsistence as—1, 2, 3, 4, 5, 6, 7, 8, 9, 10, &c. In two centuries and a quarter, the population would be to the means of subsistence as 512 to 10: in three centuries as 4096 to 13; and in two thousand years the difference would be almost incalculable, though the produce in that time would have increased to an immense extent.

No limits whatever are placed to the productions of the earth; they may increase for ever and be greater than any assignable quantity; yet still the power of population being a power of a superior order, the increase of the human species can only be kept commensurate to the increase of the means of subsistence, by the constant operation of the strong law of necessity acting as a check upon the greater power.

The effects of this check remain now to be considered.

Among plants and animals the view of the subject is simple. They are all impelled by a powerful instinct to the increase of their species; and this instinct is interrupted by no reasoning, or doubts about providing for their offspring. Wherever therefore there is liberty, the power of increase is exerted; and the superabundant effects are repressed afterwards by want of room and nourishment, which is common to animals, by becoming the prey of others.

The effects of this check on man are more complicated.

Impelled to the increase of his species by an equally powerful instinct, reason interrupts his career, and asks him whether he may not bring beings into the world, for whom he cannot provide the means of subsistence. In a state of equality, this would be the simple question. In the present state of society, other considerations occur. Will he not lower his rank in life? Will he not subject himself to greater difficulties than he at present feels? Will he not be obliged to labour harder? and if he has a large family, will his utmost exertions enable him to support them? May he not see his offspring in rags and misery, and clamouring for bread that he cannot give them? And may he not be reduced to the grating necessity of forfeiting his independence, and of being obliged to the sparing hand of charity for support?

These considerations are calculated to prevent, and certainly do prevent, a very great number in all civilized nations from pursuing the dictate of nature in an early attachment to one woman. And this restraint almost necessarily, though not absolutely so, produces vice. Yet in all societies, even those that are most vicious, the tendency to a virtuous attachment is so strong, that there is a constant effort towards an increase of population. This constant effort as constantly tends to subject the lower classes of the society to distress, and to prevent any great permanent amelioration of their condition.

The way in which these effects are produced seem to be this.

We will suppose the means of subsistence in any country just equal to the easy support of its inhabitants. The constant effort towards population, which is found to act even in the most vicious societies, increases the number of people before the means of subsistence are increased. The food therefore which before supported seven millions, must now be divided among seven millions and a half or eight millions. The poor consequently must live much worse, and many of them be reduced to severe distress. The number of labourers also being above the proportion of the work in the market, the price of labour must tend toward a decrease; while the price of provisions would at the same time tend to rise. The labourer therefore must work harder to earn the same as he did before. During this season of distress, the discouragements to marriage, and the difficulty of rearing a family are so great, that population is at a stand. In the mean time the cheapness of labour, the plenty of labourers, and the necessity of an increased industry amongst them, encourage cultivators to employ more labour upon their land; to turn up fresh soil, and to manure and improve more completely what is already in tillage; till ultimately the means of subsistence become in the same proportion to the population as at the period from which we set out. The situation of the labourer being then again tolerably comfortable, the restraints to population are in some degree loosened; and the same retrograde and progressive movements with respect to happiness are repeated.

This sort of oscillation will not be remarked by superficial observers; and it may be difficult even for the most penetrating mind to calculate its periods. Yet that in all old states some such vibration does exist; though from various transverse causes, in a much less marked, and in a much more irregular manner than I have described it, no reflecting man who considers the subject deeply can well doubt.

Many reasons occur why this oscillation has been less obvious, and less decidedly confirmed by experience, than might naturally be expected.

One principal reason is, that the histories of mankind that we possess, are histories only of the higher classes. We have but few accounts that can be depended upon of the manners and customs of that part of mankind, where these retrograde and progressive movements chiefly take place. A satisfactory history of this kind, of one people, and of one period, would require the constant and minute attention of an observing mind during a long life. Some of the objects of enquiry would be, in what proportion to the number of adults was the number of marriages: to what extent vicious customs prevailed in consequence of the restraints upon matrimony: what was the comparative mortality among the children of the most distressed part of the community, and those who lived rather more at their ease: what were the variations in the real price of labour: and what were the observable differences in the state of the lower classes of society, with respect to ease and happiness, at different times during a certain period.

Such a history would tend greatly to elucidate the manner in which the constant check upon population acts; and would probably prove the existence of the retrograde and progressive movements that have been mentioned; though the times of their vibration must necessarily be rendered irregular, from the operation of many interrupting causes; such as, the introduction or failure of certain manufactures: a greater or less prevalent spirit of agricultural enterprize: years of plenty, or years of scarcity: wars and pestilence: poor laws: the invention of processes for shortening labour without the proportional extension of the market for the commodity: and, particularly, the difference between the nominal and real price of labour; a circumstance, which has perhaps more than any other, contributed to conceal this oscillation from common view.

It very rarely happens that the nominal price of labour universally falls; but we well know that it frequently remains the same, while the nominal price of provisions has been gradually increasing. This is, in effect, a real fall in the price of labour; and during this period, the condition of the lower orders of the community must gradually grow worse and worse. But the farmers and capitalists are growing rich from the real cheapness of labour. Their increased capitals enable them to employ a greater number of men. Work therefore may be plentiful; and the price of labour would consequently rise. But the want of freedom in the market of labour, which occurs more or less in all communities, either from parish laws, or the more general cause of the facility of combination among the rich, and its difficulty among the poor, operates to prevent the price of labour from rising at the natural period, and keeps it down some time longer; perhaps, till a year of scarcity, when the clamour is too loud, and the necessity too apparent to be resisted.

The true cause of the advance in the price of labour is thus concealed; and the rich affect to grant it as an act of compassion and favour to the poor, in consideration of a year of scarcity; and when plenty returns, indulge themselves in the most unreasonable of all complaints, that the price does not again fall; when a little reflection would shew them, that it must have risen long before, but from an unjust conspiracy of their own.

But though the rich by unfair combinations, contribute frequently to prolong a season of distress among the poor; yet no possible form of society could prevent the almost constant action of misery, upon a great part of mankind, if in a state of inequality, and upon all, if all were equal.

The theory, on which the truth of this position depends, appears to me so extremely clear; that I feel at a loss to conjecture what part of it can be denied.

That population cannot increase without the means of subsistence, is a proposition so evident, that it needs no illustration.

That population does invariably increase, where there are the means of subsistence, the history of every people that have ever existed will abundantly prove.

And, that the superior power of population cannot be checked, without producing misery or vice, the ample portion of these too bitter ingredients in the cup of human life, and the continuance of the physical causes that seem to have produced them, bear too convincing a testimony.

But in order more fully to ascertain the validity of these three propositions, let us examine the different states in which mankind have been known to exist. Even a cursory review will, I think, be sufficient to convince us, that these propositions are incontrovertible truths.

HENRY THORNTON

An Enquiry into the Nature and Effects of the Paper Credit of Great Britain 1802

H enry Thornton's *Enquiry into the Nature and Effects of the Paper Credit of Great Britain* has come to be recognised as one of the outstanding works in the development of monetary theory, but its author was much more a man of affairs than a theorist. Born at Clapham in 1760, Thornton died in 1815 at Kensington Gore, in the house of his great friend and ally, William Wilberforce. Privately educated because of poor health, he entered his father's banking business in 1780, leaving in 1784 to become a partner in a merchant bank of his own. From 1783 until his death Thornton was Member of Parliament for Southwark and served on the 1804 Select Committee on the Irish currency and the famous Bullion Committee of 1810. His father had been the financial supporter of the first generation of Evangelicals and Thornton himself, along with Wilberforce, became one of the most prominent members of the group of humanitarians and evangelicals known as the 'Clapham Sect'.

In the famous Bullion Controversy of the early nineteenth century, Thornton appeared as a bullionist, identifying a fall in the exchange rate as the key test of over-issue of notes, and advocating a return to convertibility and the gold standard. Hence he has been identified as one of the architects of what, later in the century, became the accepted monetary orthodoxy; but it is now recognised that his work also included a remarkably prescient statement of the principles of short-run monetary management. In the words of J. A. Schumpeter (*History of Economic Analysis*, 689), 'no other performance of the period will bear comparison with it'.

BIBLIOGRAPHY

Thornton's *Paper Credit* was reprinted in 1939 in the 'Library of Economics', published by Allen and Unwin. The introduction to this reprint by Professor F. A. Hayek remains a principal source of reference for Thornton's economic work. The most recent specific treatment, adding much to Hayek's, is Sir John Hicks's 'Thornton's *Paper Credit*', No 10 in his *Critical Essays in Monetary Theory* (Oxford 1967).

For more general treatments of the relation of Thornton's work to that of his contemporaries and their times, see J. Viner. *Studies in the Theory of International Trade* (New York and London 1938), Chapters III and IV, 'The Bullionist Controversies'; and F. W. Fetter. *Development of British Monetary Orthodoxy 1797–1875* (Cambridge, Mass, 1965).

Until recently there has been no full biography of Henry Thornton, but the gap has now been effectively filled by Standish Meacham's *Henry Thornton of Clapham, 1760–1815* (Cambridge, Mass, 1964).

———

Chap. VIII.

Of the Tendency of a too great Issue of Bank Paper to produce an Excess of the Market Price above the Mint Price of Gold—Of the means by which it creates this Excess, namely, by its Operation on the Price of Goods and on the Course of Exchange—Errors of Dr. A. Smith on the Subject of excessive Paper—Of the Manner in which the Limitation of the Quantity of the Bank of England Paper serves to limit the Quantity and sustain the Value of all the Paper of the Kingdom.

A THIRD objection commonly made to country banks, is, the influence which their notes are supposed to have in raising the price of articles.

By the principles which shall be laid down in this Chapter, I propose to prove, that, though a general encrease of paper has this tendency, the objection, when applied to the paper of country banks, is particularly ill founded.

It will be necessary, in the discussion which is now about to take place, to join the consideration of two subjects, that of the influence which an enlarged emission of paper has in lifting up the price of commodities, and that of its influence, also, in producing an excess of the market price above the mint price of gold, and in thus exposing the bank to failure, and the country to considerable inconvenience. It is through the medium of the enhanced price of commodities that I conceive the ill effect on the mint price of gold to be brought about.

The discussion of these topics will best be introduced by a statement of the principle which regulates the value of all the articles of life.

The price of commodities in the market is formed by means of a certain struggle which takes place between the buyers and the sellers. It is commonly said, that the price of a thing is regulated by the proportion between the supply and the demand. This is, undoubtedly, true; and for the following reason. If the supply of an article or the demand for it is great, it is also known to be great; and if small, it is understood to be small. When, therefore, the supply, for example, is known to be less than the demand, the sellers judge that the buyers are in some degree at their mercy, and they insist on as favourable a price as their power over the buyers is likely to enable them to obtain. The price paid is not at all governed by the equity of the case, but entirely by the degree of command which the one party has over the other. When the demand is less than the supply, the buyers, in their turn, in some degree, command the market, giving not that sum which is calculated to indemnify the seller against loss, but so much only as they think that the seller will accept rather than not sell his article. The question of price is, therefore, in all cases, a question of power, and of power only. It is obvious, that a rise in the price of a scarce commodity will be more or less considerable in proportion as the article is felt to be one of more or less strict necessity.

The principle which has been laid down as governing the price of goods, must be considered as also regulating that of the paper for which they are sold; for it may as properly be said, on the occasion of a sale of goods, that paper is sold for goods, as that goods are sold for paper: thus the sale of a single commodity, as it is called, is a twofold transaction, though not commonly understood to be so: I mean that the price at which the exchange (or sale) takes place depends on two facts; on the proportion between the supply of the particular commodity and the demand for it, which is one question; and on the proportion, also, between the state of the general supply of the circulating medium and that of the demand for it, which is another.

Paper, moreover (of which I shall here speak as if it were the only circulating medium, it being the only one used in the larger payments), is, to some persons, somewhat in the same manner as bread is to all, an article of necessity. It is necessary to traders, partly because they have come under engagements to make payments which are only to be effected by means of their own previous receipts: and partly because they hold goods which must, within no long time, be sold for money, that is to say, for paper, since a continually growing loss accrues from the detention of them. Paper, therefore, must be bought by the trader: and if there is a difficulty in obtaining it, the buyer of it is brought under the power of the seller, and, in that case, more goods must be given for it.

Let us, now, trace carefully the steps by which an encrease of paper serves to lift up the price of articles. Let us suppose, for example, an encreased number of Bank of England notes to be issued. In such case the traders in the metropolis discover that there is a more than usual facility of obtaining notes at the bank by giving bills for them, and that they may, therefore, rely

on finding easy means of performing any pecuniary engagements into which they may enter. Every trader is encouraged,
by the knowledge of this facility of borrowing, a little to enlarge
his speculations; he is rendered, by the plenty of money, somewhat more ready to buy, and rather less eager to sell; he either
trusts that there will be a particular profit on the article which
is the object of his speculation, or else he judges, that, by extending his general purchases, he shall at least have his share of
the ordinary profit of commercial business, a profit which he
considers to be proportioned to the quantity of it. The opinion
of an encreased facility of effecting payments causes other
traders to become greater buyers for the same reason, and at
the same time. Thus an inclination to buy is created in all
quarters, and an indisposition to sell. Now, since the cost of
articles depends on the issue of that general conflict between
the buyers and sellers, which was spoken of, it follows, that any
circumstance which serves to communicate a greater degree
of eagerness to the mind of the one party than to that of the
other, will have an influence on price. It is not necessary to
suppose either a monopoly, or a combination, or the least un-
fairness, to exist, or even large and improper speculations. The
encrease in the eagerness of each buyer may be trifling. The
zeal to buy, being generally diffused, may, nevertheless, have a
sensible operation on price.

That, on the other hand, a reduction of the quantity of paper
causes a fall in the price of goods, is scarcely necessary to be
proved. It may be useful, however, in some degree, to illustrate
this point by facts. I understand, that at the time of the great
failure of paper credit in 1795, the price of corn fell, in a few
places, no less than twenty or thirty per cent. The fall arose
from the necessity of selling corn under which some farmers
were placed, in order to carry on their payments. Much of the
circulating medium being withdrawn, the demand for it was
in those places far greater than the supply; and the few persons,
therefore, who were in possession of cash, or of what would pass
as cash, having command of the market, obliged the farmers to

G

sell at a price thus greatly reduced. It was a new and sudden scarcity of cash, not any new plenty of corn, which caused the price of corn to drop.

It has been already observed, that some few days antecedently to the suspension of the cash payments of the bank, exchequer bills, as well as stocks, when sold for ready money, that is to say, for bank notes, fell in price. Not many days afterwards, although no material event had occurred except that of the stoppage of the bank, they rose. This fall and rise in the price of government securities evidently did not result from any corresponding fluctuation in the national confidence in them; for the fall took place when the national credit would naturally be the highest, namely, when the bank was as yet paying in cash, and the approaching stoppage was not known; and the rise happened when the national credit would be the lowest, namely, within a few days after that discouraging event. The reason of each of the fluctuations unquestionably was the fluctuation in the quantity of the Bank of England notes, which, as it has since appeared, were, during the day or two which preceded the suspension, about a million less than they were either a short time before or a short time afterwards. The notes being fewer during those few days, the price of them was, at the same time, higher. It was, in fact, therefore, the price of notes which rose, rather than that of stocks which fell, on the days immediately preceding the suspension; and it was the price of notes which a few days afterwards fell, rather than that of stocks which rose.[1]

[1] In the event of any great public alarm, such, for instance, as that which might be occasioned by the landing in this country of any considerable body of enemies, it is likely that the price of Bank of England notes, compared with that of stocks, or other articles for which there is a ready money market, would in like manner rise, even though the quantity of paper should continue the same: this would happen in consequence of that encreased demand for bank notes, to which it has been repeatedly observed that a state of consternation always gives occasion. Many bankers, at such a time, would feel a doubt whether they might not be drawn upon more largely than usual by some of their more timid customers; and whether, also, they might not be subjected to more than common difficulty in selling government securities,

I shall, for the present, consider the doctrine which has been laid down, as being sufficiently established, namely, that paper fluctuates in price on the same principles as any other article, its value rising as its quantity sinks, and *vice versâ*; or, in other words, that an augmentation of it has a general tendency to raise, and a diminished issue to lower, the nominal cost of commodities, although, partly for reasons which have been already touched upon, and partly for some which shall be hereafter given, an exact correspondence between the quantity of paper and the price of commodities can by no means be expected always to subsist.

The reader possibly may think that, in treating of this subject, I have been mistaking the effect for the cause, an encreased issue of paper being, in his estimation, merely a consequence which follows a rise in the price of goods, and not the circumstance which produces it. That an enlarged emission of paper may often fairly be considered as only, or chiefly, an effect of high prices, is not meant to be denied. It is, however, intended to insist, that, unquestionably, in some cases at least, the greater quantity of paper is, more properly speaking, the cause. A fuller explanation of this apparently difficult and dis-

an article which, in ordinary times, they are used to turn into cash on the shortest notice, and which, while a prompt sale of them is to be depended on, they prefer to bank notes, because an interest is gained by holding the one, and not by detaining the other.

During the short crisis of an invasion, the advantage of accruing interest would be little regarded, and each banker, therefore, would make an effort to exchange his exchequer bills, or perhaps, his stocks, for Bank of England notes, an effort which must prove generally ineffectual, supposing the quantity issued to be the same; but which, however, would have the effect of bringing down the comparative price of the article so eagerly offered in exchange for notes. Thus the price of government securities would appear to fall, when, in part at least, it would rather be the price of bank notes, which should be said to rise. Some encrease of the bank issues seems very justifiable at such a time; such an encrease, I mean, as should be sufficient only to prevent what may be termed an unnatural rise in the value of bank notes. This issue would be the means of preventing a misconception among the public respecting the degree of distrust in government securities entertained by the dealers in them, a circumstance which might be of some political importance in a moment of general consternation.

putable position will be given in the further progress of this Work.

I proceed, in the next place, to show in what manner a general rise in the cost of commodities, whether proceeding from an extravagant issue of paper, or from any other circumstance, contributes to produce an excess of the market price above the mint price of gold.

It is obvious, that, in proportion as goods are rendered dear in Great Britain, the foreigner becomes unwilling to buy them, the commodities of other countries which come into competition with our's obtaining a preference in the foreign market; and, therefore, that in consequence of a diminution of orders from abroad, our exports will be diminished; unless we assume, as we shall find it necessary to do, that some compensation in the exchange is given to the foreigner for the disadvantage attending the purchase of our articles. But not only will our exports lessen in the case supposed; our imports also will encrease; for the high British price of goods will tempt foreign commodities to come in nearly in the same degree in which it will discourage British articles from going out. I mean only, that these two effects (that of a diminished export, and that of an encreased import) will follow, provided that we suppose, what is not supposable, namely, that, at the time when the price of goods is greatly raised in Great Britain, the course of exchange suffers no alteration. For the following reason, I have said that this is not supposable. Under the circumstances which have been described of a diminished export, and an encreased import, the balance of trade must unavoidably turn against us; the consequence of which must be, that the drawers of bills on Great Britain in foreign countries will become more in number than the persons having occasion to remit bills. This disparity between the number of individuals wanting to draw, and of those wanting to remit, as was remarked in a former Chapter, must produce a fall in the price at which the overabundant bills on England sell in the foreign market. The fall in the selling price abroad of bills payable here, will operate as an advantage to the foreign buyer of our commodities in the computation of the exchangeable value of that circulating medium of his own country with which he discharges the debt in Britain contracted by his purchase. It will thus obviate the dearness of our articles: it will serve as a compensation to the foreigner for the loss which he would otherwise sustain by buying in our market. The fall of our exchange will, therefore, promote exportation and encourage importation. It will, in a great degree, prevent the high price of goods in Great Britain from producing that unfavourable balance of trade, which, for the sake of illustrating the subject, was supposed to exist.

The compensation thus made to the foreigner for the high British price of all articles is necessary as an inducement to him to take them, somewhat in the same manner as a drawback or bounty on exportation is the necessary inducement to take those particular goods which have been rendered too dear for the foreign market by taxes laid on them in this country. In each case the British consumer pays the high price, and the foreigner is spared, because otherwise he will not accept our commodities.

The fall in our exchange was just now defined to be an advantage gained in the computation of the exchangeable value of that foreign circulating medium with which the foreigner discharges his debt in Great Britain, a debt paid in the circulating medium of this country. It implies, therefore, a high valuation of his circulating medium, and a low valuation of our's; a low valuation, that is to say, both of our paper and of the coin which is interchanged with it.

Now, when coin is thus rendered cheap, it by no means follows that bullion is rendered cheap also. Coin is rendered cheap through its constituting a part of our circulating medium; but bullion does not constitute a part of it. Bullion is a commodity, and nothing but a commodity; and it rises and falls in value on the same principle as all other commodities. It becomes, like them, dear in proportion as the circulating medium for which it is exchanged is rendered cheap, and cheap in proportion as the circulating medium is rendered dear.

In the case, therefore, which has now been supposed, we are to consider coin as sinking below its proper and intrinsic worth, while bullion maintains its natural and accustomed price. Hence there arises that temptation, which was formerly noticed, either to convert back into bullion and then to export; or, which is the same thing to export and then convert back into bullion; or which is also the same thing, to convert back into bullion, and then sell to the bank, at the price which would be gained by exportation, that gold which the bank has purchased, and has converted from bullion into coin.

In this manner an encrease of paper, supposing it to be such as to raise the price of commodities in Britain above the price at which, unless there is some allowance afforded in the course of exchange, they will be received in foreign countries, contributes to produce an excess of the market price above the mint price of gold, and to prevent, therefore, the introduction of a proper supply of it into the Bank of England, as well as to draw out of its coffers, that coin which the directors of the bank would wish to keep in them.

Dr. Smith appears to me to have treated the important subject of the tendency of an excessive paper circulation to send gold out of a country, and thus to embarrass its banking establishments, in a manner which is particularly defective and unsatisfactory. It is true, that he blames the Bank of England for having contributed to bring on itself, during several successive years, a great expence in buying gold through a too great circulation of its paper; and that he also charges the Scotch banks with having had, through their excessive issues, a share in producing this evil. Thus, therefore, he seems to give to his reader some intimation of the tendency of an excessive issue of paper to create an excess of the market price above the mint price of gold.[1]

It appears, however, in some degree, from the passage in question, though much more clearly from other parts of his

[1] *Enquiry into the Nature and Causes of the Wealth of Nations*, vol. i. page 451, 4th edit. 8vo.

work, that he considers every permanent excess, whether of the market price above the mint price, or of the mint price above the market price of gold, as entirely referable to "something in the state of the coin."[1]

In one place he remarks, that a high price of bullion arises from the difference between the weight of our more light and that of our more heavy guineas; the value of the gold in the heavier guineas, as he represents the case, determining the general current value of both the lighter and the heavier pieces of coin; and the superior quantity of gold in the heavier guineas constituting, therefore, so much profit on the melting of those heavier pieces: a supposition manifestly erroneous, and contradicted by experience; for it implies that the excess of the market price above the mint price of gold both never is and never can be greater than the excess of the weight of the heavier above the lighter guineas; and, also, that the price of bullion cannot fluctuate while the state of our coinage remains in all respects the same. We have lately experienced fluctuations in our exchange, and correspondent variations in the market price, compared with the mint price of gold, amounting to no less than eight or ten per cent., the state of our coinage continuing, in all respects, the same.

Dr. Smith recommends a seignorage, as tending to raise the value both of the lighter and heavier coin; and thus, also, to diminish, if not destroy, the excess of the market price above the mint price of gold.[2]

---

[1] *Wealth of Nations*, vol i. page 69, 4th edit. 8vo. [cf. above, 33]

[2] "Were the private people who carry their gold and silver to the mint "to pay themselves for the coinage, it would add to the value of those "metals in the same manner as the fashion does to that of plate. Coined "gold and silver would be more valuable than uncoined. The seignorage, "if it was not exorbitant, would add to the bullion the whole value of the "duty, because the government having every where the exclusive privilege "of coining, no coin can come to market cheaper than they think proper to "afford it.

"A seignorage will, in many cases, take away altogether, and will in "all cases diminish, the profit of melting down the new coin. This profit "always arises from the difference between the quantity of bullion which

It is remarkable, that this Writer does not, in any degree, advert either to that more immediate cause (a fall of our exchanges), from which I have, in this as well as in a former Chapter, described the excess in question, as in all cases, arising; or to that more remote one on which I have lately dwelt, namely, a too high price of goods, which produces a fall of our exchanges.

"the common currency ought to contain, and that which it actually does "contain. If this difference is less than the seignorage, there will be loss "instead of profit. If it is equal to the seignorage, there will neither be "profit nor loss. If it is greater than the seignorage, there will, indeed, be "some profit; but less than if there were no seignorage."—*Wealth of Nations*, vol. ii. Book iv. Chap vi. pages 333, 334, and 335.

These observations, on the subject of a seignorage, seem erroneous in the following respects. Plate, when bought, is purchased in order not to be sold again, but to be retained by the possessor; and the price paid by the original buyer, may, therefore, be not unfairly considered, as it is by Dr. Smith, to be the current price of the article. Gold, on the contrary, is no sooner bought and coined, than it is sent into circulation; it is sold, that is to say (or exchanged for commodities), again and again. What we mean, therefore, by the current price of gold coin, is that price at which it passes, not in the original bargain for bullion between the seller of it, and the bank, but in the general course of this subsequent circulation. Guineas, moreover, not only circulate at home, but are liable to be sent abroad in the event of any unfavourable balance of trade. They are worth, in that case, just as much as the foreign country will give for them; and the foreign country, in estimating their value, since it means to melt them, does not at all take into its calculation the expense of the coinage of the piece of metal. It acts like a buyer not of new but of old plate, who destines it to the melting pot, and, therefore, refuses to allow any thing for "the fashion."

This foreign price of our coin principally determines the current value of the price of coin in England. It appears to me to do this in the following manner.

When the price which our coin will fetch in foreign countries is such as to tempt it out of the kingdom, the directors of the bank naturally diminish, in some degree, the quantity of their paper, through an anxiety for the safety of their establishment. By diminishing their paper they raise its value; and in raising its value, they raise also the value in England of the current coin which is exchanged for it. Thus the value of our gold coin conforms itself to the value of the current paper, and the current paper is rendered by the bank directors of that value which it is necessary that it should bear in order to prevent large exportations; a value sometimes rising a little above, and sometimes falling a little below, the price which our coin bears abroad; a price, in the formation of which no regard is had to the fashion.

Dr. Smith does not, in any of his observations on this subject, proceed sufficiently, as I conceive, on the practical principle of shewing how it is through the medium of prices (of the prices of goods in general, and of bullion in particular, compared with the price of the current circulating medium), that the operations of importing and exporting gold are brought about. He considers our coin as going abroad simply in consequence of our circulation at home being over full. Payment in coin, according to his doctrine is demanded of every bank for as much of its paper as is excessive, because the excessive paper can neither be sent abroad nor turned to any use at home; whereas, when it is changed into coin, the coin may be transmitted to a foreign part, and may there be advantageously employed.[1]

The reader will perceive, that, according to the principle which I have endeavoured to establish, coin does not merely leave the country because, the circulation being full, no use can be found at home for additional circulating medium; but that every encrease of paper has been represented as enhancing the price of goods, which advanced price of goods affords employment to a larger quantity of circulating medium, so that

A seignorage, nevertheless, might add to the current value of the coin of the kingdom for the following reason. It might incline the directors of the bank to improve the value of their paper by a stricter limitation of it, for the sake of more effectually exempting themselves from an occasional burthen, which is now borne for them by the government. The point *below* which they would wish to prevent their paper from falling would still be the same as it is now, namely, the selling price of our coin when melted and carried to foreign countries: the care, however, which they would take to prevent its falling below that price would, perhaps, be greater, and would be such as to raise its average price, if, in the event of each depression, they should be subject not only as they are now, to loss in the purchase of gold, but to a further loss in coining it. There seems no reason, however, to suppose, that the degree of fluctuation which is now apt to subsist between the market price and mint price of gold could, by any efforts of the bank, be materially lessened. It results from the fluctuations in the exchange; and those fluctuations, in general, proceed from variations in the markets of Europe, which affect the balance of trade, and cannot by any management of bank paper, be exactly counteracted.

[1] *Wealth of Nations*, vol. i. page 450.

the circulation can never be said to be over full. This advanced price of goods is the same thing as a reduced price of coin; the coin, therefore, in consequence of its reduced price, is carried out of the country for the sake of obtaining for it a better market. The heavier pieces, undoubtedly, will be preferred, if there is a facility of obtaining and transporting them; but the lighter guineas will also be exported, when the state of the exchange shall be sufficiently low to afford a profit on such a transaction. One of the consequences of Dr. Smith's mode of treating the subject, is, that the reader is led into the error of thinking, that when, through an excessive issue of paper, gold has been made to flow away from us, the expence of restoring it consists merely in the charge of collecting it and transporting it from the place to which it is gone. It follows, on the contrary, from the principles which I have laid down, that, in order to bring back gold, the expence not only of importing it may be to be incurred, but that also of purchasing it at a loss, and at a loss which may be either more or less considerable: a circumstance of great importance in the question. If this loss should ever become extremely great, the difficulties of restoring the value of our paper might not easily be surmounted, and a current discount or difference between the coin and paper of the country would scarcely be avoidable.

Dr. Smith, indeed, represents the expence of bringing back gold as considerable; but he seems to impute the greatness of it to the circumstance of its recurring again and again: and he describes it as continuing to recur in the case of each individual bank, whether in town or country, which persists in the false policy of issuing more paper than is sufficient to fill the circulation of the neighbouring district. I shall here take occasion to notice some great inaccuracies in one part of his reasoning upon this point.

He says—"A banking company which issues more paper "than can be employed in the circulation of the country, and "of which the excess is continually returning upon them for "payment, ought to encrease the quantity of gold and silver

"which they keep at all times in their coffers, not only in propor-
"tion to this excess, but to a much greater proportion. Suppose,
"for instance, all the paper of a particular bank, which the
"circulation of the country can easily absorb, amounts to forty
"thousand pounds, and the bank keeps usually ten thousand
"pounds in gold and silver for its occasional demands. If this
"bank should attempt to circulate forty-four thousand pounds,
"the excess of four thousand pounds will return as fast as it is
"issued. Fourteen thousand pounds must then be kept instead
"of ten thousand pounds, and the bank will gain nothing by
"the excessive circulation. On the contrary, it will lose the
"whole expence of continually collecting four thousand pounds
"in gold and silver, which will be continually going out of its
"coffers as fast as they are brought in."

He then adds—"Had every particular bank always under-
"stood and attended to its own interest, the circulation would
"never have been overstocked with paper money."

There is, no doubt, some sort of ground for saying that an
excess of paper will come back upon the banks which issue it,
and that, in coming back, it will involve the issuing banks in
expence. Much exception, however, might be taken against Dr.
Smith's mode of estimating the expence which the quantity
which would come back would bring upon the issuing banks.
But the objection which I shall, in the first place, urge against
the remark of Dr. Smith, is, that, even granting it to be just, it
can be just only in a case which can scarcely ever occur among
the country banks of this kingdom. I mean, that it can apply
solely to the case of a single bank of which the paper circulates
exclusively through a surrounding district: it obviously cannot
hold in the case of many banks, the paper of all of which circulates in the same district.

In order to explain this clearly, let us make the following
supposition. Let us imagine the circulation of country bank
paper which a certain district will bear to be one hundred
thousand pounds, and ten banks to be in that district, each
usually circulating and able to keep in circulation ten thousand

pounds. Let us also suppose an excessive issue of four thousand
pounds, and let us allow the effect of this on the ten banks
to be that which Dr. Smith describes, a point which might
certainly be disputed, namely, that a necessity will arise for
always keeping (for this is what Dr. Smith's language implies)
an additional stock of gold amounting to exactly four thousand
pounds, and also that a reiterated expence will be incurred (Dr.
Smith does not say how frequently reiterated) in collecting and
transporting these four thousand pounds of gold. Still it must
be observed, that we may suppose the issue of the four thousand pounds excessive paper to be made by some one only of
the ten banks, while the charge incurred by such issue may be
divided among them all. It may, therefore, on Dr. Smith's own
principles, answer to one of several banks emitting paper which
circulates in the same place, to issue the paper which is considered by him as excessive; and the practice of doing so may be
owing to the country banker's too well knowing his own interest, and not, as Dr. Smith supposes, to his too ill understanding it.

But the case which I have supposed has been put merely by
way of illustration. When many banks issue notes circulating
over the same district, it is impossible to say whose paper constitutes the excess. Whatever temptation to excess exists, must
be a general one. It is, however, counteracted not only by the
charge of transporting gold on which alone Dr. Smith dwells,
but likewise by all the other charges, as well as by all the risks
to which country bank notes subject the issuers; not to mention the difficulty of finding a channel through which a quantity
of paper much larger than common can be sent by the country
bank into circulation.

Dr. Smith supposes, in the passage which has just been
quoted, that, when there is an excessive circulation of country
bank paper, the excess returns upon the banks to be exchanged
for gold and silver. The fact is, that it returns to be exchanged
not for gold and silver only, but either for gold and silver, or
for bills on London. A bill on London is an order to receive in

London, after a certain interval, either gold or Bank of England notes. This order imposes on the country banker the task of providing a fund in London sufficient to answer his draft; it serves, however, to spare that expence of transporting gold, as well as to lessen that necessity of maintaining a stock of guineas, which Dr. Smith assumes to be the consequence of every excessive emission of notes, and to be the certain means, if bankers do but understand their interest, of limiting their issue.

The remark which has just been made derives particular importance from the circumstances of the period through which we have passed. For, if the usual means of preventing an excess of country bank notes were nothing else than the liability of the issuers to be called upon for a money payment of them, it might be fairly assumed, that, at a time when the money payment of them has been suspended, we must necessarily have been exposed to the greatest inundation of country paper, and to a proportionate depreciation of it. The unbounded issue of country bank notes has been restrained by the obligation under which country bankers have considered themselves to be of granting bills on London; that is to say, orders to receive in London Bank of England paper in exchange for their notes, if required to do so: and it is certain that they would be required to do so whenever the quantity of their notes should be much greater in proportion to the occasion for them, than the quantity of the notes of the Bank of England in proportion to the occasion for those notes.

For the sake of explaining this, let it be admitted, for a moment, that a country bank has issued a very extraordinary quantity of notes. We must assume these to be employed by the holders of them in making purchases in the place in which alone the country bank paper passes, namely, in the surrounding district. The effect of such purchases, according to the principles established in this Chapter, must be a great local rise in the price of articles. But to suppose a great and merely local rise, is to suppose that which can never happen or which, at least, cannot long continue to exist; for every purchaser will discover that he can buy commodities elsewhere at a cheaper rate; and he will not fail to procure them in the quarter in which they are cheap, and to transport them to the spot in which they are dear, for the sake of the profit on the transaction. In order that he may be enabled to do this, he will demand to have the notes which pass current in the place in which we have supposed goods to have been rendered dear by the extraordinary emission of paper, converted into the circulating medium of the place in which goods are cheap: he will, therefore, require to have his country bank note turned into a Bank of England note, or into a bill on London, which is nearly the same thing, provided Bank of England notes are fewer in proportion to the occasion for them than the country bank notes; that is to say, provided Bank of England notes have less lifted up the price of goods in London than country bank notes have lifted up the price of goods in the country.

This point may be still more fully illustrated in the following manner. Let us imagine a mercantile house to consist of two branches, the one placed in the metropolis, the other in the country, and each branch to be accustomed to make certain payments in the spot in which it is situated, each, however, to be in the habit of borrowing as largely as it is able, the one of a neighbouring country bank, the other of the Bank of England, and of applying these loans to the joint use of the trading concern. Let us next suppose an extraordinary facility of borrowing at the country bank to arise, while the opportunities of obtaining loans at the Bank of England remain the same.[1] In such

[1] The case here put is assumed to exist only by way of argument. The point intended to be shewn, is, that the case cannot happen; or, at least, that such cannot be the case, at the same time, of all the country banks in the kingdom. A single individual, it is true, may find his means of borrowing at a particular country bank to encrease in the manner which is here supposed; for he may obtain a preference over other borrowers. A single bank, also, may find its means of lending to encrease; for its notes may usurp the place of those of other banks. There can, however, be no material enlargement on the whole of the paper of the country, while the facility of borrowing in London remains the same.

case the mercantile house, provided its London payments continue to bear the same proportion as before to its country payments, which will hardly fail to be the case, will exchange some
part of its encreased loans in the country, consisting in country
bank notes, for bills on London, or, in other words, for Bank of
England notes. It will thus adjust, with the greatest nicety, the
quantity of London and of country paper to the amount of
the pecuniary demands upon it in each quarter; and, in doing
so, it will contribute to prevent the supply of notes in either
place from becoming greater in proportion to the demand than
in the other. What has been supposed of one house, may be
supposed of many similar ones; and not only of houses of the
particular description which has been spoken of, but also of the
several independent establishments in the two distant places
which have pecuniary transactions together, and have an interest in accommodating each other. Their general operations,
of a pecuniary kind, must be such as always to check a local
rise in the price of commodities in either place, while it is as
yet so small as to be scarcely perceptible. In this manner,
therefore, the exchangeableness of country paper for London
paper will never fail very nearly to equalize the value of them
both. It is, moreover, important clearly to point out that their
value will be equalized, or nearly equalized, not by a tendency
in the London paper to partake in a low value which the country
paper has acquired in consequence of its not being limited by
any voluntary act of the issuers; nor by a tendency in each to
approximate in value to the other; but by a tendency in the
country paper to take exactly the high value which the London
paper bears in consequence of its being restricted by the issuers.
That this must be the case is plain, from the remark which has
just been made; for it has been shewn, that the country paper,
however it may fail to be limited in quantity by any moderation
or prudence of the issuers, becomes no less effectually limited
through the circumstance of their being compelled by the
holders to exchange as much of it as is excessive for the London
paper which is limited; which is limited, I mean, in consequence

of a principle of limitation which the directors of the Bank of England have prescribed to themselves.

The country paper, let it then be observed, does not add any thing to the quantity of the London paper; for the effectual limitation of the London paper is the great point, which it must be borne in mind, that we have assumed. The country paper, therefore, does not in any degree diminish the price of the London paper; for its price must remain fixed so long as its quantity continues fixed, supposing, as we do in our present argument, that the demand for it is the same. It has been proved, however, that the country paper is rendered, by its exchangeableness with the London paper, almost exactly equal to it in value. It is, then, rendered almost exactly equal in value to a paper of which the value is completely sustained. Thus, therefore, the limitation of the supply of the single article of London paper, of which, however, we are taking for granted that the demand continues the same, is the means both of sustaining the value of London paper, and also of sustaining the value as well as limiting the quantity of the whole paper of the country.

It is, however, necessary here to point out to the reader, that, in the immediately preceding observations, we have assumed certain facts to exist, for the sake of stating clearly a general principle. It will be the object of a succeeding Chapter to shew in what respects the case which has been supposed differs from the actual one.

JEAN-BAPTISTE SAY

A Treatise on Political Economy 1803

Jean-Baptiste Say became perhaps the best known French economist of the nineteenth century. He was born at Lyons in 1767, died at Paris in 1832, and was the head of a whole family of economists—his brother Louis, his son Horace and his grandson Léon all gained some reputation as writers on political economy.

Napoleon Bonaparte appointed J.-B. Say a member of the Tribunat in 1799, but when Say refused to support Napoleon's fiscal policy in his *Traité d'Économie Politique* in 1803 he was relieved of his office. For some years after this Say engaged in business, becoming a substantial cotton manufacturer, but after the fall of the Empire in 1815, he returned to Paris and offered the first formal course of lectures on political economy to be given in France. In 1819 he was given a chair at the Conservatoire des Arts et Métiers and became Professor at the Collège de France in 1830.

A believer in natural law and *laissez faire*, Say was the founder of the optimistic liberal school of economics in France. Unlike his classical contemporaries in Britain he based his explanation of value mainly on utility. Much that afterwards became widely accepted in economic thinking derived originally from Say— such as the division of political economy into the branches of production, distribution and consumption, and the concept of the *entrepreneur*; but his most important contribution by far was his Law of Markets, which gave rise to controversy in his own time, and has continued to do so at the present day. Many students of economics have talked glibly of 'Say's Law' without having read what Say himself wrote on the subject in Chapter XV of his *Traité d'Économie Politique*, here reproduced from the English translation of 1821 by C. R. Prinsep.

BIBLIOGRAPHY

The best account of the orthodox classical position on the 'Law of Markets' is that given by J. S. Mill in his essay 'On the Influence of Consumption Upon Production', *Essays on Some Unsettled Questions of Political Economy* (1844, reprinted 1948) 47–74. For a statement on the opposing view, see the extract from Malthus's *Principles of Political Economy* given on pp 203–20.

For the modern discussion and reinterpretation of Say's Law, the fundamental sources are G. S. Becker and W. J. Baumol. 'The Classical Monetary Theory: the outcome of the discussion', *Economica*, XIX (1952), 355–76; and D. Patinkin. *Money, Interest and Prices* (2nd edition, New York 1965).

More general surveys are numerous. Among the best are M. Blaug. *Economic Theory in Retrospect* (2nd edition, London 1968), Chapter 5: 'Say's Law and Classical Monetary Theory'; W. J. Fellner. *Emergence and Content of Modern Economic Analysis* (New York 1960), Chapter 8: 'Say's Law and the Question of Full Employment'; and J. A. Schumpeter. *History of Economic Analysis* (New York 1954), Part III, Chapter 6, Section 4: 'Say's Law of Markets'.

For a more comprehensive study of the work of Say, reference may be made to E. Teilhac, *L'Oeuvre Économique de J.-B. Say* (Paris 1927).

Book I

CHAPTER XV.

OF THE DEMAND OR MARKET FOR PRODUCTS.

It is common to hear adventurers in the different channels of industry assert, that their difficulty lies not in the production, but in the disposal of commodities; that products would always be abundant, if there were but a ready demand, or market for them. When the demand for their commodities is slow, difficult, and productive of little advantage, they pronounce money to be scarce; the grand object of their desire is, a consumption brisk enough to quicken sales and keep up prices. But ask them what peculiar causes and circumstances facilitate the demand for their products, and you will soon perceive that most of them have extremely vague notions of these matters; that their observation of facts is imperfect, and their explanation still more so; that they treat doubtful points as matter of certainty, often pray for what is directly opposite to their interests, and importunately solicit from authority a protection of the most mischievous tendency.

To enable us to form clear and correct practical notions in regard to markets for the products of industry, we must carefully analyse the best established and most certain facts, and apply to them the inferences we have already deduced from a similar way of proceeding; and thus perhaps we may arrive at new and important truths, that may serve to enlighten the views of the agents of industry, and to give confidence to the measures of governments anxious to afford them encouragement.

A man who applies his labour to the investing of objects with value by the creation of utility of some sort, can not expect such a value to be appreciated and paid for, unless where other men have the means of purchasing it. Now, of what do these means consist? Of other values of other products, likewise the fruits of industry, capital, and land. Which leads us to a conclusion that may at first sight appear paradoxical, namely, that it is production which opens a demand for products.

Should a tradesman say, "I do not want other products for my woollens, I want money," there could be little difficulty in convincing him that his customers could not pay him in money, without having first procured it by the sale of some other commodities of their own. "Yonder farmer," he may be told, "will buy your woollens, if his crops be good, and will buy more or less according to their abundance or scantiness; he can buy none at all, if his crops fail altogether. Neither can you buy his wool nor his corn yourself, unless you contrive to get woollens or some other article to buy withal. You say, you only want money; I say, you want other commodities, and not money. For what, in point of fact, do you want the money? Is it not for the purchase of raw materials or stock for your trade, or victuals for your support?[1] Wherefore, it is products that you want, and not money. The silver coin you will have received on the sale of your own products, and given in the purchase of those of other people, will the next moment execute the same office between other contracting parties, and so from one to another to infinity; just as a public vehicle successively transports objects one after another. If you can not find a ready sale for your commodity, will you say, it is merely for want of a vehicle to transport it? For, after all, money is but the agent of the transfer of values. Its whole utility has consisted in conveying to your hands the value of the commodities, which your customer has sold, for the purpose of buying again from you; and the very next purchase you make, it will again convey to a third person the value of the products you may have sold to others. So that you will have bought, and every body must buy, the objects of want or desire, each with the value of his respec-

[1] Even when money is obtained with a view to hoard or bury it, the ultimate object is always to employ it in a purchase of some kind. The heir of the lucky finder uses it in that way, if the miser do not; for money, as money, has no other use than to buy with.

tive products transformed into money for the moment only.
Otherwise, how could it be possible that there should now be
bought and sold in France five or six times as many commodities, as in the miserable reign of Charles VI.? Is it not obvious,
that five or six times as many commodities must have been
produced, and that they must have served to purchase one or
the other?"

Thus, to say that sales are dull, owing to the scarcity of money,
is to mistake the means for the cause; an error that proceeds
from the circumstance, that almost all produce is in the first
instance exchanged for money, before it is ultimately converted
into other produce: and the commodity, which recurs so repeatedly in use, appears to vulgar apprehensions the most important of commodities, and the end and object of all transactions, whereas it is only the medium. Sales cannot be said to be
dull because money is scarce, but because other products are so.
There is always money enough to conduct the circulation and
mutual interchange of other values, when those values really
exist. Should the increase of traffic require more money to
facilitate it, the want is easily supplied, and is a strong indication of prosperity—a proof that a great abundance of values
has been created, which it is wished to exchange for other
values. In such cases, merchants know well enough how to find
substitutes for the product serving as the medium of exchange
or money:[1] and money itself soon pours in, for this reason, that
all produce naturally gravitates to that place where it is most
in demand. It is a good sign when the business is too great for
the money; just in the same way as it is a good sign when the
goods are too plentiful for the warehouses.

When a superabundant article can find no vent, the scarcity
of money has so little to do with the obstruction of its sale, that
the sellers would gladly receive its value in goods for their own
consumption at the current price of the day: they would not
ask for money, or have any occasion for that product, since the

---

[1] By bills at sight, or after date, bank-notes, running-credits, write-offs,
&c. as at London and Amsterdam.

only use they could make of it would be to convert it forthwith into articles of their own consumption.[1]

This observation is applicable to all cases, where there is a supply of commodities or of services in the market. They will universally find the most extensive demand in those places, where the most of values are produced; because in no other places are the sole means of purchase created, that is, values. Money performs but a momentary function in this double exchange; and when the transaction is finally closed, it will always be found, that one kind of commodity has been exchanged for another.

It is worth while to remark, that a product is no sooner created, than it, from that instant, affords a market for other products to the full extent of its own value. When the producer has put the finishing hand to his product, he is most anxious to sell it immediately, lest its value should diminish in his hands. Nor is he less anxious to dispose of the money he may get for it; for the value of money is also perishable. But the only way of getting rid of money is in the purchase of some product or other. Thus, the mere circumstance of the creation of one product immediately opens a vent for other products.

For this reason, a good harvest is favourable, not only to the agriculturist, but likewise to the dealers in all commodities generally. The greater the crop, the larger are the purchases of the growers. A bad harvest, on the contrary, hurts the sale of commodities at large. And so it is also with the products of manufacture and commerce. The success of one branch of commerce supplies more ample means of purchase, and consequently opens a market for the products of all the other branches; on the other hand, the stagnation

---

[1] I speak here of their aggregate consumption, whether unproductive and designed to satisfy the personal wants of themselves and their families, or expended in the sustenance of reproductive industry. The woollen or cotton manufacturer operates a two-fold consumption of wool and cotton: 1. For his personal wear. 2. For the supply of his manufacture; but, be the purpose of his consumption what it may, whether personal gratification or reproduction, he must needs buy what he consumes with what he produces.

of one channel of manufacture, or of commerce, is felt in all the rest.

But it may be asked, if this be so, how does it happen, that there is at times so great a glut of commodities in the market, and so much difficulty in finding a vent for them. Why cannot one of these superabundant commodities be exchanged for another? I answer that the glut of a particular commodity arises from its having outrun the total demand for it in one of two ways; either because it has been produced in excessive abundance, or because the production of other commodities has fallen short.

It is because the production of some commodities has declined, that other commodities are superabundant. To use a more hackneyed phrase, people have bought less, because they have made less profit:[1] and they have made less profit for one of two causes; either they have found difficulties in the employment of their productive means, or these means have themselves been deficient.

It is observable, moreover, that precisely at the same time that one commodity makes a loss, another commodity is making excessive profit.[2] And, since such profits must operate as a powerful stimulus to the cultivation of that particular kind of products, there must needs be some violent means, or some extraordinary cause, a political or natural convulsion, or the avarice or ignorance of authority, to perpetuate this scarcity on the one hand, and consequent glut on the other. No sooner is the cause of this political disease removed, than the means of production feel a natural impulse towards the vacant channels,

[1] Individual profits must, in every description of production, from the general merchant to the common artisan, be derived from the participation in the values produced. The ratio of that participation will form the subject of Book II., *infrà*.

[2] The reader may easily apply these maxims to any time or country he is acquainted with. We have had a striking instance in France during the years 1811, 1812, and 1813; when the high prices of colonial produce of wheat, and other articles, went hand-in-hand with the low price of many others that could find no advantageous market.

the replenishment of which restores activity to all the others. One kind of production would seldom outstrip every other, and its products be disproportionately cheapened, were production left entirely free.[1]

[1] These considerations have hitherto been almost wholly overlooked, though forming the basis of correct conclusions in matters of commerce, and of its regulation by the national authority. The right course where it has, by good luck been pursued, appears to have been selected by accident, or, at most, by a confused idea of its propriety, without either self-conviction, or the ability to convince other people.

Sismondi, who seems not to have very well understood the principles laid down in this and the three first chapters of Book II. of this work, instances the immense quantity of manufactured products with which England has of late inundated the markets of other nations, as a proof, that it is impossible for industry to be too productive. (Nouv. Prin. liv. iv. c. 4.) But the glut thus occasioned proves nothing more than the feebleness of production in those countries that have been thus glutted with English manufactures. Did Brazil produce wherewithal to purchase the English goods exported thither, those goods would not glut her market. Were England to admit the import of the products of the United States, she would find a better market for her own in those States. The English government, by the exorbitance of its taxation upon import and consumption, virtually interdicts to its subjects many kinds of importation, thus obliging the merchant to offer to foreign countries a higher price for those articles, whose import is practicable, as sugar, coffee, gold, silver, &c. for the price of the precious metals to them is enhanced by the low price of their commodities, which accounts for the ruinous returns of their commerce.

I would not be understood to maintain in this chapter, that one product can not be raised in too great abundance, in relation to all others; but merely that nothing is more favourable to the demand of one product, than the supply of another; that the import of English manufactures into Brazil would cease to be excessive and be rapidly absorbed, did Brazil produce on her side returns sufficiently ample; to which end it would be necessary that the legislative bodies of either country should consent, the one to free production, the other to free importation. In Brazil every thing is grasped by monopoly, and property is not exempt from the invasion of the government. In England, the heavy duties are a serious obstruction to the foreign commerce of the nation, inasmuch as they circumscribe the choice of returns. I happen myself to know of a most valuable and scientific collection of natural history, which could not be imported from Brazil into England by reason of the exorbitant duties.*

* The views of Sismondi, in this particular, have been since adopted by our own Malthus, and those of our author by Ricardo. This difference of opinion has given rise to an interesting discussion between our author and Malthus, to whom he has recently addressed a correspondence on this and

Should a producer imagine, that many other classes, yielding no material products, are his customers and consumers equally with the classes that raise themselves a product of their own; as, for example, public functionaries, physicians, lawyers, churchmen, &c., and thence infer, that there is a class of demand other than that of the actual producers, he would but expose the shallowness and superficiality of his ideas. A priest goes to a shop to buy a gown or a surplice; he takes the value, that is to make the purchase, in the form of money. Whence had he that money? From some tax-gatherer who has taken it from a tax-payer. But whence did this latter derive it? From the value he has himself produced. This value, first produced by the tax-payer, and afterwards turned into money, and given to the priest for his salary, has enabled him to make the purchase. The priest stands in the place of the producer, who might himself have laid the value of his product on his own account, in the purchase, perhaps, not of a gown or surplice, but of some other more serviceable product. The consumption of the particular product, the gown or surplice, has but supplanted that of some other product. It is quite impossible that the purchase of one product can be affected, otherwise than by the value of another.[1]

From this important truth may be deduced the following important conclusions:—

1. That, in every community the more numerous are the producers, and the more various their productions, the more

other parts of the science. Were any thing wanting to confirm the arguments of this chapter, it would be supplied by a reference to his *Lettre* 1, *à M. Malthus*. *Sismondi* has vainly attempted to answer Ricardo, but has made no mention of his original antagonist. *Vide Annales de Legislation*, No. 1. art. 3. Geneve, 1820. [*Translator*]

[1] The capitalist, in spending the interest of his capital, spends his portion of the products raised by the employment of that capital. The general rules that regulate the ratio he receives will be investigated in Book II., *infrà*. Should he ever spend the principal, still he consumes products only; for capital consists of products, devoted indeed to reproductive, but susceptible of unproductive consumption; to which it is in fact consigned whenever it is wasted or dilapidated.

prompt, numerous, and extensive are the markets for those
productions; and, by a natural consequence, the more profitable
are they to the producers; for price rises with the demand. But
this advantage is to be derived from real production alone,
and not from a forced circulation of products; for a value once
created is not augmented in its passage from one hand to
another, nor by being seized and expended by the government,
instead of by an individual. The man, that lives upon the productions of other people, originates no demand for those productions; he merely puts himself in the place of the producer,
to the great injury of production, as we shall presently see.

2. That each individual is interested in the general prosperity
of all, and that the success of one branch of industry promotes
that of all the others. In fact, whatever profession or line of
business a man may devote himself to, he is the better paid and
the more readily finds employment, in proportion as he sees
others thriving equally around him. A man of talent, that
scarcely vegetates in a retrograde state of society, would find a
thousand ways of turning his faculties to account in a thriving
community that could afford to employ and reward his ability.
A merchant established in a rich and populous town, sells to
a much larger amount than one who sets up in a poor district,
with a population sunk in indolence and apathy. What could
an active manufacturer, or an intelligent merchant, do in a
small deserted and semi-barbarous town in a remote corner of
Poland or Westphalia? Though in no fear of a competitor, he
could sell but little, because little was produced; whilst at
Paris, Amsterdam, or London, in spite of the competition of a
hundred dealers in his own line, he might do business on the
largest scale. The reason is obvious: he is surrounded with
people who produce largely in an infinity of ways, and who
make purchases, each with his respective products, that is to
say, with the money arising from the sale of what he may have
produced.

This is the true source of the gains made by the towns'
people out of the country people, and again by the latter out of

the former; both of them have wherewith to buy more largely, the more amply they themselves produce. A city, standing in the centre of a rich surrounding country, feels no want of rich and numerous customers, and, on the other hand, the vicinity of an opulent city gives additional value to the produce of the country. The division of nations into agricultural, manufacturing, and commercial, is idle enough. For the success of a people in agriculture is a stimulus to its manufacturing and commercial prosperity; and the flourishing condition of its manufacture and commerce reflects a benefit upon its agriculture also.[1]

The position of a nation, in respect of its neighbours, is analogous to the relation of one of its provinces to the others, or of the country to the town; it has an interest in their prosperity, being sure to profit by their opulence. The government of the United States, therefore, acted most wisely, in their attempt, about the year 1802, to civilize their savage neighbours, the Creek Indians. The design was to introduce habits of industry amongst them, and make them producers capable of carrying on a barter trade with the States of the Union; for there is nothing to be got by dealing with a people that have nothing to pay. It is useful and honourable to mankind, that one nation among so many should conduct itself uniformly upon liberal principles. The brilliant results of this enlightened policy will demonstrate, that the systems and theories really destructive and fallacious, are the exclusive and jealous maxims

[1] A productive establishment on a large scale is sure to animate the industry of the whole neighbourhood. "In Mexico," says Humboldt, "the best cultivated tract, and that which brings to the recollection of the traveller the most beautiful part of French scenery, is the level country extending from Salamanca as far as Silao, Guanaxuato, and Villa de Leon, and encircling the richest mines of the known world. Wherever the veins of precious metal have been discovered and worked, even in the most desert part of the Cordilleras, and in the most barren and insulated spots, the working of the mines, instead of interrupting the business of superficial cultivation, has given it more than usual activity. The opening of a considerable vein is sure to be followed by the immediate erection of a town; farming concerns are established in the vicinity; and the spot so lately insulated in the midst of wild and desert mountains, is soon brought into contact with the tracts before in tillage." *Essai pol. sur. la Nouv. Espagne.*

acted upon by the old European governments, and by them most impudently styled *practical truths*, for no other reason, as it would seem, than because they have the misfortune to put them in practice. The United States will have the honour of proving experimentally, that true policy goes hand-in-hand with moderation and humanity.[1]

3. From this fruitful principle, we may draw this further conclusion, that it is no injury to the internal or national industry and production to buy and import commodities from abroad; for nothing can be bought from strangers, except with native products, which find a vent in this external traffic. Should it be objected, that this foreign produce may have been bought with specie, I answer, specie is not always a native product, but must have been bought itself with the products of native industry; so that, whether the foreign articles be paid for in specie or in home products, the vent for national industry is the same in both cases.[2]

4. The same principle leads to the conclusion, that the en-

[1] It is only by the recent advances of political economy, that these most important truths have been made manifest, not to vulgar apprehension alone, but even to the most distinguished and enlightened observers. We read in Voltaire that "such is the lot of humanity, that the patriotic desire for one's country's grandeur, is but a wish for the humiliation of one's neighbours;—that it is clearly impossible for one country to gain, except by the loss of another." (*Dict. Phil. Art. Patrie.*) By a continuation of the same false reasoning, he goes on to declare, that a thorough citizen of the world cannot wish his country to be greater or less, richer or poorer. It is true, that he would not desire her to extend the limits of her dominion, because, in so doing, she might endanger her own well-being; but he will desire her to progress in wealth, for her progressive prosperity promotes that of all other nations.

[2] This effect has been sensibly experienced in Brazil of late years. The large imports of European commodities, which the freedom of navigation directed to the markets of Brazil, has been so favourable to its native productions and commerce, that Brazilian products never found so good a sale. So there is an instance of a national benefit arising from importation. By the way, it might have perhaps been better for Brazil if the prices of her products and the profits of her producers had risen more slowly and gradually; for exorbitant prices never lead to the establishment of a permanent commercial intercourse; it is better to gain by the multiplication of one's own products than by their increased price.

couragement of mere consumption is no benefit to commerce; for the difficulty lies in supplying the means, not in stimulating the desire of consumption; and we have seen that production alone, furnishes those means. Thus, it is the aim of good government to stimulate production, of bad government to encourage consumption.

For the same reason that the creation of a new product is the opening of a new market for other products, the consumption or destruction of a product is the stoppage of a vent for them. This is no evil where the end of the product has been answered by its destruction, which end is the satisfying of some human want, or the creation of some new product designed for such a satisfaction. Indeed, if the nation be in a thriving condition, the gross national re-production exceeds the gross consumption. The consumed products have fulfilled their office, as it is natural and fitting they should; the consumption, however, has opened no new market, but just the reverse.[2]

Having once arrived at the clear conviction, that the general demand for products is brisk in proportion to the activity of production, we need not trouble ourselves much to inquire towards what channel of industry production may be most advantageously directed. The products created give rise to various degrees of demand, according to the wants, the manners, the comparative capital, industry, and natural resources of each country; the article most in request, owing to the competition of buyers, yields the best interest of money to the capitalist, the largest profits to the adventurer, and the best wages to the labourer; and the agency of their respective services is naturally attracted by these advantages towards those particular channels.

In a community, city, province, or nation, that produces abundantly, and adds every moment to the sum of its products,

[2] If the barren consumption of a product be of itself adverse to re-production, and a diminution *pro tanto* of the existing demand or vent for produce, how shall we designate that degree of insanity, which would induce a government deliberately to burn and destroy the imports of foreign products, and thus to annihilate the sole advantage accruing from unproductive consumption, that is to say the gratification of the wants of the consumer?

almost all the branches of commerce, manufacture, and generally of industry, yield handsome profits, because the demand is great, and because there is always a large quantity of products in the market, ready to bid for new productive services. And, *vice versâ*, wherever, by reason of the blunders of the nation or its government, production is stationary, or does not keep pace with consumption, the demand gradually declines, the value of the product is less than the charges of its production; no productive exertion is properly rewarded; profits and wages decrease; the employment of capital becomes less advantageous and more hazardous; it is consumed piecemeal, not through extravagance, but through necessity, and because the sources of profit are dried up.[1] The labouring classes experience a want of work; families before in tolerable circumstances, are more cramped and confined; and those before in difficulties are left altogether destitute. Depopulation, misery, and returning barbarism, occupy the place of abundance and happiness.

Such are the concomitants of declining production, which are only to be remedied by frugality, intelligence, activity, and freedom.

---

[1] Consumption of this kind gives no encouragement to future production, but devours products already in existence. No additional demand can be created until there be new products raised; there is only an exchange of one product for another. Neither can one branch of industry suffer without affecting the rest.

DAVID RICARDO

The Principles of Political Economy and Taxation

1871

D avid Ricardo has been referred to as 'the economist's economist', because of the rigour and
abstraction of his theories; yet, paradoxically,
he lacked any academic background and was
highly successful in practical affairs.

Born in 1772, Ricardo was the third child of a prosperous
Jewish broker who had emigrated from Amsterdam to London.
At the early age of fourteen he began to work for his father on
the Stock Exchange, and at twenty-one he set up his own
stockbroking firm. Such were his abilities and reputation for
integrity that within a few years he had made a substantial
fortune, which gave him leisure to cultivate his own interests.
Of these, political economy became the chief.

Ricardo first established a reputation as a writer on monetary
questions in the years 1809–10, when he emerged as one of the
ablest exponents of the bullionist viewpoint, though less flexible
and perceptive than Henry Thornton. These writings brought
him into contact with the philosophical radical James Mill,
who urged him to write a full-scale treatise—the result was
The Principles of Political Economy and Taxation, first published
in 1817.

By this time Ricardo had retired completely from business and bought a considerable landed estate. In 1819 he entered the House of Commons and from then until his death in 1823 he divided his time between parliamentary duties and economic studies.

Although his *Principles of Political Economy* went through three editions in his lifetime, it was at first a controversial and never a popular book. Nevertheless its doctrines were so effectively propagated by James Mill and other disciples of Ricardo that the work eventually became one of the cornerstones of classical economics.

In it Ricardo attempted a new analysis of what he considered to be 'the principal problem of Political Economy'—to 'determine the laws' regulating the distribution of the national income between landlords, capitalists and labourers and the changes in that distribution in the progress of society. Ricardo saw that for the solution of this problem in a complex economy a theory of value was essential. In particular he required an invariable measure of value for the various products of the economy; this, combined with his interest in long-term aspects, led him towards the idea of labour as both the measure and the ultimate cause of value. Neither of these propositions could he establish to his own satisfaction and the opening chapter of his *Principles* shows Ricardo grappling with the difficulties of a labour theory of value in a manner which demonstrates both his power of abstract analysis and his intellectual candour.

For these reasons, this chapter has retained its fascination for economic theorists even at the present day, when the doctrine it presents has long been discarded. On the other hand, the two additional chapters of the *Principles* reprinted here contain ideas which have been and still are of permanent significance in economic thought—the theory of differential rent—perhaps the best known of all Ricardo's theories, though not originated by him—and the theory of comparative costs in international trade.

BIBLIOGRAPHY

The Works and Correspondence of David Ricardo (10 vols, Cambridge 1951–5), edited by P. Sraffa and M. H. Dobb, is now the standard edition. *The Principles of Political Economy and Taxation* forms Volume I of the set, and the introduction to this by Mr Sraffa has become the starting point for most interpretations and criticisms of Ricardo.

Such interpretations are many: among the most useful are O. St Clair. *A Key to Ricardo* (London 1957); M. Blaug. *Ricardian Economics* (New Haven 1958), which also contains a useful bibliography; and the same author's *Economic Theory in Retrospect* also contains a valuable chapter (4) on 'Ricardo's System', with a useful reading list.

On the labour theory of value see G. J. Stigler. 'Ricardo and the 93% Labour Theory of Value', *American Economic Review*, 48 (June 1958), 357–67; and D. F. Gordon. 'What Was the Labour Theory of Value?', *American Economic Review* (Supplement), 49 (May 1959), 462–72.

On the doctrine of comparative cost, the standard source is J. Viner. *Studies in the Theory of International Trade* (New York and London 1937), Chapter 8.

For the theory of rent, the best treatment is still D. H. Buchanan. 'The Historical Approach to Rent and Price Theory', *Economica*, IX (June 1929), 123–55. (Reprinted in *Readings in the Theory of Income Distribution* (1946), 599–637.)

There is no full biography of Ricardo, but most of the available material is assembled in Volume X of the *Works and Correspondence*, 'Biographical Miscellany'. There is also a biographical sketch in J. H. Hollander. *David Ricardo: A Centenary Estimate* (Baltimore 1910).

PRINCIPLES OF POLITICAL ECONOMY

CHAPTER I

ON VALUE

SECTION I

The value of a commodity, or the quantity of any other commodity for which it will exchange, depends on the relative quantity of labour which is necessary for its production, and not on the greater or less compensation which is paid for that labour

IT has been observed by Adam Smith that "the word Value has two different meanings, and sometimes expresses the utility of some particular object, and sometimes the power of purchasing other goods which the possession of that object conveys. The one may be called *value in use*; the other *value in exchange*. The things," he continues, "which have the greatest value in use, have frequently little or no value in exchange; and, on the contrary, those which have the greatest value in exchange, have little or no value in use." Water and air are abundantly useful; they are indeed indispensable to existence, yet, under ordinary circumstances, nothing can be obtained in exchange for them. Gold, on the contrary, though of little use compared with air or water, will exchange for a great quantity of other goods.

Utility then is not the measure of exchangeable value, although it is absolutely essential to it. If a commodity were in no way useful—in other words, if it could in no way contribute to our gratification—it would be destitute of exchangeable value, however scarce it might be, or whatever quantity of labour might be necessary to procure it.

Possessing utility, commodities derive their exchangeable value from two sources: from their scarcity, and from the quantity of labour required to obtain them.

There are some commodities, the value of which is determined by their scarcity alone. No labour can increase the quantity of such goods, and therefore their value cannot be lowered by an increased supply. Some rare statues and pictures, scarce books and coins, wines of a peculiar quality, which can be made only from grapes grown on a particular soil, of which there is a very limited quantity, are all of this description. Their value is wholly independent of the quantity of labour originally necessary to produce them, and varies with the varying wealth and inclinations of those who are desirous to possess them.

These commodities, however, form a very small part of the mass of commodities daily exchanged in the market. By far the greatest part of those goods which are the objects of desire are procured by labour; and they may be multiplied, not in one country alone, but in many, almost without any assignable limit, if we are disposed to bestow the labour necessary to obtain them.

In speaking, then, of commodities, of their exchangeable value, and of the laws which regulate their relative prices, we mean always such commodities only as can be increased in quantity by the exertion of human industry, and on the production of which competition operates without restraint.

In the early stages of society, the exchangeable value of these commodities, or the rule which determines how much of one shall be given in exchange for another, depends almost exclusively on the comparative quantity of labour expended on each.

"The real price of everything," says Adam Smith, "what everything really costs to the man who wants to acquire it, is the toil and trouble of acquiring it. What everything is really worth to the man who has acquired it, and who wants to dispose of it, or exchange it for something else, is the toil and trouble which it can save to himself, and which it can impose upon other people." "Labour was the first price—the original purchase-money that was paid for all things." Again, "in that early and rude state of society which precedes both the accumulation of stock and the appropriation of land, the proportion between the quantities of labour necessary for acquiring different objects seems to be the only circumstance which can afford any rule for exchanging them for one another. If, among a nation of hunters, for example, it usually cost twice the labour to kill a beaver which it does to kill a deer, one beaver should naturally exchange for, or be worth, two deer. It is natural that what is usually the produce of two days' or two hours' labour should be worth double of what is usually the produce of one day's or one hour's labour."[1]

That this is really the foundation of the exchangeable value of all things, excepting those which cannot be increased by human industry, is a doctrine of the utmost importance in political economy; for from no source do so many errors, and so much difference of opinion in that science proceed, as from the vague ideas which are attached to the word value.

If the quantity of labour realised in commodities regulate their exchangeable value, every increase of the quantity of labour must augment the value of that commodity on which it is exercised, as every diminution must lower it.

Adam Smith, who so accurately defined the original source of exchangeable value, and who was bound in consistency to maintain that all things become more or less valuable in proportion as more or less labour was bestowed on their production, has himself erected another standard measure of value, and speaks of things being more or less valuable in proportion as they will exchange for more or less of this standard measure. Sometimes he speaks of corn, at other times of labour, as a standard measure; not the quantity of labour bestowed on the production of any object, but the quantity which it can command in the market: as if these were two equivalent expressions, and as if, because a man's labour had become doubly efficient, and he could therefore produce twice the quantity of a commodity, he would necessarily receive twice the former quantity in exchange for it.

---

[1] Book i. chap. 5. [cf. above, 16, 34]

If this indeed were true, if the reward of the labourer were always in proportion to what he produced, the quantity of labour bestowed on a commodity, and the quantity of labour which that commodity would purchase, would be equal, and either might accurately measure the variations of other things; but they are not equal; the first is under many circumstances an invariable standard, indicating correctly the variations of other things; the latter is subject to as many fluctuations as the commodities compared with it. Adam Smith, after most ably showing the insufficiency of a variable medium, such as gold and silver, for the purpose of determining the varying value of other things, has himself, by fixing on corn or labour, chosen a medium no less variable.

Gold and silver are no doubt subject to fluctuations from the discovery of new and more abundant mines; but such discoveries are rare, and their effects, though powerful, are limited to periods of comparatively short duration. They are subject also to fluctuation from improvements in the skill and machinery with which the mines may be worked; as in consequence of such improvements a greater quantity may be obtained with the same labour. They are further subject to fluctuation from the decreasing produce of the mines, after they have yielded a supply to the world for a succession of ages. But from which of these sources of fluctuation is corn exempted? Does not that also vary, on one hand, from improvements in agriculture, from improved machinery and implements used in husbandry, as well as from the discovery of new tracts of fertile land, which in other countries may be taken into cultivation, and which will affect the value of corn in every market where importation is free? Is it not on the other hand subject to be enhanced in value from prohibitions of importation, from increasing population and wealth, and the greater difficulty of obtaining the increased supplies, on account of the additional quantity of labour which the cultivation of inferior land requires? Is not the value of labour equally variable; being not only affected, as all other things are, by the proportion between the supply and demand, which uniformly varies with every change in the condition of the community, but also by the varying price of food and other necessaries, on which the wages of labour are expended?

In the same country double the quantity of labour may be required to produce a given quantity of food and necessaries at one time that may be necessary at another and a distant time; yet the labourer's reward may possibly be very little diminished. If the labourer's wages at the former period were a certain quantity of food and necessaries, he probably could not have subsisted if that quantity had been reduced. Food and necessaries in this case will have risen 100 per cent. if estimated by the *quantity* of labour necessary to their production, while they will scarcely have increased in value if measured by the quantity of labour for which they will *exchange*.

The same remark may be made respecting two or more countries. In America and Poland, on the land last taken into cultivation, a year's labour of any given number of men will produce much more corn than on land similarly circumstanced in England. Now, supposing all other necessaries to be equally cheap in those three countries, would it not be a great mistake to conclude that the quantity of corn awarded to the labourer would in each country be in proportion to the facility of production?

If the shoes and clothing of the labourer could, by improvements in machinery, be produced by one-fourth of the labour now necessary to their production, they would probably fall 75 per cent.; but so far is it from being true that the labourer would thereby be enabled permanently to consume four coats, or four pair of shoes, instead of one, that it is probable his wages would in no long time be adjusted by the effects of competition, and the stimulus to population, to the new value of the necessaries on which they were expended. If these improvements extended to all the objects of the labourer's consumption, we should find him probably, at the end of a very few years, in possession of only a small, if any, addition to his enjoyments, although the exchangeable value of those commodities, compared with any other commodity, in the manufacture of which no such improvement were made, had sustained a very considerable reduction; and though they were the produce of a very considerably diminished quantity of labour.

It cannot then be correct to say with Adam Smith, "that as labour may sometimes *purchase* a greater and sometimes a smaller quantity of goods, it is their value which varies, not that of the labour which purchases them;" and therefore, "that labour, *alone never varying in its own value*, is alone the ultimate and real standard by which the value of all commodities can at all times and places be estimated and compared;"—but it is correct to say, as Adam Smith had previously said, "that the proportion between the quantities of labour necessary for acquiring different objects seems to be the only circumstance which can afford any rule for exchanging them for one another;" or in other words that it is the comparative quantity of commodities which labour will produce that determines their present or past relative value, and not the comparative quantities of commodities which are given to the labourer in exchange for his labour.

Two commodities vary in relative value, and we wish to know in which the variation has really taken place. If we compare the present value of one with shoes, stockings, hats, iron, sugar, and all other commodities, we find that it will exchange for precisely the same quantity of all these things as before. If we compare the other with the same commodities, we find it has varied with respect to them all: we may then with great probability infer that the variation has been in this commodity, and not in the commodities with which we have compared it. If on examining still more particularly into all the circumstances connected with the production of these various commodities, we find that precisely the same quantity of labour and capital are necessary to the production of the shoes, stockings, hats, iron, sugar, etc.; but that the same quantity as before is not necessary to produce the single commodity whose relative value is altered, probability is changed into certainty, and we are

sure that the variation is in the single commodity: we then
discover also the cause of its variation.

If I found that an ounce of gold would exchange for a less
quantity of all the commodities above enumerated and many
others; and if, moreover, I found that by the discovery of a
new and more fertile mine, or by the employment of machinery
to great advantage, a given quantity of gold could be obtained
with a less quantity of labour, I should be justified in saying
that the cause of the alteration in the value of gold relatively
to other commodities was the greater facility of its production,
or the smaller quantity of labour necessary to obtain it. In like
manner, if labour fell very considerably in value, relatively to
all other things, and if I found that its fall was in consequence
of an abundant supply, encouraged by the great facility with
which corn, and the other necessaries of the labourer, were
produced, it would, I apprehend, be correct for me to say that
corn and necessaries had fallen in value in consequence of less
quantity of labour being necessary to produce them, and that
this facility of providing for the support of the labourer had been
followed by a fall in the value of labour. No, say Adam Smith
and Mr. Malthus, in the case of the gold you were correct in
calling its variation a fall of its value, because corn and labour
had not then varied; and as gold would command a less quantity of them, as well as of all other things, than before, it was
correct to say that all things had remained stationary and that
gold only had varied; but when corn and labour fall, things
which we have selected to be our standard measure of value,
notwithstanding all the variations to which we acknowledge
they are subject, it would be highly improper to say so; the
correct language will be to say that corn and labour have remained stationary, and all other things have risen in value.

Now it is against this language that I protest. I find that
precisely, as in the case of the gold, the cause of the variation
between corn and other things is the smaller quantity of labour
necessary to produce it, and therefore, by all just reasoning, I
am bound to call the variation of corn and labour a fall in their

value, and not a rise in the value of the things with which they are compared. If I have to hire a labourer for a week, and instead of ten shillings I pay him eight, no variation having taken place in the value of money, the labourer can probably obtain more food and necessaries with his eight shillings than he before obtained for ten: but this is owing, not to a rise in the real value of his wages, as stated by Adam Smith, and more recently by Mr. Malthus, but to a fall in the value of the things on which his wages are expended, things perfectly distinct; and yet for calling this a fall in the real value of wages, I am told that I adopt new and unusual language, not reconcilable with the true principles of the science. To me it appears that the unusual and, indeed, inconsistent language is that used by my opponents.

Suppose a labourer to be paid a bushel of corn for a week's work when the price of corn is 80s. per quarter, and that he is paid a bushel and a quarter when the price falls to 40s. Suppose, too, that he consumes half a bushel of corn a week in his own family, and exchanges the remainder for other things, such as fuel, soap, candles, tea, sugar, salt, etc. etc.; if the three-fourths of a bushel which will remain to him, in one case, cannot procure him as much of the above commodities as half a bushel did in the other, which it will not, will labour have risen or fallen in value? Risen, Adam Smith must say, because his standard is corn, and the labourer receives more corn for a week's labour. Fallen, must the same Adam Smith say, "because the value of a thing depends on the power of purchasing other goods which the possession of that object conveys," and labour has a less power of purchasing such other goods.

SECTION II

Labour of different qualities differently rewarded. This no cause of variation in the relative value of commodities

In speaking, however, of labour, as being the foundation of all value, and the relative quantity of labour as almost exclusively determining the relative value of commodities, I must not be supposed to be inattentive to the different qualities of labour, and the difficulty of comparing an hour's or a day's labour in one employment with the same duration of labour in another. The estimation in which different qualities of labour are held comes soon to be adjusted in the market with sufficient precision for all practical purposes, and depends much on the comparative skill of the labourer and intensity of the labour performed. The scale, when once formed, is liable to little variation. If a day's labour of a working jeweller be more valuable than a day's labour of a common labourer, it has long ago been adjusted and placed in its proper position in the scale of value.[1]

In comparing, therefore, the value of the same commodity at different periods of time, the consideration of the comparative skill and intensity of labour required for that particular commodity needs scarcely to be attended to, as it operates equally at both periods. One description of labour at one time is compared with the same description of labour at another; if a tenth, a fifth, or a fourth has been added or taken away, an effect proportioned to the cause will be produced on the relative value of the commodity.

If a piece of cloth be now of the value of two pieces of linen,

---

[1] "But though labour be the real measure of the exchangeable value of all commodities, it is not that by which their value is commonly estimated. It is often difficult to ascertain the proportion between two different quantities of labour. The time spent in two different sorts of work will not always alone determine this proportion. The different degrees of hardship endured, and of ingenuity exercised, must likewise be taken into account. There may be more labour in an hour's hard work than in two hours' easy business; or in an hour's application to a trade, which it costs ten years' labour to learn, than in a month's industry at an ordinary and obvious employment. But it is not easy to find any accurate measure, either of hardship or ingenuity. In exchange, indeed, the different productions of different sorts of labour for one another, some allowance is commonly made for both. It is adjusted, however, not by any accurate measure, but by the higgling and bargaining of the market, according to that sort of rough equality which, though not exact, is sufficient for carrying on the business of common life."—*Wealth of Nations*, book i. chap. 5. [above, 17]

and if, in ten years hence, the ordinary value of a piece of cloth should be four pieces of linen, we may safely conclude that either more labour is required to make the cloth, or less to make the linen, or that both causes have operated.

As the inquiry to which I wish to draw the reader's attention relates to the effect of the variations in the relative value of commodities, and not in their absolute value, it will be of little importance to examine into the comparative degree of estimation in which the different kinds of human labour are held. We may fairly conclude that whatever inequality there might originally have been in them, whatever the ingenuity, skill, or time necessary for the acquirement of one species of manual dexterity more than another, it continues nearly the same from one generation to another; or at least that the variation is very inconsiderable from year to year, and therefore can have little effect, for short periods, on the relative value of commodities.

"The proportion between the different rates both of wages and profit in the different employments of labour and stock seems not to be much affected, as has already been observed, by the riches or poverty, the advancing, stationary, or declining state of the society. Such revolutions in the public welfare, though they affect the general rates both of wages and profit, must in the end affect them equally in all different employments. The proportion between them therefore must remain the same, and cannot well be altered, at least for any considerable time, by any such revolutions."[1]

SECTION III

Not only the labour applied immediately to commodities affect their value, but the labour also which is bestowed on the implements, tools, and buildings, with which such labour is assisted

EVEN in that early state to which Adam Smith refers, some capital, though possibly made and accumulated by the hunter himself, would be necessary to enable him to kill his game.

[2] *Wealth of Nations*, book i. chap. 10.

Without some weapon, neither the beaver nor the deer could be destroyed, and therefore the value of these animals would be regulated, not solely by the time and labour necessary to their destruction, but also by the time and labour necessary for providing the hunter's capital, the weapon, by the aid of which their destruction was effected.

Suppose the weapon necessary to kill the beaver was constructed with much more labour than that necessary to kill the deer, on account of the greater difficulty of approaching near to the former animal, and the consequent necessity of its being more true to its mark; one beaver would naturally be of more value than two deer, and precisely for this reason, that more labour would, on the whole, be necessary to its destruction. Or suppose that the same quantity of labour was necessary to make both weapons, but that they were of very unequal durability; of the durable implement only a small portion of its value would be transferred to the commodity, a much greater portion of the value of the less durable implement would be realised in the commodity which it contributed to produce.

All the implements necessary to kill the beaver and deer might belong to one class of men, and the labour employed in their destruction might be furnished by another class; still, their comparative prices would be in proportion to the actual labour bestowed, both on the formation of the capital and on the destruction of the animals. Under different circumstances of plenty or scarcity of capital, as compared with labour, under different circumstances of plenty or scarcity of the food and necessaries essential to the support of men, those who furnished an equal value of capital for either one employment or for the other might have a half, a fourth, or an eighth of the produce obtained, the remainder being paid as wages to those who furnished the labour; yet this division could not affect the relative value of these commodities, since whether the profits of capital were greater or less, whether they were 50, 20, or 10 per cent., or whether the wages of labour were high or low, they would operate equally on both employments.

If we suppose the occupations of the society extended, that some provide canoes and tackle necessary for fishing, others the seed and rude machinery first used in agriculture, still the same principle would hold true, that the exchangeable value of the commodities produced would be in proportion to the labour bestowed on their production; not on their immediate production only, but on all those implements or machines required to give effect to the particular labour to which they were applied.

If we look to a state of society in which greater improvements have been made, and in which arts and commerce flourish, we shall still find that commodities vary in value conformably with this principle: in estimating the exchangeable value of stockings, for example, we shall find that their value, comparatively with other things, depends on the total quantity of labour necessary to manufacture them and bring them to market. First, there is the labour necessary to cultivate the land on which the raw cotton is grown; secondly, the labour of conveying the cotton to the country where the stockings are to be manufactured, which includes a portion of the labour bestowed in building the ship in which it is conveyed, and which is charged in the freight of the goods; thirdly, the labour of the spinner and weaver; fourthly, a portion of the labour of the engineer, smith, and carpenter, who erected the buildings and and machinery, by the help of which they are made; fifthly, the labour of the retail dealer, and of many others, whom it is unnecessary further to particularise. The aggregate sum of these various kinds of labour determines the quantity of other things for which these stockings will exchange, while the same consideration of the various quantities of labour which have been bestowed on those other things will equally govern the portion of them which will be given for the stockings.

To convince ourselves that this is the real foundation of exchangeable value, let us suppose any improvement to be made in the means of abridging labour in any one of the various processes through which the raw cotton must pass before the manufactured stockings come to the market to be exchanged

for other things, and observe the effects which will follow. If
fewer men were required to cultivate the raw cotton, or if fewer
sailors were employed in navigating, or shipwrights in construct-
ing the ship, in which it was conveyed to us; if fewer hands
were employed in raising the buildings and machinery, or if
these, when raised, were rendered more efficient, the stockings
would inevitably fall in value, and consequently command less
of other things. They would fall, because a less quantity of
labour was necessary to their production, and would therefore
exchange for a smaller quantity of those things in which no such
abridgment of labour had been made.

Economy in the use of labour never fails to reduce the relative
value of a commodity, whether the saving be in the labour
necessary to the manufacture of the commodity itself, or in
that necessary to the formation of the capital by the aid of
which it is produced. In either case the price of stockings would
fall, whether there were fewer men employed as bleachers,
spinners, and weavers, persons immediately necessary to their
manufacture; or as sailors, carriers, engineers, and smiths,
persons more indirectly concerned. In the one case, the whole
saving of labour would fall on the stockings, because that
portion of labour was wholly confined to the stockings; in the
other, a portion only would fall on the stockings, the remainder
being applied to all those other commodities, to the production
of which the buildings, machinery, and carriage were sub-
servient.

Suppose that, in the early stages of society, the bows and
arrows of the hunter were of equal value, and of equal durability, with the canoe and implements of the fisherman, both
being the produce of the same quantity of labour. Under such
circumstances the value of the deer, the produce of the hunter's
day's labour, would be exactly equal to the value of the fish, the
produce of the fisherman's day's labour. The comparative
value of the fish and the game would be entirely regulated by
the quantity of labour realised in each, whatever might be the
quantity of production or however high or low general wages

or profits might be. If, for example, the canoes and implements of the fisherman were of the value of £100, and were calculated to last for ten years, and he employed ten men, whose annual labour cost £100, and who in one day obtained by their labour twenty salmon: If the weapons employed by the hunter were also of £100 value, and calculated to last ten years, and if he also employed ten men, whose annual labour cost £100, and who in one day procured him ten deer; then the natural price of a deer would be two salmon, whether the proportion of the whole produce bestowed on the men who obtained it were large or small. The proportion which might be paid for wages is of the utmost importance in the question of profits; for it must at once be seen that profits would be high or low exactly in proportion as wages were low or high; but it could not in the least affect the relative value of fish and game, as wages would be high or low at the same time in both occupations. If the hunter urged the plea of his paying a large proportion, or the value of a large proportion of his game for wages, as an inducement to the fisherman to give him more fish in exchange for his game, the latter would state that he was equally affected by the same cause; and therefore, under all variations of wages and profits, under all the effects of accumulation of capital, as long as they continued by a day's labour to obtain respectively the same quantity of fish and the same quantity of game, the natural rate of exchange would be one deer for two salmon.

If with the same quantity of labour a less quantity of fish or a greater quantity of game were obtained, the value of fish would rise in comparison with that of game. If, on the contrary, with the same quantity of labour a less quantity of game or a greater quantity of fish was obtained, game would rise in comparison with fish.

If there were any other commodity which was invariable in its value, we should be able to ascertain, by comparing the value of fish and game with this commodity, how much of the variation was to be attributed to a cause which affected the value of fish, and how much to a cause which affected the value of game.

Suppose money to be that commodity. If a salmon were worth £1 and a deer £2, one deer would be worth two salmon. But a deer might become of the value of three salmon, for more labour might be required to obtain the deer, or less to get the salmon, or both these causes might operate at the same time. If we had this invariable standard, we might easily ascertain in what degree either of these causes operated. If salmon continued to sell for £1 whilst deer rose to £3, we might conclude that more labour was required to obtain the deer. If deer continued at the same price of £2 and salmon sold for 13s. 4d., we might then be sure that less labour was required to obtain the salmon; and if deer rose to £2 10s. and salmon fell to 16s. 8d., we should be convinced that both causes had operated in producing the alteration of the relative value of these commodities.

No alteration in the wages of labour could produce any alteration in the relative value of these commodities; for suppose them to rise, no greater quantity of labour would be required in any of these occupations but it would be paid for at a higher price, and the same reasons which should make the hunter and fisherman endeavour to raise the value of their game and fish would cause the owner of the mine to raise the value of his gold. This inducement acting with the same force on all these three occupations, and the relative situation of those engaged in them being the same before and after the rise of wages, the relative value of game, fish, and gold would continue unaltered. Wages might rise twenty per cent., and profits consequently fall in a greater or less proportion, without occasioning the least alteration in the relative value of these commodities.

Now suppose that, with the same labour and fixed capital, more fish could be produced, but no more gold or game, the relative value of fish would fall in comparison with gold or game. If, instead of twenty salmon, twenty-five were the produce of one day's labour, the price of a salmon would be sixteen shillings instead of a pound, and two salmon and a half, instead of two salmon, would be given in exchange for one deer, but the price of deer would continue at £2 as before. In the same manner, if fewer fish could be obtained with the same capital and labour, fish would rise in comparative value. Fish then would rise or fall in exchangeable value, only because more or less labour was required to obtain a given quantity; and it never could rise or fall beyond the proportion of the increased or diminished quantity of labour required.

If we had then an invariable standard, by which we could measure the variation in other commodities, we should find that the utmost limit to which they could permanently rise, if produced under the circumstances supposed, was proportioned to the additional quantity of labour required for their production; and that unless more labour were required for their production they could not rise in any degree whatever. A rise of wages would not raise them in money value, nor relatively to any other commodities, the production of which required no additional quantity of labour, which employed the same proportion of fixed and circulating capital, and fixed capital of the same durability. If more or less labour were required in the production of the other commodity, we have already stated that this will immediately occasion an alteration in its relative value, but such alteration is owing to the altered quantity of requisite labour, and not to the rise of wages.

SECTION IV

The principle that the quantity of labour bestowed on the production of commodities regulates their relative value considerably modified by the employment of machinery and other fixed and durable capital

IN the former section we have supposed the implements and weapons necessary to kill the deer and salmon to be equally durable, and to be the result of the same quantity of labour, and we have seen that the variations in the relative value of deer and salmon depended solely on the varying quantities of labour necessary to obtain them, but in every state of society, the tools, implements, buildings, and machinery employed in different trades may be of various degrees of durability, and

K

may require different portions of labour to produce them. The proportions, too, in which the capital that is to support labour, and the capital that is invested in tools, machinery, and buildings, may be variously combined. This difference in the degree of durability of fixed capital, and this variety in the proportions in which the two sorts of capital may be combined, introduce another cause, besides the greater or less quantity of labour necessary to produce commodities, for the variations in their relative value—this cause is the rise or fall in the value of labour.

The food and clothing consumed by the labourer, the buildings in which he works, the implements with which his labour is assisted, are all of a perishable nature. There is, however, a vast difference in the time for which these different capitals will endure: a steam-engine will last longer than a ship, a ship than the clothing of the labourer, and the clothing of the labourer longer than the food which he consumes.

According as capital is rapidly perishable, and requires to be frequently reproduced, or is of slow consumption, it is classed under the heads of circulating or of fixed capital.[1] A brewer whose buildings and machinery are valuable and durable is said to employ a large portion of fixed capital: on the contrary, a shoemaker, whose capital is chiefly employed in the payment of wages, which are expended on food and clothing, commodities more perishable than buildings and machinery, is said to employ a large proportion of his capital as circulating capital.

It is also to be observed that the circulating capital may circulate, or be returned to its employer, in very unequal times. The wheat bought by a farmer to sow is comparatively a fixed capital to the wheat purchased by a baker to make into loaves. One leaves it in the ground and can obtain no return for a year; the other can get it ground into flour, sell it as bread to his customers, and have his capital free to renew the same or commence any other employment in a week.

---

[1] A division not essential, and in which the line of demarcation cannot be accurately drawn.

Two trades then may employ the same amount of capital; but it may be very differently divided with respect to the portion which is fixed and that which is circulating.

In one trade very little capital may be employed as circulating capital, that is to say, in the support of labour—it may be principally invested in machinery, implements, buildings, etc., capital of a comparatively fixed and durable character. In another trade the same amount of capital may be used, but it may be chiefly employed in the support of labour, and very little may be invested in implements, machines, and buildings. A rise in the wages of labour cannot fail to affect unequally commodities produced under such different circumstances.

Again, two manufacturers may employ the same amount of fixed and the same amount of circulating capital; but the durability of their fixed capitals may be very unequal. One may have steam-engines of the value of £10,000, the other, ships of the same value.

If men employed no machinery in production but labour only, and were all the same length of time before they brought their commodities to market, the exchangeable value of their goods would be precisely in proportion to the quantity of labour employed.

If they employed fixed capital of the same value and of the same durability, then, too, the value of the commodities produced would be the same, and they would vary with the greater or less quantity of labour employed on their production.

But although commodities produced under similar circumstances would not vary with respect to each other from any cause but an addition or diminution of the quantity of labour necessary to produce one or other of them, yet, compared with others not produced with the same proportionate quantity of fixed capital, they would vary from the other cause also which I have before mentioned, namely, a rise in the value of labour, although neither more nor less labour were employed in the production of either of them. Barley and oats would continue to bear the same relation to each other under any variation of wages.

Cotton goods and cloth would do the same, if they also were produced under circumstances precisely similar to each other, but yet with a rise or fall of wages barley might be more or less valuable compared with cotton goods and oats compared with cloth.

Suppose two men employ one hundred men each for a year in the construction of two machines, and another man employs the same number of men in cultivating corn, each of the machines at the end of the year will be of the same value as the corn, for they will each be produced by the same quantity of labour. Suppose one of the owners of one of the machines to employ it, with the assistance of one hundred men, the following year in making cloth, and the owner of the other machine to employ his also, with the assistance likewise of one hundred men, in making cotton goods, while the farmer continues to employ one hundred men as before in the cultivation of corn. During the second year they will all have employed the same quantity of labour, but the goods and machine together of the clothier, and also of the cotton manufacturer, will be the result of the labour of two hundred men employed for a year; or, rather, of the labour of one hundred men for two years; whereas the corn will be produced by the labour of one hundred men for one year, consequently if the corn be of the value of £500, the machine and cloth of the clothier together ought to be of the value of £1000, and the machine and cotton goods of the cotton manufacturer ought to be also of twice the value of the corn. But they will be of more than twice the value of the corn, for the profit on the clothier's and cotton manufacturer's capital for the first year has been added to their capitals, while that of the farmer has been expended and enjoyed. On account then of the different degrees of durability of their capitals, or, which is the same thing, on account of the time which must elapse before one set of commodities can be brought to market, they will be valuable, not exactly in proportion to the quantity of labour bestowed on them—they will not be as two to one, but something more, to compensate for the greater length of time which must elapse before the most valuable can be brought to market.

Suppose that for the labour of each workman £50 per annum were paid, or that £5000 capital were employed and profits were 10 per cent., the value of each of the machines as well as of the corn, at the end of the first year, would be £5500. The second year the manufacturers and farmers will again employ £5000 each in the support of labour, and will therefore again sell their goods for £5500; but the men using the machines, to be on a par with the farmer, must not only obtain £5500 for the equal capitals of £5000 employed on labour, but they must obtain a further sum of £550 for the profit on £5500, which they have invested in machinery, and consequently their goods must sell for £6050. Here, then, are capitalists employing precisely the same quantity of labour annually on the production of their commodities, and yet the goods they produce differ in value on account of the different quantities of fixed capital, or accumulated labour, employed by each respectively. The cloth and cotton goods are of the same value, because they are the produce of equal quantities of labour and equal quantities of fixed capital; but corn is not of the same value as these commodities, because it is produced, as far as regards fixed capital, under different circumstances.

But how will their relative value be affected by a rise in the value of labour? It is evident that the relative values of cloth and cotton goods will undergo no change, for what affects one must equally affect the other under the circumstances supposed; neither will the relative values of wheat and barley undergo any change, for they are produced under the same circumstances as far as fixed and circulating capital are concerned; but the relative value of corn to cloth, or to cotton goods, must be altered by a rise of labour.

There can be no rise in the value of labour without a fall of profits. If the corn is to be divided between the farmer and the labourer, the larger the proportion that is given to the latter the less will remain for the former. So, if cloth or cotton goods be divided between the workman and his employer, the larger the proportion given to the former the less remains for the latter. Suppose then, that owing to a rise of wages, profits fall from 10 to 9 per cent., instead of adding £550 to the common price of their goods (to £5500) for the profits on their fixed capital, the manufacturers would add only 9 per cent. on that sum, or £495, consequently the price would be £5995 instead of £6050. As the corn would continue to sell for £5500 the manufactured goods in which more fixed capital was employed would fall relatively to corn or to any other goods in which a less portion of fixed capital entered. The degree of alteration in the relative value of goods, on account of a rise or fall of labour, would depend on the proportion which the fixed capital bore to the whole capital employed. All commodities which are produced by very valuable machinery, or in very valuable buildings, or which require a great length of time before they can be brought to market, would fall in relative value, while all those which were chiefly produced by labour, or which would be speedily brought to market, would rise in relative value.

The reader, however, should remark that this cause of the variation of commodities is comparatively slight in its effects. With such a rise of wages as should occasion a fall of 1 per cent. in profits, goods produced under the circumstances I have supposed vary in relative value only 1 per cent.; they fall with so great a fall of profits from £6050 to £5995. The greatest effects which could be produced on the relative prices of these goods from a rise of wages could not exceed 6 or 7 per cent.; for profits could not, probably, under any circumstances, admit of a greater general and permanent depression than to that amount.

Not so with the other great cause of the variation in the value of commodities, namely, the increase or diminution in the quantity of labour necessary to produce them. If to produce the corn, eighty, instead of one hundred men, should be required, the value of the corn would fall 20 per cent., or from £5500 to £4400. If to produce the cloth, the labour of eighty instead of one hundred men would suffice, cloth would fall from £6050 to £4950. An alteration in the permanent rate of profits, to any great amount, is the effect of causes which do not operate but in the course of years, whereas alterations in the quantity of labour necessary to produce commodities are of daily occurrence. Every improvement in machinery, in tools, in buildings, in raising the raw material, saves labour, and enables us to produce the commodity to which the improvement is applied with more facility, and consequently its value alters. In estimating, then, the causes of the variations in the value of commodities, although it would be wrong wholly to omit the consideration of the effect produced by a rise or fall of labour, it would be equally incorrect to attach much importance to it; and consequently, in the subsequent part of this work, though I shall occasionally refer to this cause of variation, I shall consider all the great variations which take place in the relative value of commodities to be produced by the greater or less quantity of labour which may be required from time to time to produce them.

It is hardly necessary to say that commodities which have the same quantity of labour bestowed on their production will differ in exchangeable value if they cannot be brought to market in the same time.

Suppose I employ twenty men at an expense of £1000 for a year in the production of a commodity, and at the end of the year I employ twenty men again for another year, at a further expense of £1000 in finishing or perfecting the same commodity, and that I bring it to market at the end of two years, if profits be 10 per cent., my commodity must sell for £2310; for I have employed £1000 capital for one year, and £2100 capital for one year more. Another man employs precisely the same quantity of labour, but he employs it all in the first year; he employs forty men at an expense of £2000, and at the end of the first year he sells it with 10 per cent. profit, or for £2200. Here, then, are two commodities having precisely the same quantity of labour bestowed on them, one of which sells for £2310—the other for £2200.

This case appears to differ from the last, but is, in fact, the same. In both cases the superior price of one commodity is owing to the greater length of time which must elapse before it can be brought to market. In the former case the machinery and cloth were more than double the value of the corn, although only double the quantity of labour was bestowed on them. In the second case, one commodity is more valuable than the other, although no more labour was employed on its production. The difference in value arises in both cases from the profits being accumulated as capital, and is only a just compensation for the time that the profits were withheld.

It appears, then, that the division of capital into different proportions of fixed and circulating capital, employed in different trades, introduces a considerable modification to the rule, which is of universal application when labour is almost exclusively employed in production; namely, that commodities never vary in value unless a greater or less quantity of labour be bestowed on their production, it being shown in this section that, without any variation in the quantity of labour, the rise of its value merely will occasion a fall in the exchangeable value of those goods in the production of which fixed capital is employed; the larger the amount of fixed capital, the greater will be the fall.

SECTION V

The principle that value does not vary with the rise or fall of wages, modified also by the unequal durability of capital, and by the unequal rapidity with which it is returned to its employer

IN the last section we have supposed that, of two equal capitals, in two different occupations, the proportions of fixed and circulating capitals were unequal; now let us suppose them to be in the same proportion, but of unequal durability. In proportion as fixed capital is less durable it approaches to the nature of circulating capital. It will be consumed and its value reproduced in a shorter time, in order to preserve the capital of the manufacturer. We have just seen that in proportion as fixed capital preponderates in a manufacture, when wages rise the value of commodities produced in that manufacture is relatively lower than that of commodities produced in manufactures where circulating capital preponderates. In proportion to the less durability of fixed capital, and its approach to the nature of circulating capital, the same effect will be produced by the same cause.

If fixed capital be not of a durable nature it will require a great quantity of labour annually to keep it in its original state of efficiency; but the labour so bestowed may be considered as really expended on the commodity manufactured, which must bear a value in proportion to such labour. If I had a machine worth £20,000 which with very little labour was efficient to the production of commodities, and if the wear and tear of such machine were of trifling amount, and the general rate of profit 10 per cent., I should not require much more than £2000 to be added to the price of the goods, on account of the employment of my machine; but if the wear and tear of the machine were great, if the quantity of labour requisite to keep it in an efficient state were that of fifty men annually, I should require an additional price for my goods equal to that which would be obtained by any other manufacturer who employed fifty men in the production of other goods, and who used no machinery at all.

But a rise in the wages of labour would not equally affect commodities produced with machinery quickly consumed, and commodities produced with machinery slowly consumed. In the production of the one, a great deal of labour would be continually transferred to the commodity produced—in the other very little would be so transferred. Every rise of wages, therefore, or, which is the same thing, every fall of profits, would lower the relative value of those commodities which were produced with a capital of a durable nature, and would proportionally elevate those which were produced with capital more perishable. A fall of wages would have precisely the contrary effect.

I have already said that fixed capital is of various degrees of durability—suppose now a machine which could in any particular trade be employed to do the work of one hundred men for a year, and that it would last only for one year. Suppose, too, the machine to cost £5000, and the wages annually paid to one hundred men to be £5000, it is evident that it would be a matter of indifference to the manufacturer whether he bought the machine or employed the men. But suppose labour to rise, and consequently the wages of one hundred men for a year to amount to £5500, it is obvious that the manufacturer would now no longer hesitate, it would be for his interest to buy the machine and get his work done for £5000. But will not the machine rise in price, will not that also be worth £5500 in consequence of the rise of labour? It would rise in price if there were no stock employed on its construction, and no profits to be paid to the maker of it. If, for example, the machine were the produce of the labour of one hundred men, working one year upon it with wages of £50 each, and its price were consequently £5000; should those wages rise to £55, its price would be £5500, but this cannot be the case; less than one hundred men are employed or it could not be sold for £5000, for out of the £5000 must be paid the profits of stock which employed the men. Suppose then that only eighty-five men were employed at an expense of £50 each, or £4250 per annum, and that the £750 which the sale of the machine would produce over and above the wages advanced to the men constituted the profits of the engineer's stock. When wages rose 10 per cent., he would be obliged to employ an additional capital of £425, and would therefore employ £4675 instead of £4250, on which capital he would only get a profit of £325 if he continued to sell his machine for £5000; but this is precisely the case of all manufacturers and capitalists; the rise of wages affects them all. If therefore the maker of the machine should raise the price of it in consequence of a rise of wages, an unusual quantity of capital would be employed in the construction of such machines, till their price afforded only the common rate of profits.[1] We see then that machines would not rise in price in consequence of a rise of wages.

The manufacturer, however, who in a general rise of wages can have recourse to a machine which shall not increase the charge of production on his commodity, would enjoy peculiar advantages if he could continue to charge the same price for his goods; but he, as we have already seen, would be obliged to lower the price of his commodities, or capital would flow to his trade till his profits had sunk to the general level. Thus then is the public benefited by machinery: these mute agents are always the produce of much less labour than that which they displace, even when they are of the same money value. Through their influence an increase in the price of provisions which raises wages will affect fewer persons; it will reach, as in the above instance, eighty-five men instead of a hundred, and the saving which is the consequence shows itself in the reduced price of the commodity manufactured. Neither machines, nor the commodities made by them, rise in real value, but all commodities made by machines fall, and fall in proportion to their durability.

It will be seen then, that in the early stages of society, before much machinery or durable capital is used, the commodities produced by equal capitals will be nearly of equal value, and will rise or fall only relatively to each other on account of more or less labour being required for their production; but after the introduction of these expensive and durable instruments, the commodities produced by the employment of equal capitals will be of very unequal value, and although they will still be liable to rise or fall relatively to each other, as more or less

---

[1] We here see why it is that old countries are constantly impelled to employ machinery, and new countries to employ labour. With every difficulty of providing for the maintenance of men, labour necessarily rises, and with every rise in the price of labour, new temptations are offered to the use of machinery. This difficulty of providing for the maintenance of men is in constant operation in old countries; in new ones a very great increase in the population may take place without the least rise in the wages of labour. It may be as easy to provide for the seventh, eighth, and ninth million of men as for the second, third, and fourth.

labour becomes necessary to their production, they will be subject to another, though a minor variation, also from the rise or fall of wages and profits. Since goods which sell for £5000 may be the produce of a capital equal in amount to that from which are produced other goods which sell for £10,000, the profits on their manufacture will be the same; but those profits would be unequal if the prices of the goods did not vary with a rise or fall in the rate of profits.

It appears, too, that in proportion to the durability of capital employed in any kind of production the relative prices of those commodities on which such durable capital is employed will vary inversely as wages; they will fall as wages rise, and rise as wages fall; and, on the contrary, those which are produced chiefly by labour with less fixed capital, or with fixed capital of a less durable character than the medium in which price is estimated, will rise as wages rise, and fall as wages fall.

SECTION VI

On an invariable measure of value

WHEN commodities varied in relative value it would be desirable to have the means of ascertaining which of them fell and which rose in real value, and this could be effected only by comparing them one after another with some invariable standard measure of value, which should itself be subject to none of the fluctuations to which other commodities are exposed. Of such a measure it is impossible to be possessed, because there is no commodity which is not itself exposed to the same variations as the things the value of which is to be ascertained; that is, there is none which is not subject to require more or less labour for its production. But if this cause of variation in the value of a medium could be removed—if it were possible that in the production of our money, for instance, the same quantity of labour should at all times be required, still it would not be a perfect standard or invariable measure of value, because, as I have already endeavoured to explain, it would be subject to relative variations from a rise or fall of wages, on account of the different proportions of fixed capital which might be necessary to produce it, and to produce those other commodities whose alteration of value we wished to ascertain. It might be subject to variations, too, from the same cause, on account of the different degrees of durability of the fixed capital employed on it, and the commodities to be compared with it—or the time necessary to bring the one to market might be longer or shorter than the time necessary to bring the other commodities to market, the variations of which were to be determined; all which circumstances disqualify any commodity that can be thought of from being a perfectly accurate measure of value.

If, for example, we were to fix on gold as a standard, it is evident that it is but a commodity obtained under the same contingencies as every other commodity, and requiring labour and fixed capital to produce it. Like every other commodity, improvements in the saving of labour might be applied to its production, and consequently it might fall in relative value to other things merely on account of the greater facility of producing it.

If we suppose this cause of variation to be removed, and the same quantity of labour to be always required to obtain the same quantity of gold, still gold would not be a perfect measure of value, by which we could accurately ascertain the variations in all other things, because it would not be produced with precisely the same combinations of fixed and circulating capital as all other things; nor with fixed capital of the same durability; nor would it require precisely the same length of time before it could be brought to market. It would be a perfect measure of value for all things produced under the same circumstances precisely as itself, but for no others. If, for example, it were produced under the same circumstances as we have supposed necessary to produce cloth and cotton goods, it would be a perfect measure of value for those things, but not so for corn, for coals, and other commodities produced with either a less or a greater proportion of fixed capital, because, as we have shown, every alteration in the permanent rate of profits would have some effect on the relative value of all these goods, independently of any alteration in the quantity of labour employed on their production. If gold were produced under the same circumstances as corn, even if they never changed, it would not, for the same reasons, be at all times a perfect measure of the value of cloth and cotton goods. Neither gold, then, nor any other commodity, can ever be a perfect measure of value for all things; but I have already remarked that the effect on the relative prices of things, from a variation in profits, is comparatively slight; that by far the most important effects are produced by the varying quantities of labour required for production; and therefore, if we suppose this important cause of variation removed from the production of gold, we shall probably possess as near an approximation to a standard measure of value as can be theoretically conceived. May not gold be considered as a commodity produced with such proportions of the two kinds of capital as approach nearest to the average quantity employed in the production of most commodities? May not these proportions be so nearly equally distant from the two extremes, the one where little fixed capital is used, the other where little labour is employed, as to form a just mean between them?

If, then, I may suppose myself to be possessed of a standard so nearly approaching to an invariable one, the advantage is that I shall be enabled to speak of the variations of other things without embarrassing myself on every occasion with the consideration of the possible alteration in the value of the medium in which price and value are estimated.

To facilitate, then, the object of this inquiry, although I fully allow that money made of gold is subject to most of the variations of other things, I shall suppose it to be invariable, and therefore all alterations in price to be occasioned by some alteration in the value of the commodity of which I may be speaking.

Before I quit this subject, it may be proper to observe that

Adam Smith, and all the writers who have followed him, have, without one exception that I know of, maintained that a rise in the price of labour would be uniformly followed by a rise in the price of all commodities. I hope I have succeeded in showing that there are no grounds for such an opinion, and that only those commodities would rise which had less fixed capital employed upon them than the medium in which price was estimated, and that all those which had more would positively fall in price when wages rose. On the contrary, if wages fell, those commodities only would fall which had a less proportion of fixed capital employed on them than the medium in which price was estimated; all those which had more would positively rise in price.

It is necessary for me also to remark that I have not said, because one commodity has so much labour bestowed upon it as will cost £1000, and another so much as will cost £2000, that therefore one would be of the value of £1000, and the other of the value of £2000; but I have said that their value will be to each other as two to one, and that in those proportions they will be exchanged. It is of no importance to the truth of this doctrine whether one of these commodities sells for £1100 and the other for £2200, or one for £1500 and the other for £3000; into that question I do not at present inquire; I affirm only that their relative values will be governed by the relative quantities of labour bestowed on their production.[1]

[1] Mr. Malthus remarks on this doctrine, "We have the power indeed, arbitrarily, to call the labour which has been employed upon a commodity its real value, but in so doing we use words in a different sense from that in which they are customarily used; we confound at once the very important distinction between *cost* and *value*; and render it almost impossible to explain with clearness the main stimulus to the production of wealth, which in fact depends upon this distinction."

Mr. Malthus appears to think that it is a part of my doctrine that the cost and value of a thing should be the same; it is, if he means by cost, "cost of production" including profits. In the above passage, this is what he does not mean, and therefore he has not clearly understood me.

SECTION VII

Different effects from the alteration in the value of money, the medium in
which PRICE is always expressed, or from the alteration in the value
of the commodities which money purchases

ALTHOUGH I shall, as I have already explained, have occasion
to consider money as invariable in value, for the purpose of
more distinctly pointing out the causes of relative variations in
the value of other things, it may be useful to notice the different
effects which will follow from the prices of goods being altered
by the causes to which I have already adverted, namely, the
different quantities of labour required to produce them, and their
being altered by a variation in the value of money itself.

Money being a variable commodity, the rise of money-wages
will be frequently occasioned by a fall in the value of money.
A rise of wages from this cause will, indeed, be invariably accompanied by a rise in the price of commodities; but in such
cases it will be found that labour and all commodities have not
varied in regard to each other, and that the variation has been
confined to money.

Money, from its being a commodity obtained from a foreign
country, from its being the general medium of exchange between
all civilised countries, and from its being also distributed among
those countries in proportions which are ever changing with
every improvement in commerce and machinery, and with every
increasing difficulty of obtaining food and necessaries for an
increasing population, is subject to incessant variations. In
stating the principles which regulate exchangeable value and
price, we should carefully distinguish between those variations
which belong to the commodity itself, and those which are
occasioned by a variation in the medium in which value is
estimated or price expressed.

A rise in wages, from an alteration in the value of money,
produces a general effect on price, and for that reason it produces no real effect whatever on profits. On the contrary, a

rise of wages, from the circumstance of the labourer being more liberally rewarded, or from a difficulty of procuring the necessaries on which wages are expended, does not, except in some instances, produce the effect of raising price, but has a great effect in lowering profits. In the one case, no greater proportion of the annual labour of the country is devoted to the support of the labourers; in the other case, a larger portion is so devoted.

It is according to the division of the whole produce of the land of any particular farm, between the three classes, of landlord, capitalist, and labourer, that we are to judge of the rise or fall of rent, profit, and wages, and not according to the value at which that produce may be estimated in a medium which is confessedly variable.

It is not by the absolute quantity of produce obtained by either class that we can correctly judge of the rate of profit, rent, and wages, but by the quantity of labour required to obtain that produce. By improvements in machinery and agriculture the whole produce may be doubled; but if wages, rent, and profit be also doubled, these three will bear the same proportions to one another as before, and neither could be said to have relatively varied. But if wages partook not of the whole of this increase; if they, instead of being doubled, were only increased one-half; if rent, instead of being doubled, were only increased three-fourths, and the remaining increase went to profit, it would, I apprehend, be correct for me to say that rent and wages had fallen while profits had risen; for if we had an invariable standard by which to measure the value of this produce we should find that a less value had fallen to the class of labourers and landlords, and a greater to the class of capitalists, than had been given before. We might find, for example, that though the absolute quantity of commodities had been doubled, they were the produce of precisely the former quantity of labour. Of every hundred hats, coats, and quarters of corn produced, if

L

The labourers had before	.	.	.	25
The landlords	.	.	.	.	25
And the capitalists	.	.	.	50

$$100:$$

And if, after these commodities were double the quantity, of every 100

The labourers had only	.	.	.	22
The landlords	.	.	.	22
And the capitalists	.	.	.	56

$$100:$$

In that case I should say that wages and rent had fallen and profits risen; though, in consequence of the abundance of commodities, the quantity paid to the labourer and landlord would have increased in the proportion of 25 to 44. Wages are to be estimated by their real value, viz., by the quantity of labour and capital employed in producing them, and not by their nominal value either in coats, hats, money, or corn. Under the circumstances I have just supposed, commodities would have fallen to half their former value, and if money had not varied, to half their former price also. If then in this medium, which had not varied in value, the wages of the labourer should be found to have fallen, it will not the less be a real fall because they might furnish him with a greater quantity of cheap commodities than his former wages.

The variation in the value of money, however great, makes no difference in the *rate* of profits; for suppose the goods of the manufacturer to rise from £1000 to £2000, or 100 per cent., if his capital, on which the variations of money have as much effect as on the value of produce, if his machinery, buildings, and stock in trade rise also a 100 per cent., his rate of profits will be the same, and he will have the same quantity, and no more, of the produce of the labour of the country at his command.

If, with a capital of a given value, he can, by economy in labour, double the quantity of produce, and it fall to half its former price, it will bear the same proportion to the capital that produced it which it did before, and consequently profits will still be at the same rate.

If, at the same time that he doubles the quantity of produce by the employment of the same capital, the value of money is by any accident lowered one half, the produce will sell for twice the money value that it did before; but the capital employed to produce it will also be of twice its former value; and therefore in this case, too, the value of the produce will bear the same proportion to the value of the capital as it did before; and although the produce be doubled, rent, wages, and profits will only vary as the proportions vary, in which this double produce may be divided among the three classes that share it.

CHAPTER II

ON RENT

IT remains however to be considered whether the appropriation of land, and the consequent creation of rent, will occasion any variation in the relative value of commodities independently of the quantity of labour necessary to production. In order to understand this part of the subject we must inquire into the nature of rent, and the laws by which its rise or fall is regulated.

Rent is that portion of the produce of the earth which is paid to the landlord for the use of the original and indestructible powers of the soil. It is often, however, confounded with the interest and profit of capital, and, in popular language, the term is applied to whatever is annually paid by a farmer to his landlord. If, of two adjoining farms of the same extent, and of the same natural fertility, one had all the conveniences of farming buildings, and, besides, were properly drained and manured, and advantageously divided by hedges, fences, and walls, while the other had none of these advantages, more remuneration would naturally be paid for the use of one than for the use of the other; yet in both cases this remuneration would be called rent. But it is evident that a portion only of the money annually to be paid for the improved farm would be given for the original and indestructible powers of the soil; the other portion would be paid for the use of the capital which had been employed in ameliorating the quality of the land, and in erecting such buildings as were necessary to secure and preserve the produce. Adam Smith sometimes speaks of rent in the strict sense to which I am desirous of confining it, but more often in the popular sense in which the term is usually employed. He tells us that the demand for timber, and its consequent high price, in the more southern countries of Europe caused a rent to be paid for forests in Norway which could before afford no rent. Is it not, however, evident that the person who paid what he thus calls rent, paid it in consideration of the valuable commodity which was then standing on the land, and that he actually repaid himself with a profit by the sale of the timber? If, indeed, after the timber was removed, any compensation were paid to the landlord for the use of the land, for the purpose of growing timber or any other produce, with a view to future demand, such compensation might justly be called rent, because it would be paid for the productive powers of the land; but in the case stated by Adam Smith, the compensation was paid for the liberty of removing and selling the timber, and not for the liberty of growing it. He speaks also of the rent of coal mines, and of stone quarries, to which the same observation applies—that the compensation given for the mine or quarry is paid for the value of the coal or stone which can be removed from them, and has no connection with the original and indestructible powers of the land. This is a distinction of great importance in an inquiry concerning rent and profits; for it is found that the laws which regulate the progress of rent are widely different from those which regulate the progress of profits, and seldom operate in the same direction. In all improved countries, that which is annually paid to the landlord, partaking of both characters, rent and profit, is sometimes kept stationary by the effects of opposing causes; at other times advances or recedes as one or the other of these causes preponderates. In the future pages of this work, then, whenever I speak of the rent of land, I wish to be understood as speaking of that compensation which is paid to the owner of land for the use of its original and indestructible powers.

On the first settling of a country in which there is an abundance of rich and fertile land, a very small proportion of which is required to be cultivated for the support of the actual population, or indeed can be cultivated with the capital which the population can command, there will be no rent; for no one would pay for the use of land when there was an abundant quantity not yet appropriated, and, therefore, at the disposal of whosoever might choose to cultivate it.

On the common principles of supply and demand, no rent could be paid for such land, for the reason stated why nothing is given for the use of air and water, or for any other of the gifts of nature which exist in boundless quantity. With a given quantity of materials, and with the assistance of the pressure of the atmosphere, and the elasticity of steam, engines may perform work, and abridge human labour to a very great extent; but no charge is made for the use of these natural aids, because they are inexhaustible and at every man's disposal. In the same manner, the brewer, the distiller, the dyer, make incessant use of the air and water for the production of their commodities; but as the supply is boundless, they bear no price.[1] If all land had the same properties, if it were unlimited in quantity, and

[1] "The earth, as we have already seen, is not the only agent of nature which has a productive power; but it is the only one, or nearly so, that one set of men take to themselves to the exclusion of others; and of which, consequently, they can appropriate the benefits. The waters of rivers, and of the sea, by the power which they have of giving movement to our machines, carrying our boats, nourishing our fish, have also a productive power; the wind which turns our mills, and even the heat of the sun, work for us; but happily no one has yet been able to say, the 'wind and the sun are mine, and the service which they render must be paid for.' "—*Économie Politique*, par J. B. Say, vol. ii. p. 124.

uniform in quality, no charge could be made for its use, unless where it possessed peculiar advantages of situation. It is only, then, because land is not unlimited in quantity and uniform in quality, and because, in the progress of population, land of an inferior quality, or less advantageously situated, is called into cultivation, that rent is ever paid for the use of it. When, in the progress of society, land of the second degree of fertility is taken into cultivation, rent immediately commences on that of the first quality, and the amount of that rent will depend on the difference in the quality of these two portions of land.

When land of the third quality is taken into cultivation, rent immediately commences on the second, and it is regulated as before by the difference in their productive powers. At the same time, the rent of the first quality will rise, for that must always be above the rent of the second by the difference between the produce which they yield with a given quantity of capital and labour. With every step in the progress of population, which shall oblige a country to have recourse to land of a worse quality, to enable it to raise its supply of food, rent, on all the more fertile land, will rise.

Thus suppose land—No. 1, 2, 3—to yield, with an equal employment of capital and labour, a net produce of 100, 90, and 80 quarters of corn. In a new country, where there is an abundance of fertile land compared with the population, and where therefore it is only necessary to cultivate No. 1, the whole net produce will belong to the cultivator, and will be the profits of the stock which he advances. As soon as population had so far increased as to make it necessary to cultivate No. 2, from which ninety quarters only can be obtained after supporting the labourers, rent would commence on No. 1; for either there must be two rates of profit on agricultural capital, or ten quarters, or the value of ten quarters must be withdrawn from the produce of No. 1 for some other purpose. Whether the proprietor of the land, or any other person, cultivated No. 1, these ten quarters would equally constitute rent; for the cultivator of No. 2 would get the same result with his capital whether he cultivated No 1, paying ten quarters for rent, or continued to cultivate No. 2, paying no rent. In the same manner it might be shown that when No. 3 is brought into cultivation, the rent of No. 2 must be ten quarters, or the value of ten quarters, whilst the rent of No. 1 would rise to twenty quarters; for the cultivator of No. 3 would have the same profits whether he paid twenty quarters for the rent of No. 1, ten quarters for the rent of No. 2, or cultivated No. 3 free of all rent.

It often, and, indeed, commonly happens, that before No. 2, 3, 4, or 5, or the inferior lands are cultivated, capital can be employed more productively on those lands which are already in cultivation. It may perhaps be found that by doubling the original capital employed on No. 1, though the produce will not be doubled, will not be increased by 100 quarters, it may be increased by eighty-five quarters, and that this quantity exceeds what could be obtained by employing the same capital on land No. 3.

In such case, capital will be preferably employed on the old land, and will equally create a rent; for rent is always the difference between the produce obtained by the employment of two equal quantities of capital and labour. If, with a capital of £1000 a tenant obtain 100 quarters of wheat from his land, and by the employment of a second capital of £1000 he obtain a further return of eighty-five, his landlord would have the power, at the expiration of his lease, of obliging him to pay fifteen quarters or an equivalent value for additional rent; for there cannot be two rates of profit. If he is satisfied with a diminution of fifteen quarters in the return for his second £1000, it is because no employment more profitable can be found for it. The common rate of profit would be in that proportion, and if the original tenant refused, some other person would be found willing to give all which exceeded that rate of profit to the owner of the land from which he derived it.

In this case, as well as in the other, the capital last employed pays no rent. For the greater productive powers of the first £1000, fifteen quarters, is paid for rent, for the employment of the second £1000 no rent whatever is paid. If a third £1000 be employed on the same land, with a return of seventy-five quarters, rent will then be paid for the second £1000, and will be equal to the difference between the produce of these two, or ten quarters; and at the same time the rent for the first £1000 will rise from fifteen to twenty-five quarters; while the last £1000 will pay no rent whatever.

If, then, good land existed in a quantity much more abundant than the production of food for an increasing population required, or if capital could be indefinitely employed without a diminished return on the old land, there could be no rise of rent; for rent invariably proceeds from the employment of an additional quantity of labour with a proportionally less return.

The most fertile and most favourably situated land will be first cultivated, and the exchangeable value of its produce will be adjusted in the same manner as the exchangeable value of all other commodities, by the total quantity of labour necessary in various forms, from first to last, to produce it and bring it to market. When land of an inferior quality is taken into cultivation, the exchangeable value of raw produce will rise, because more labour is required to produce it.

The exchangeable value of all commodities, whether they be manufactured, or the produce of the mines, or the produce of land, is always regulated, not by the less quantity of labour that will suffice for their production under circumstances highly favourable, and exclusively enjoyed by those who have peculiar facilities of production; but by the greater quantity of labour necessarily bestowed on their production by those who have no such facilities; by those who continue to produce them under the most unfavourable circumstances; meaning—by the most unfavourable circumstances, the most unfavourable under which the quantity of produce required renders it necessary to carry on the production.

Thus, in a charitable institution, where the poor are set to work with the funds of benefactors, the general prices of the commodities, which are the produce of such work, will not be governed by the peculiar facilities afforded to these workmen, but by the common, usual, and natural difficulties which every other manufacturer will have to encounter. The manufacturer enjoying none of these facilities might indeed be driven altogether from the market if the supply afforded by these favoured workmen were equal to all the wants of the community; but if he continued the trade, it would be only on condition that he should derive from it the usual and general rate of profits on stock; and that could only happen when his commodity sold for a price proportioned to the quantity of labour bestowed on its production.[1]

It is true, that on the best land, the same produce would still be obtained with the same labour as before, but its value would be enhanced in consequence of the diminished returns obtained by those who employed fresh labour and stock on the less fertile land. Notwithstanding, then, that the advantages of fertile over inferior lands are in no case lost, but only transferred from the cultivator, or consumer, to the landlord, yet, since more labour is required on the inferior lands, and since it is from such land

[1] Has not M. Say forgotten, in the following passage, that it is the cost of production which ultimately regulates price? "The produce of labour employed on the land has this peculiar property, that it does not become more dear by becoming more scarce, because population always diminishes at the same time that food diminishes, and consequently the quantity of these products *demanded* diminishes at the same time as the quantity supplied. Besides, it is not observed that corn is more dear in those places where there is plenty of uncultivated land, than in completely cultivated countries. England and France were much more imperfectly cultivated in the middle ages than they are now; they produced much less raw produce: nevertheless, from all that we can judge by a comparison with the value of other things, corn was not sold at a dearer price. If the produce was less, so was the population; the weakness of the demand compensated the feebleness of the supply" (vol. ii. 338). M. Say being impressed with the opinion that the price of commodities is regulated by the price of labour, and justly supposing that charitable institutions of all sorts tend to increase the population beyond what it otherwise would be, and therefore to lower wages, says, "I suspect that the cheapness of the goods which come from England is partly caused by the numerous charitable institutions which exist in that country" (vol. ii. 277). This is a consistent opinion in one who maintains that wages regulate price.

only that we are enabled to furnish ourselves with the additional supply of raw produce, the comparative value of that produce will continue permanently above its former level, and make it exchange for more hats, cloth, shoes, etc., etc., in the production of which no such additional quantity of labour is required.

The reason, then, why raw produce rises in comparative value is because more labour is employed in the production of the last portion obtained, and not because a rent is paid to the landlord. The value of corn is regulated by the quantity of labour bestowed on its production on that quality of land, or with that portion of capital, which pays no rent. Corn is not high because a rent is paid, but a rent is paid because corn is high; and it has been justly observed that no reduction would take place in the price of corn although landlords should forego the whole of their rent. Such a measure would only enable some farmers to live like gentlemen, but would not diminish the quantity of labour necessary to raise raw produce on the least productive land in cultivation.

Nothing is more common than to hear of the advantages which the land possesses over every other source of useful produce, on account of the surplus which it yields in the form of rent. Yet when land is most abundant, when most productive, and most fertile, it yields no rent; and it is only when its powers decay, and less is yielded in return for labour, that a share of the original produce of the more fertile portions is set apart for rent. It is singular that this quality in the land, which should have been noticed as an imperfection compared with the natural agents by which manufacturers are assisted, should have been pointed out as constituting its peculiar pre-eminence. If air, water, the elasticity of steam, and the pressure of the atmosphere were of various qualities; if they could be appropriated, and each quality existed only in moderate abundance, they, as well as the land, would afford a rent, as the successive qualities were brought into use. With every worse quality employed, the value of the commodities in the manufacture of which they were used would rise, because equal quantities of labour would be less productive. Man would do more by the sweat of his brow and nature perform less; and the land would be no longer pre-eminent for its limited powers.

If the surplus produce which land affords in the form of rent be an advantage, it is desirable that, every year, the machinery newly constructed should be less efficient than the old, as that would undoubtedly give a greater exchangeable value to the goods manufactured, not only by that machinery but by all the other machinery in the kingdom; and a rent would be paid to all those who possessed the most productive machinery.[1]

[1] "In agriculture, too," says Adam Smith, "nature labours along with man; and though her labour costs no expense, its produce has its value, as well as that of the most expensive workman." The labour of nature is paid, not because she does much, but because she does little. In proportion as she becomes niggardly in her gifts she exacts a greater price for her work. Where she is munificently beneficent she always works gratis. "The labouring cattle employed in agriculture not only occasion, like the workmen in manufactures, the reproduction of a value equal to their own consumption, or to the capital which employs them, together with its owner's profits, but of a much greater value. Over and above the capital of the farmer and all its profits, they regularly occasion the reproduction of the rent of the landlord. This rent may be considered as the produce of those powers of nature, the use of which the landlord lends to the farmer. It is greater or smaller according to the supposed extent of those powers, or, in other words, according to the supposed natural or improved fertility of the land. It is the work of nature which remains, after deducting or compensating everything which can be regarded as the work of man. It is seldom less than a fourth, and frequently more than a third of the whole produce. No equal quantity of productive labour employed in manufactures can ever occasion so great a reproduction. *In them nature does nothing, man does all*; and the reproduction must always be in proportion to the strength of the agents that occasion it. The capital employed in agriculture, therefore, not only puts into motion a greater quantity of productive labour than any equal capital employed in manufactures, but in proportion, too, to the quantity of the productive labour which it employs it adds a much greater value to the annual produce of the land and labour of the country, to the *real* wealth and revenue of its inhabitants. Of all the ways in which a capital can be employed, it is by far the most advantageous to the society."—Book II. chap. v.

Does nature nothing for man in manufactures? Are the powers of wind and water, which move our machinery and assist navigation, nothing? The pressure of the atmosphere and the elasticity of steam, which enable us to work the most stupendous engines—are they not the gifts of nature?

The rise of rent is always the effect of the increasing wealth of the country, and of the difficulty of providing food for its augmented population. It is a symptom, but it is never a cause of wealth; for the wealth often increases most rapidly while rent is either stationary, or even falling. Rent increases most rapidly as the disposable land decreases in its productive powers. Wealth increases most rapidly in those countries where the disposable land is most fertile, where importation is least restricted, and where, through agricultural improvements, productions can be multiplied without any increase in the proportional quantity of labour, and where consequently the progress of rent is slow.

If the high price of corn were the effect, and not the cause of rent, price would be proportionally influenced as rents were high or low, and rent would be a component part of price. But that corn which is produced by the greatest quantity of labour is the regulator of the price of corn; and rent does not and cannot enter in the least degree as a component part of its price.[1]

To say nothing of the effects of the matter of heat in softening and melting metals, of the decomposition of the atmosphere in the process of dyeing and fermentation. There is not a manufacture which can be mentioned in which nature does not give her assistance to man, and give it, too, generously and gratuitously.

In remarking on the passage which I have copied from Adam Smith, Mr. Buchanan observes, "I have endeavoured to show, in the observations on productive and unproductive labour, contained in the fourth volume, that agriculture adds no more to the national stock than any other sort of industry. In dwelling on the reproduction of rent as so great an advantage to society, Dr. Smith does not reflect that rent is the effect of high price, and that what the landlord gains in this way he gains at the expense of the community at large. There is no absolute gain to the society by the reproduction of rent; it is only one class profiting at the expense of another class. The notion of agriculture yielding a produce, and a rent in consequence, because nature concurs with human industry in the process of cultivation, is a mere fancy. It is not from the produce, but from the price at which the produce is sold, that the rent is derived; and this price is got not because nature assists in the production, but because it is the price which suits the consumption to the supply."

[1] The clearly understanding this principle is, I am persuaded, of the utmost importance to the science of political economy.

Adam Smith, therefore, cannot be correct in supposing that the original rule which regulated the exchangeable value of commodities, namely, the comparative quantity of labour by which they were produced, can be at all altered by the appropriation of land and the payment of rent. Raw material enters into the composition of most commodities, but the value of that raw material, as well as corn, is regulated by the productiveness of the portion of capital last employed on the land and paying no rent; and therefore rent is not a component part of the price of commodities.

We have been hitherto considering the effects of the natural progress of wealth and population on rent in a country in which the land is of variously productive powers, and we have seen that with every portion of additional capital which it becomes necessary to employ on the land with a less productive return rent would rise. It follows from the same principles that any circumstances in the society which should make it unnecessary to employ the same amount of capital on the land, and which should therefore make the portion last employed more productive, would lower rent. Any great reduction in the capital of a country which should materially diminish the funds destined for the maintenance of labour, would naturally have this effect. Population regulates itself by the funds which are to employ it, and therefore always increases or diminishes with the increase or diminution of capital. Every reduction of capital is therefore necessarily followed by a less effective demand for corn, by a fall of price, and by diminished cultivation. In the reverse order to that in which the accumulation of capital raises rent will the diminution of it lower rent. Land of a less unproductive quality will be in succession relinquished, the exchangeable value of produce will fall, and land of a superior quality will be the land last cultivated, and that which will then pay no rent.

The same effects may, however, be produced when the wealth and population of a country are increased, if that increase is accompanied by such marked improvements in agriculture as shall have the same effect of diminishing the necessity of cultivating the poorer lands, or of expending the same amount or capital on the cultivation of the more fertile portions.

If a million of quarters of corn be necessary for the support of a given population, and it be raised on land of the qualities of No. 1, 2, 3; and if an improvement be afterwards discovered by which it can be raised on No. 1 and 2, without employing No. 3, it is evident that the immediate effect must be a fall of rent; for No. 2, instead of No. 3, will then be cultivated without paying any rent; and the rent of No. 1, instead of being the difference between the produce of No. 3 and No. 1, will be the difference only between No. 2 and 1. With the same population, and no more, there can be no demand for any additional quantity of corn; the capital and labour employed on No. 3 will be devoted to the production of other commodities desirable to the community, and can have no effect in raising rent, unless the raw material from which they are made cannot be obtained without employing capital less advantageously on the land, in which case No. 3 must again be cultivated.

It is undoubtedly true that the fall in the relative price of raw produce, in consequence of the improvement in agriculture, or rather in consequence of less labour being bestowed on its production, would naturally lead to increased accumulation; for the profits of stock would be greatly augmented. This accumulation would lead to an increased demand for labour, to higher wages, to an increased population, to a further demand for raw produce, and to an increased cultivation. It is only, however, after the increase in the population that rent would be as high as before; that is to say, after No. 3 was taken into cultivation. A considerable period would have elapsed, attended with a positive diminution of rent.

But improvements in agriculture are of two kinds: those which increase the productive powers of the land and those which enable us, by improving our machinery, to obtain its produce with less labour. They both lead to a fall in the price of raw produce; they both affect rent, but they do not affect it equally. If they did not occasion a fall in the price of raw produce they would not be improvements; for it is the essential quality of an improvement to diminish the quantity of labour before required to produce a commodity; and this diminution cannot take place without a fall of its price or relative value.

The improvements which increased the productive powers of the land are such as the more skilful rotation of crops or the better choice of manure. These improvements absolutely enable us to obtain the same produce from a smaller quantity of land. If, by the introduction of a course of turnips, I can feed my sheep besides raising my corn, the land on which the sheep were before fed becomes unnecessary, and the same quantity of raw produce is raised by the employment of a less quantity of land. If I discover a manure which will enable me to make a piece of land produce 20 per cent. more corn, I may withdraw at least a portion of my capital from the most unproductive part of my farm. But, as I before observed, it is not necessary that land should be thrown out of cultivation in order to reduce rent: to produce this effect, it is sufficient that successive portions of capital are employed on the same land with different results, and that the portion which gives the least result should be withdrawn. If, by the introduction of the turnip husbandry, or by the use of a more invigorating manure, I can obtain the same produce with less capital, and without disturbing the difference between the productive powers of the successive portions of capital, I shall lower rent; for a different and more productive portion will be that which will form the standard from which every other will be reckoned. If, for example, the successive portions of capital yielded 100, 90, 80, 70; whilst I employed these four portions, my rent would be 60, or the difference between

$$\left.\begin{array}{l}
70 \text{ and } 100 = 30 \\
70 \text{ and } 90 = 20 \\
70 \text{ and } 80 = 10 \\
\\
\phantom{70 \text{ and } 80 = }60
\end{array}\right\} \text{ whilst the produce would be } 340 \left\{\begin{array}{l}
100 \\
90 \\
80 \\
70 \\
\hline
340
\end{array}\right.$$

and while I employed these portions, the rent would remain the same, although the produce of each should have an equal augmentation. If, instead of 100, 90, 80, 70, the produce should be increased to 125, 115, 105, 95, the rent would still be 60, or the difference between

$$
\left.\begin{array}{l}
95 \text{ and } 125 = 30 \\
95 \text{ and } 115 = 20 \\
95 \text{ and } 105 = 10 \\
\overline{} \\
60
\end{array}\right\}
\begin{array}{c}
\text{whilst the produce would be} \\
\text{increased to } 440
\end{array}
\left\{\begin{array}{l}
125 \\
115 \\
105 \\
95 \\
\overline{} \\
440
\end{array}\right.
$$

But with such an increase of produce, without an increase of demand,[1] there could be no motive for employing so much capital on the land; one portion would be withdrawn, and consequently the last portion of capital would yield 105 instead of 95, and rent would fall to 30, or the difference between

$$
\left.\begin{array}{l}
105 \text{ and } 125 = 20 \\
105 \text{ and } 115 = 10 \\
\overline{} \\
30
\end{array}\right\}
\begin{array}{c}
\text{whilst the produce will be still} \\
\text{adequate to the wants of the} \\
\text{population, for it would be } 345 \\
\text{quarters, or}
\end{array}
\left\{\begin{array}{l}
125 \\
115 \\
105 \\
\overline{} \\
345
\end{array}\right.
$$

the demand being only for 340 quarters.—But there are improvements which may lower the relative value of produce without lowering the corn rent, though they will lower the money rent of land. Such improvements do not increase the productive powers of the land, but they enable us to obtain its produce with less labour. They are rather directed to the forma-

---

[1] I hope I am not understood as undervaluing the importance of all sorts of improvement in agriculture to landlords—their immediate effect is to lower rent; but as they give a great stimulus to population, and at the same time enable us to cultivate poorer lands with less labour, they are ultimately of immense advantage to landlords. A period, however, must elapse during which they are positively injurious to him.

tion of the capital applied to the land than to the cultivation of the land itself. Improvements in agricultural implements, such as the plough and the thrashing machine, economy in the use of horses employed in husbandry, and a better knowledge of the veterinary art, are of this nature. Less capital, which is the same thing as less labour, will be employed on the land; but to obtain the same produce, less land cannot be cultivated. Whether improvements of this kind, however, affect corn rent, must depend on the question whether the difference between the produce obtained by the employment of different portions of capital be increased, stationary, or diminished. If four portions of capital, 50, 60, 70, 80, be employed on the land, giving each the same results, and any improvement in the formation of such capital should enable me to withdraw 5 from each, so that they should be 45, 55, 65, and 75, no alteration would take place in the corn rent; but if the improvements were such as to enable me to make the whole saving on that portion of capital which is least productively employed, corn rent would immediately fall, because the difference between the capital most productive and the capital least productive would be diminished; and it is this difference which constitutes rent.

Without multiplying instances, I hope enough has been said to show that whatever diminishes the inequality in the produce obtained from successive portions of capital employed on the same or on new land tends to lower rent; and that whatever increases that inequality, necessarily produces an opposite effect, and tends to raise it.

In speaking of the rent of the landlord, we have rather considered it as the proportion of the produce, obtained with a given capital on any given farm, without any reference to its exchangeable value; but since the same cause, the difficulty of production, raises the exchangeable value of raw produce, and raises also the proportion of raw produce paid to the landlord for rent, it is obvious that the landlord is doubly benefited by difficulty of production. First, he obtains a greater

M

share, and, secondly, the commodity in which he is paid is of greater value.[1]

CHAPTER VII

ON FOREIGN TRADE

No extension of foreign trade will immediately increase the amount of value in a country, although it will very powerfully contribute to increase the mass of commodities, and therefore the sum of enjoyments. As the value of all foreign goods is measured by the quantity of the produce of our land and labour which is given in exchange for them, we should have no greater value if, by the discovery of new markets, we obtained double the quantity of foreign goods in exchange for a given quantity of ours. If by the purchase of English goods to the amount of £1000 a merchant can obtain a quantity of foreign goods, which he can sell in the English market for £1200, he will

---

[1] To make this obvious, and to show the degrees in which corn and money rent will vary, let us suppose that the labour of ten men will, on land of a certain quality, obtain 180 quarters of wheat, and its value to be £4 per quarter, or £720; and that the labour of ten additional men will, on the same or any other land, produce only 170 quarters in addition; wheat would rise from £4 to £4 4s. 8d. for 170: 180: :£4: £4 4s. 8d.; or, as in the production of 170 quarters, the labour of 10 men is necessary in one case, and only of 9.44 in the other, the rise would be as 9.44 to 10, or as £4 to £4 4s. 8d. If 10 men be further employed, and the return be

$$
\begin{array}{lll}
160 & \text{the price will rise to } £4 & 10 \ \ 0 \\
150 \quad \text{,,} & \text{,,} \quad 4 & 16 \ \ 0 \\
140 \quad \text{,,} & \text{,,} \quad 5 & 2 \ 10 \\
\end{array}
$$

Now, if no rent was paid for the land which yielded 180 quarters, when corn was at £4 per quarter, the value of 10 quarters would be paid as rent when only 170 could be procured, which at £4 4s. 8d. would £42 7s. 6d.

$$
\begin{array}{llllll}
20 \text{ quarters when } 160 \text{ were produced, which at } £4 & 10 & 0 \text{ would be } £ & 90 & 0 & 0 \\
30 \text{ quarters} \quad \text{,,} \quad 150 & \text{,,} & \text{,,} \quad £4 & 16 & 0 \quad \text{,,} & 144 & 0 & 0 \\
40 \text{ quarters} \quad \text{,,} \quad 140 & \text{,,} & \text{,,} \quad 5 & 2 & 10 \quad \text{,,} & 205 & 13 & 4 \\
\end{array}
$$

Corn rent would increase in the proportion of $\begin{Bmatrix} 100 \\ 200 \\ 300 \\ 400 \end{Bmatrix}$ and money rent in the proportion of $\begin{Bmatrix} 100 \\ 212 \\ 340 \\ 485 \end{Bmatrix}$

obtain 20 per cent. profit by such an employment of his capital; but neither his gains, nor the value of the commodities imported, will be increased or diminished by the greater or smaller quantity of foreign goods obtained. Whether, for example, he imports twenty-five or fifty pipes of wine, his interest can be no way affected if at one time the twenty-five pipes, and at another the fifty pipes, equally sell for £1200. In either case his profit will be limited to £200, or 20 per cent. on his capital; and in either case the same value will be imported into England. If the fifty pipes sold for more than £1200, the profits of this individual merchant would exceed the general rate of profits, and capital would naturally flow into this advantageous trade, till the fall of the price of wine had brought everything to the former level.

It has indeed been contended that the great profits which are sometimes made by particular merchants in foreign trade will elevate the general rate of profits in the country, and that the abstraction of capital from other employments, to partake of the new and beneficial foreign commerce, will raise prices generally, and thereby increase profits. It has been said, by high authority, that less capital being necessarily devoted to the growth of corn, to the manufacture of cloth, hats, shoes, etc., while the demand continues the same, the price of these commodities will be so increased, that the farmer, hatter, clothier, and shoemaker will have an increase of profits as well as the foreign merchant.[1]

They who hold this argument agree with me that the profits of different employments have a tendency to conform to one another; to advance and recede together. Our variance consists in this: They contend that the equality of profits will be brought about by the general rise of profits; and I am of opinion that the profits of the favoured trade will speedily subside to the general level.

For, first, I deny that less capital will necessarily be devoted to the growth of corn, to the manufacture of cloth, hats, shoes,

[1] See Adam Smith, book i. chap. 9.

etc., unless the demand for these commodities be diminished; and if so, their price will not rise. In the purchase of foreign commodities, either the same, a larger, or a less portion of the produce of the land and labour of England will be employed. If the same portion be so employed, then will the same demand exist for cloth, shoes, corn, and hats as before, and the same portion of capital will be devoted to their production. If, in consequence of the price of foreign commodities being cheaper, a less portion of the annual produce of the land and labour of England is employed in the purchase of foreign commodities, more will remain for the purchase of other things. If there be a greater demand for hats, shoes, corn, etc., than before, which there may be, the consumers of foreign commodities having an additional portion of their revenue disposable, the capital is also disposable with which the greater value of foreign commodities was before purchased; so that with the increased demand for corn, shoes, etc., there exists also the means of procuring an increased supply, and therefore neither prices nor profits can permanently rise. If more of the produce of the land and labour of England be employed in the purchase of foreign commodities, less can be employed in the purchase of other things, and therefore fewer hats, shoes, etc., will be required. At the same time that capital is liberated from the production of shoes, hats, etc., more must be employed in manufacturing those commodities with which foreign commodities are purchased; and, consequently, in all cases the demand for foreign and home commodities together, as far as regards value, is limited by the revenue and capital of the country. If one increases the other must diminish. If the quantity of wine imported in exchange for the same quantity of English commodities be doubled, the people of England can either consume double the quantity of wine that they did before, or the same quantity of wine and a greater quantity of English commodities. If my revenue had been £1000 with which I purchased annually one pipe of wine for £100, and a certain quantity of English commodities for £900; when wine fell to £50 per pipe, I might lay out the £50 saved, either in the purchase of an additional pipe of wine or in the purchase of more English commodities. If I bought more wine, and every wine-drinker did the same, the foreign trade would not be in the least disturbed; the same quantity of English commodities would be exported in exchange for wine, and we should receive double the quantity, though not double the value of wine. But if I, and others, contented ourselves with the same quantity of wine as before, fewer English commodities would be exported, and the wine-drinkers might either consume the commodities which were before exported, or any others for which they had an inclination. The capital required for their production would be supplied by the capital liberated from the foreign trade.

There are two ways in which capital may be accumulated; it may be saved either in consequence of increased revenue or of diminished consumption. If my profits are raised from £1000 to £1200, while my expenditure continues the same, I accumulate annually £200 more than I did before. If I save £200 out of my expenditure, while my profits continue the same, the same effect will be produced; £200 per annum will be added to my capital. The merchant who imported wine after profits had been raised from 20 per cent. to 40 per cent., instead of purchasing his English goods for £1000, must purchase them for £857 2s. 10d., still selling the wine which he imports in return for those goods for £1200; or, if he continued to purchase his English goods for £1000, must raise the price of his wine to £1400; he would thus obtain 40 instead of 20 per cent. profit on his capital; but if, in consequence of the cheapness of all the commodities on which his revenue was expended, he and all other consumers could save the value of £200 out of every £1000 they before expended, they would more effectually add to the real wealth of the country; in one case, the savings would be made in consequence of an increase of revenue, in the other, in consequence of diminished expenditure.

If, by the introduction of machinery, the generality of the commodities on which revenue was expended fell 20 per cent.

in value, I should be enabled to save as effectually as if my revenue had been raised 20 per cent.; but in one case the rate of profits is stationary, in the other it is raised 20 per cent.—If, by the introduction of cheap foreign goods, I can save 20 per cent. from my expenditure, the effect will be precisely the same as if machinery had lowered the expense of their production, but profits would not be raised.

It is not, therefore, in consequence of the extension of the market that the rate of profit is raised, although such extension may be equally efficacious in increasing the mass of commodities, and may thereby enable us to augment the funds destined for the maintenance of labour, and the materials on which labour may be employed. It is quite as important to the happiness of mankind that our enjoyments should be increased by the better distribution of labour, by each country producing those commodities for which by its situation, its climate, and its other natural or artificial advantages it is adapted, and by their exchanging them for the commodities of other countries, as that they should be augmented by a rise in the rate of profits.

It has been my endeavour to show throughout this work that the rate of profits can never be increased but by a fall in wages, and that there can be no permanent fall of wages but in consequence of a fall of the necessaries on which wages are expended. If, therefore, by the extension of foreign trade, or by improvements in machinery, the food and necessaries of the labourer can be brought to market, at a reduced price, profits will rise. If, instead of growing our own corn, or manufacturing the clothing and other necessaries of the labourer, we discover a new market from which we can supply ourselves with these commodities at a cheaper price, wages will fall and profits rise; but if the commodities obtained at a cheaper rate, by the extension of foreign commerce, or by the improvement of machinery, be exclusively the commodities consumed by the rich, no alteration will take place in the rate of profits. The rate of wages would not be affected, although wine, velvets, silks, and other expensive commodities should fall 50 per cent., and consequently profits would continue unaltered.

Foreign trade, then, though highly beneficial to a country, as it increases the amount and variety of the objects on which revenue may be expended, and affords, by the abundance and cheapness of commodities, incentives to saving, and to the accumulation of capital, has no tendency to raise the profits of stock unless the commodities imported be of that description on which the wages of labour are expended.

The remarks which have been made respecting foreign trade apply equally to home trade. The rate of profits is never increased by a better distribution of labour, by the invention of machinery, by the establishment of roads and canals, or by any means of abridging labour either in the manufacture or in the conveyance of goods. These are causes which operate on price, and never fail to be highly beneficial to consumers; since they enable them, with the same labour, or with the value of the produce of the same labour, to obtain in exchange a greater quantity of the commodity to which the improvement is applied; but they have no effect whatever on profit. On the other hand, every diminution in the wages of labour raises profits, but produces no effect on the price of commodities. One is advantageous to all classes, for all classes are consumers; the other is beneficial only to producers; they gain more, but everything remains at its former price. In the first case they get the same as before; but everything on which their gains are expended is diminished in exchangeable value.

The same rule which regulates the relative value of commodities in one country does not regulate the relative value of the commodities exchanged between two or more countries.

Under a system of perfectly free commerce, each country naturally devotes its capital and labour to such employments as are most beneficial to each. This pursuit of individual advantage is admirably connected with the universal good of the whole. By stimulating industry, by rewarding ingenuity, and by using most efficaciously the peculiar powers bestowed by nature, it distributes labour most effectively and most economically: while, by increasing the general mass of productions, it diffuses general benefit, and binds together, by one common tie of interest and intercourse, the universal society of nations throughout the civilised world. It is this principle which determines that wine shall be made in France and Portugal, that corn shall be grown in America and Poland, and that hardware and other goods shall be manufactured in England.

In one and the same country, profits are, generally speaking, always on the same level; or differ only as the employment of capital may be more or less secure and agreeable. It is not so between different countries. If the profits of capital employed in Yorkshire should exceed those of capital employed in London, capital would speedily move from London to Yorkshire, and an equality of profits would be effected; but if in consequence of the diminished rate of production in the lands of England from the increase of capital and population wages should rise and profits fall, it would not follow that capital and population would necessarily move from England to Holland, or Spain, or Russia, where profits might be higher.

If Portugal had no commercial connection with other countries, instead of employing a great part of her capital and industry in the production of wines, with which she purchases for her own use the cloth and hardware of other countries, she would be obliged to devote a part of that capital to the manufacture of those commodities, which she would thus obtain probably inferior in quality as well as quantity.

The quantity of wine which she shall give in exchange for the cloth of England is not determined by the respective quantities of labour devoted to the production of each, as it would be if both commodities were manufactured in England, or both in Portugal.

England may be so circumstanced that to produce the cloth may require the labour of 100 men for one year; and if she attempted to make the wine, it might require the labour of 120 men for the same time. England would therefore find it her interest to import wine, and to purchase it by the exportation of cloth.

To produce the wine in Portugal might require only the labour of 80 men for one year, and to produce the cloth in the same country might require the labour of 90 men for the same time. It would therefore be advantageous for her to export wine in exchange for cloth. This exchange might even take place notwithstanding that the commodity imported by Portugal could be produced there with less labour than in England. Though she could make the cloth with the labour of 90 men, she would import it from a country where it required the labour of 100 men to produce it, because it would be advantageous to her rather to employ her capital in the production of wine, for which she would obtain more cloth from England, than she could produce by diverting a portion of her capital from the cultivation of vines to the manufacture of cloth.

Thus England would give the produce of the labour of 100 men for the produce of the labour of 80. Such an exchange could not take place between the individuals of the same country. The labour of 100 Englishmen cannot be given for that of 80 Englishmen, but the produce of the labour of 100 Englishmen may be given for the produce of the labour of 80 Portuguese, 60 Russians, or 120 East Indians. The difference in this respect, between a single country and many, is easily accounted for, by considering the difficulty with which capital moves from one country to another, to seek a more profitable employment, and the activity with which it invariably passes from one province to another in the same country.[1]

[1] It will appear, then, that a country possessing very considerable advantages in machinery and skill, and which may therefore be enabled to manufacture commodities with much less labour than her neighbours, may, in return for such commodities, import a portion of the corn required for its consumption, even if its land were more fertile and corn could be grown with less labour than in the country from which it was imported. Two men can both make shoes and hats, and one is superior to the other in both employments; but in making hats he can only exceed his competitor by one-fifth or 20 per cent., and in making shoes he can excel him by one-third

It would undoubtedly be advantageous to the capitalists of England, and to the consumers in both countries, that under such circumstances the wine and the cloth should both be made in Portugal, and therefore that the capital and labour of England employed in making cloth should be removed to Portugal for that purpose. In that case, the relative value of these commodities would be regulated by the same principle as if one were the produce of Yorkshire and the other of London: and in every other case, if capital freely flowed towards those countries where it could be most profitably employed, there could be no difference in the rate of profit, and no other difference in the real or labour price of commodities than the additional quantity of labour required to convey them to the various markets where they were to be sold.

Experience, however, shows that the fancied or real insecurity of capital, when not under the immediate control of its owner, together with the natural disinclination which every man has to quit the country of his birth and connections, and intrust himself, with all his habits fixed, to a strange government and new laws, check the emigration of capital. These feelings, which I should be sorry to see weakened, induce most men of property to be satisfied with a low rate of profits in their own country, rather than seek a more advantageous employment for their wealth in foreign nations.

Gold and silver having been chosen for the general medium of circulation, they are, by the competition of commerce, distributed in such proportions amongst the different countries of the world as to accommodate themselves to the natural traffic which would take place if no such metals existed, and the trade between countries were purely a trade of barter.

Thus, cloth cannot be imported into Portugal unless it sell there for more gold than it cost in the country from which it was imported; and wine cannot be imported into England unless

or 33 per cent.;—will it not be for the interest of both that the superior man should employ himself exclusively in making shoes, and the inferior man in making hats?

it will sell for more there than it cost in Portugal. If the trade were purely a trade of barter, it could only continue whilst England could make cloth so cheap as to obtain a greater quantity of wine with a given quantity of labour by manufacturing cloth than by growing vines; and also whilst the industry of Portugal were attended by the reverse effects. Now suppose England to discover a process for making wine, so that it should become her interest rather to grow it than import it; she would naturally divert a portion of her capital from the foreign trade to the home trade; she would cease to manufacture cloth for exportation, and would grow wine for herself. The money price of these commodities would be regulated accordingly; wine would fall here while cloth continued at its former price, and in Portugal no alteration would take place in the price of either commodity. Cloth would continue for some time to be exported from this country, because its price would continue to be higher in Portugal than here; but money instead of wine would be given in exchange for it, till the accumulation of money here, and its diminution abroad, should so operate on the relative value of cloth in the two countries that it would cease to be profitable to export it. If the improvement in making wine were of a very important description, it might become profitable for the two countries to exchange employments; for England to make all the wine, and Portugal all the cloth consumed by them; but this could be effected only by a new distribution of the precious metals, which should raise the price of cloth in England and lower it in Portugal. The relative price of wine would fall in England in consequence of the real advantage from the improvement of its manufacture; that is to say, its natural price would fall; the relative price of cloth would rise there from the accumulation of money.

Thus, suppose before the improvement in making wine in England the price of wine here were £50 per pipe, and the price of a certain quantity of cloth were £45, whilst in Portugal the price of the same quantity of wine was £45, and that of the same quantity of cloth £50; wine would be exported from

Portugal with a profit of £5, and cloth from England with a profit of the same amount.

Suppose that, after the improvement, wine falls to £45 in England, the cloth continuing at the same price. Every transaction in commerce is an independent transaction. Whilst a merchant can buy cloth in England for £45, and sell it with the usual profit in Portugal, he will continue to export it from England. His business is simply to purchase English cloth, and to pay for it by a bill of exchange, which he purchases with Portuguese money. It is to him of no importance what becomes of this money: he has discharged his debt by the remittance of the bill. His transaction is undoubtedly regulated by the terms on which he can obtain this bill, but they are known to him at the time; and the causes which may influence the market price of bills, or the rate of exchange, is no consideration of his.

If the markets be favourable for the exportation of wine from Portugal to England, the exporter of the wine will be a seller of a bill, which will be purchased either by the importer of the cloth, or by the person who sold him his bill; and thus, without the necessity of money passing from either country, the exporters in each country will be paid for their goods. Without having any direct transaction with each other, the money paid in Portugal by the importer of cloth will be paid to the Portuguese exporter of wine; and in England by the negotiation of the same bill the exporter of the cloth will be authorised to receive its value from the importer of wine.

But if the prices of wine were such that no wine could be exported to England, the importer of cloth would equally purchase a bill; but the price of that bill would be higher, from the knowledge which the seller of it would possess that there was no counter bill in the market by which he could ultimately settle the transactions between the two countries; he might know that the gold or silver money which he received in exchange for his bill must be actually exported to his correspondent in England, to enable him to pay the demand which he had authorised to be made upon him, and he might therefore charge in the price of his bill all the expenses incurred, together with his fair and usual profit.

If then this premium for a bill on England should be equal to the profit on importing cloth, the importation would of course cease; but if the premium on the bill were only 2 per cent., if to be enabled to pay a debt in England of £100, £102 should be paid in Portugal, whilst cloth which cost £45 would sell for £50, cloth would be imported, bills would be bought, and money would be exported, till the diminution of money in Portugal, and its accumulation in England, had produced such a state of prices as would make it no longer profitable to continue these transactions.

But the diminution of money in one country, and its increase in another, do not operate on the price of one commodity only, but on the prices of all, and therefore the price of wine and cloth will be both raised in England and both lowered in Portugal. The price of cloth, from being £45 in one country and £50 in the other, would probably fall to £49 or £48 in Portugal, and rise to £46 or £47 in England, and not afford a sufficient profit after paying a premium for a bill to induce any merchant to import that commodity.

It is thus that the money of each country is apportioned to it in such quantities only as may be necessary to regulate a profitable trade of barter. England exported cloth in exchange for wine because, by so doing, her industry was rendered more productive to her; she had more cloth and wine than if she had manufactured both for herself; and Portugal imported cloth and exported wine because the industry of Portugal could be more beneficially employed for both countries in producing wine. Let there be more difficulty in England in producing cloth, or in Portugal in producing wine, or let there be more facility in England in producing wine, or in Portugal in producing cloth, and the trade must immediately cease.

No change whatever takes place in the circumstances of Portugal; but England finds that she can employ her labour more productively in the manufacture of wine, and instantly the trade of barter between the two countries changes. Not only is the exportation of wine from Portugal stopped, but a new distribution of the precious metals takes place, and her importation of cloth is also prevented.

Both countries would probably find it their interest to make their own wine and their own cloth; but this singular result would take place: in England, though wine would be cheaper, cloth would be elevated in price, more would be paid for it by the consumer; while in Portugal the consumers, both of cloth and of wine, would be able to purchase those commodities cheaper. In the country where the improvement was made prices would be enhanced; in that where no change had taken place, but where they had been deprived of a profitable branch of foreign trade, prices would fall.

This, however, is only a seeming advantage to Portugal, for the quantity of cloth and wine together produced in that country would be diminished, while the quantity produced in England would be increased. Money would in some degree have changed its value in the two countries; it would be lowered in England and raised in Portugal. Estimated in money, the whole revenue of Portugal would be diminished; estimated in the same medium the whole revenue of England would be increased.

Thus, then, it appears that the improvement of a manufacture in any country tends to alter the distribution of the precious metals amongst the nations of the world: it tends to increase the quantity of commodities, at the same time that it raises general prices in the country where the improvement takes place.

To simplify the question, I have been supposing the trade between two countries to be confined to two commodities—to wine and cloth; but it is well known that many and various articles enter into the list of exports and imports. By the abstraction of money from one country, and the accumulation of it in another, all commodities are affected in price, and consequently encouragement is given to the exportation of many more commodities besides money, which will therefore prevent so great an effect from taking place on the value of money in the two countries as might otherwise be expected.

Beside the improvements in arts and machinery, there are various other causes which are constantly operating on the natural course of trade, and which interfere with the equilibrium and the relative value of money. Bounties on exportation or importation, new taxes on commodities, sometimes by their direct, and at other times by their indirect operation, disturb the natural trade of barter, and produce a consequent necessity of importing or exporting money, in order that prices may be accommodated to the natural course of commerce; and this effect is produced not only in the country where the disturbing cause takes place, but, in a greater or less degree, in every country of the commercial world.

This will in some measure account for the different value of money in different countries; it will explain to us why the prices of home commodities, and those of great bulk, though of comparatively small value, are, independently of other causes, higher in those countries where manufactures flourish. Of two countries having precisely the same population, and the same quantity of land of equal fertility in cultivation, with the same knowledge too of agriculture, the prices of raw produce will be highest in that where the greater skill and the better machinery is used in the manufacture of exportable commodities. The rate of profits will probably differ but little; for wages, or the real reward of the labourer, may be the same in both; but those wages, as well as raw produce, will be rated higher in money in that country, into which, from the advantages attending their skill and machinery, an abundance of money is imported in exchange for their goods.

Of these two countries, if one had the advantage in the manufacture of goods of one quality, and the other in the manufacture of goods of another quality, there would be no decided influx of the precious metals into either; but if the advantage very heavily preponderated in favour of either, that effect would be inevitable.

In the former part of this work, we have assumed, for the purpose of argument, that money always continued of the same value; we are now endeavouring to show that, besides the ordinary variations in the value of money, and those which are common to the whole commercial world, there are also partial variations to which money is subject in particular countries; and to the fact that the value of money is never the same in any two countries, depending as it does on relative taxation, on manufacturing skill, on the advantages of climate, natural productions, and many other causes.

Although, however, money is subject to such perpetual variations, and consequently the prices of the commodities which are common to most countries are also subject to considerable difference, yet no effect will be produced on the rate of profits, either from the influx or efflux of money. Capital will not be increased because the circulating medium is augmented. If the rent paid by the farmer to his landlord, and the wages to his labourers, be 20 per cent. higher in one country than another, and if at the same time the nominal value of the farmer's capital be 20 per cent. more, he will receive precisely the same rate of profits, although he should sell his raw produce 20 per cent. higher.

Profits, it cannot be too often repeated, depend on wages; not on nominal, but real wages; not on the number of pounds that may be annually paid to the labourer, but on the number of days' work necessary to obtain those pounds. Wages may therefore be precisely the same in two countries; they may bear, too, the same proportion to rent, and to the whole produce obtained from the land, although in one of those countries the labourer should receive ten shillings per week and in the other twelve.

In the early states of society, when manufactures have made little progress, and the produce of all countries is nearly similar, consisting of the bulky and most useful commodities, the value of money in different countries will be chiefly regulated by their distance from the mines which supply the precious metals; but as the arts and improvements of society advance, and different nations excel in particular manufactures, although distance will still enter into the calculation, the value of the precious metals will be chiefly regulated by the superiority of those manufactures.

Suppose all nations to produce corn, cattle, and coarse clothing only, and that it was by the exportation of such commodities that gold could be obtained from the countries which produced them, or from those who held them in subjection; gold would naturally be of greater exchangeable value in Poland than in England, on account of the greater expense of sending such a bulky commodity as corn the more distant voyage, and also the greater expense attending the conveying of gold to Poland.

This difference in the value of gold, or, which is the same thing, this difference in the price of corn in the two countries, would exist, although the facilities of producing corn in England should far exceed those of Poland, from the greater fertility of the land and the superiority in the skill and implements of the labourer.

If, however, Poland should be the first to improve her manufactures, if she should succeed in making a commodity which was generally desirable, including great value in little bulk, or if she should be exclusively blessed with some natural production, generally desirable, and not possessed by other countries, she would obtain an additional quantity of gold in exchange for this commodity, which would operate on the price of her corn, cattle, and coarse clothing. The disadvantage of distance would probably be more than compensated by the advantage of having an exportable commodity of great value, and money would be permanently of lower value in Poland than in England. If, on the contrary, the advantage of skill and machinery were possessed by England, another reason would be added to that which before existed why gold should be less valuable in England than in Poland, and why corn, cattle, and clothing should be at a higher price in the former country.

These I believe to be the only two causes which regulate the comparative value of money in the different countries of the world; for although taxation occasions a disturbance of the

N

equilibrium of money, it does so by depriving the country in which it is imposed of some of the advantages attending skill, industry, and climate.

It has been my endeavour carefully to distinguish between a low value of money and a high value of corn, or any other commodity with which money may be compared. These have been generally considered as meaning the same thing; but it is evident that when corn rises from five to ten shillings a bushel, it may be owing either to a fall in the value of money or to a rise in the value of corn. Thus we have seen that, from the necessity of having recourse successively to land of a worse and worse quality, in order to feed an increasing population, corn must rise in relative value to other things. If therefore money continue permanently of the same value, corn will exchange for more of such money, that is to say, it will rise in price. The same rise in the price of corn will be produced by such improvement of machinery in manufactures as shall enable us to manufacture commodities with peculiar advantages: for the influx of money will be the consequence; it will fall in value, and therefore exchange for less corn. But the effects resulting from a high price of corn when produced by the rise in the value of corn, and when caused by a fall in the value of money, are totally different. In both cases the money price of wages will rise, but if it be in consequence of the fall in the value of money, not only wages and corn, but all other commodities will rise. If the manufacturer has more to pay for wages he will receive more for his manufactured goods, and the rate of profits will remain unaffected. But when the rise in the price of corn is the effect of the difficulty of production, profits will fall; for the manufacturer will be obliged to pay more wages, and will not be enabled to remunerate himself by raising the price of his manufactured commodity.

Any improvement in the facility of working the mines, by which the precious metals may be produced with a less quantity of labour, will sink the value of money generally. It will then exchange for fewer commodities in all countries; but when any particular country excels in manufactures, so as to occasion an influx of money towards it, the value of money will be lower, and the prices of corn and labour will be relatively higher in that country than in any other.

This higher value of money will not be indicated by the exchange; bills may continue to be negotiated at par, although the prices of corn and labour should be 10, 20, or 30 per cent. higher in one country than another. Under the circumstances supposed, such a difference of prices is the natural order of things, and the exchange can only be at par when a sufficient quantity of money is introduced into the country excelling in manufactures, so as to raise the price of its corn and labour. If foreign countries should prohibit the exportation of money, and could successfully enforce obedience to such a law, they might indeed prevent the rise in the prices of the corn and labour of the manufacturing country; for such rise can only take place after the influx of the precious metals, supposing paper money not to be used; but they could not prevent the exchange from being very unfavourable to them. If England were the manufacturing country, and it were possible to prevent the importation of money, the exchange with France, Holland, and Spain might be 5, 10, or 20 per cent. against those countries.

Whenever the current of money is forcibly stopped, and when money is prevented from setting at its just level, there are no limits to the possible variations of the exchange. The effects are similar to those which follow when a paper money, not exchangeable for specie at the will of the holder, is forced into circulation. Such a currency is necessarily confined to the country where it is issued: it cannot, when too abundant, diffuse itself generally amongst other countries. The level of circulation is destroyed, and the exchange will inevitably be unfavourable to the country where it is excessive in quantity: just so would be the effects of a metallic circulation if by forcible means, by laws which could not be evaded, money should be detained in a country, when the stream of trade gave it an impetus towards other countries.

When each country has precisely the quantity of money which it ought to have, money will not indeed be of the same value in each, for with respect to many commodities it may differ 5, 10, or even 20 per cent., but the exchange will be at par. One hundred pounds in England, or the silver which is in £100, will purchase a bill of £100, or an equal quantity of silver in France, Spain, or Holland.

In speaking of the exchange and the comparative value of money in different countries, we must not in the least refer to the value of money estimated in commodities in either country. The exchange is never ascertained by estimating the comparative value of money in corn, cloth, or any commodity whatever, but by estimating the value of the currency of one country in the currency of another.

It may also be ascertained by comparing it with some standard common to both countries. If a bill on England for £100 will purchase the same quantity of goods in France or Spain that a bill on Hamburgh for the same sum will do, the exchange between Hamburgh and England is at par; but if a bill on England for £130 will purchase no more than a bill on Hamburgh for £100, the exchange is 30 per cent. against England.

In England £100 may purchase a bill, or the right of receiving £101 in Holland, £102 in France, and £105 in Spain. The exchange with England is, in that case, said to be 1 per cent. against Holland, 2 per cent. against France, and 5 per cent. against Spain. It indicates that the level of currency is higher than it should be in those countries, and the comparative value of their currencies, and that of England, would be immediately restored to par by extracting from theirs or by adding to that of England.

Those who maintain that our currency was depreciated during the last ten years, when the exchange varied from 20 to 30 per cent. against this country, have never contended, as they have been accused of doing, that money could not be more valuable in one country than another as compared with various commodities; but they did contend that £130 could not be detained in England unless it was depreciated, when it was of no more value, estimated in the money of Hamburgh or of Holland, than the bullion in £100.

By sending 130 good English pounds sterling to Hamburgh, even at an expense of £5, I should be possessed there of £125; what then could make me consent to give £130 for a bill which would give me £100 in Hamburgh, but that my pounds were not good pounds sterling?—they were deteriorated, were degraded in intrinsic value below the pounds sterling of Hamburgh, and if actually sent there, at an expense of £5, would sell only for £100. With metallic pounds sterling, it is not denied that my £130 would procure me £125 in Hamburgh, but with paper pounds sterling I can only obtain £100; and yet it was maintained that £130 in paper was of equal value with £130 in silver or gold.

Some indeed more reasonably maintained that £130 in paper was not of equal value with £130 in metallic money; but they said that it was the metallic money which had changed its value and not the paper money. They wished to confine the meaning of the word depreciation to an actual fall of value, and not to a comparative difference between the value of money and the standard by which by law it is regulated. One hundred pounds of English money was formerly of equal value with and could purchase £100 of Hamburgh money: in any other country a bill of £100 on England, or on Hamburgh, could purchase precisely the same quantity of commodities. To obtain the same things, I was lately obliged to give £130 English money, when Hamburgh could obtain them for £100 Hamburgh money. If English money was of the same value then as before, Hamburgh money must have risen in value. But where is the proof of this? How is it to be ascertained whether English money has fallen or Hamburgh money has risen? there is no standard by which this can be determined. It is a plea which admits of no proof, and can neither be positively affirmed nor positively contradicted. The nations of the world must have been early convinced that there was no standard of value in nature to which they might unerringly refer, and therefore chose a medium which on the whole appeared to them less variable than any other commodity.

To this standard we must conform till the law is changed, and till some other commodity is discovered by the use of which we shall obtain a more perfect standard than that which we have established. While gold is exclusively the standard in this country money will be depreciated when a pound sterling is not of equal value with 5 dwts. and 3 grs. of standard gold, and that whether gold rises or falls in general value.

THOMAS ROBERT MALTHUS

The Principles of Political Economy considered with a view to their Practical Application 1820

The extract from Malthus's *Essay on the Principle of Population* given above (Chapter II) showed him as a fundamental contributor to the fabric of classical economics. The reading given here from his *Principles of Political Economy* (1st edition 1820, 2nd edition 1836) shows him in his other role as a fundamental critic of some of its main doctrines.

Virtually all the classical economists accepted the proof of the 'impossibility of general over-production' given by J.-B. Say (see Chapter IV, 113–24); Malthus was the only major figure of the school who called it into question. His belief that Say's doctrine was 'utterly unfounded' and that there could be a deficiency of 'effectual demand' leading to a general glut of commodities led him into a prolonged controversy with his friend Ricardo, as well as with Say himself. In this controversy the evidence of facts was on Malthus's side, but Ricardo had the advantage of greater logic and consistency in analysis, with the result that, in the words of Keynes, 'Ricardo conquered England as completely as the Holy Inquisition conquered Spain' (*General Theory of Employment, Interest and Money*, 32).

For a full century Say's Law of Markets became the accepted orthodoxy and Malthus's ideas became part of the underworld of economic heresies. With the publication of Keynes's *General Theory* came a rehabilitation both by Keynes himself and others who saw in Malthus an anticipator of Keynesian doctrines. However, as the sections reprinted here make plain, Malthus's theories of accumulation and gluts were part of a much wider treatment of the causes of 'the Progress of Wealth' and whether they can or cannot be properly regarded as anticipating the Keynesian approach to problems of saving, investment and employment has remained a matter of controversy.

BIBLIOGRAPHY

Most of the references given above (112) in connection with Say's Law are relevant here also. The fullest account of the whole debate is that given by B. A. Corry. *Money, Saving and Investment in English Classical Economics, 1800–1850*. Corry comes down against the 'Keynesian' interpretation of Malthus: so also does J. Sowell. 'The General Glut Controversy Reconsidered', *Oxford Economic Papers*, XV (November 1963), 193–203.

For the opposite view, see M. Paglin. *Malthus and Lauderdale: the Anti-Ricardian Tradition* (New York 1961); also P. Lambert. 'The Law of Markets prior to J.-B. Say and the Say–Malthus Debate', *International Economic Papers*, No 6, 7–22, and 'Lauderdale, Malthus and Keynes', *Annals of Public and Co-Operative Economy*, XXXVII, No 1 (January 1966), 3–23.

CHAPTER VII.

ON THE IMMEDIATE CAUSES OF THE PROGRESS OF WEALTH

SECTION I.

Statement of the particular Object of Inquiry.

THERE is scarcely any inquiry more curious, or, from its importance, more worthy of attention, than that which traces the causes which practically check the progress of wealth in different countries, and stop it, or make it proceed very slowly, while the power of production remains comparatively undiminished, or at least would furnish the means of a great and abundant increase of produce and population.

In a former work[1] I endeavoured to trace the causes which practically keep down the population of a country to the level of its actual supplies. It is now my object to shew what are the causes which chiefly influence these supplies, or call the powers of production forth into the shape of increasing wealth.

Among the primary and most important causes which influence the wealth of nations, must unquestionably be placed, those which come under the head of politics and morals. Security of property, without a certain degree of which, there can be no encouragement to individual industry, depends mainly upon the political constitution of a country, the excellence of its laws and the manner in which they are administered. And those habits which are the most favourable to regular exertions as well as to general rectitude of character, and are consequently most favourable to the production and maintenance of wealth, depend chiefly upon the same causes, combined with moral and religious instruction. It is not however my intention at present to enter fully into these causes, important and effective as they are; but to confine myself chiefly to the more immediate

---

[1] *Essay on the Principle of Population.*

and proximate causes of increasing wealth, whether they may have their origin in these political and moral sources, or in any others more specifically and directly within the province of political economy.

It is obviously true that there are many countries, not essentially different either in the degree of security which they afford to property, or in the moral and religious instruction received by the people, which yet, with nearly equal natural capabilities, make a very different progress in wealth. It is the principal object of the present inquiry to explain this; and to furnish some solution of certain phenomena frequently obtruded upon our attention, whenever we take a view of the different states of Europe, or of the world; namely, countries with great powers of production comparatively poor, and countries with small powers of production comparatively rich.

If the actual riches of a country not subject to repeated violences and a frequent destruction of produce, be not after a certain period in some degree proportioned to its power of producing riches, this deficiency must have arisen from the want of an adequate stimulus to continued production. The practical question then for our consideration is, what are the most immediate and effective stimulants to the continued creation and progress of wealth.

SECTION II.

Of the Increase of Population considered as a Stimulus to the continued Increase of Wealth.

Many writers have been of opinion that an increase of population is the sole stimulus necessary to the increase of wealth, because population, being the great source of consumption, must in their opinion necessarily keep up the demand for an increase of produce, which will naturally be followed by a continued increase of supply.

That a permanent increase of population is a powerful and necessary element of increasing demand, will be most readily allowed; but that the increase of population alone, or, more properly speaking, the pressure of the population hard against the limits of subsistence, does not furnish an effective stimulus to the continued increase of wealth, is not only evident in theory, but is confirmed by universal experience. If want alone, or the desire of the labouring classes to possess the necessaries and conveniences of life, were a sufficient stimulus to production, there is no state in Europe, or in the world, that would have found any other practical limit to its wealth than its power to produce; and the earth would probably before this period have contained, at the very least, ten times as many inhabitants as are supported on its surface at present.

But those who are acquainted with the nature of effective demand, will be fully aware that, where the right of private property is established, and the wants of society are supplied by industry and barter, the desire of any individual to possess the necessary conveniences and luxuries of life, however intense, will avail nothing towards their production, if there be no where a reciprocal demand for something which he possesses. A man whose only possession is his labour has, or has not, an effective demand for produce according as his labour is, or is not, in demand by those who have the disposal of produce. And no productive labour will ever be in demand unless the produce when obtained is of greater value than the labour which obtained it. No fresh hands can be employed in any sort of industry merely in consequence of the demand for its produce occasioned by the persons employed. No farmer will take the trouble of superintending the labour of ten additional men merely because his whole produce will then sell in the market at an advanced price just equal to what he had paid his additional labourers. There must be something in the previous state of the demand and supply of the commodity in question, or in its price, antecedent to and independently of the demand occasioned by the new labourers, in order to warrant the employment of an additional number of people in its production.

It will be said perhaps that the increase of population will lower wages, and, by thus diminishing the costs of production, will increase the profits of the capitalists and the encouragement to produce. Some temporary effect of this kind may no doubt take place, but it is evidently very strictly limited. The fall of wages cannot go on beyond a certain point without not only stopping the progress of the population but making it even retrograde; and before this point is reached, it will probably happen that the increase of produce occasioned by the labour of the additional number of persons will have so lowered its value, as more than to counterbalance the fall of wages, and thus to diminish instead of increase the profits of the capitalists and the power and will to employ more labour.

It is obvious then in theory that an increase of population, when an additional quantity of labour is not wanted, will soon be checked by want of employment, and the scanty support of those employed, and will not furnish the required stimulus to an increase of wealth proportioned to the power of production.

But, if any doubts should remain with respect to the *theory* on the subject, they will surely be dissipated by a reference to *experience*. It is scarcely possible to cast our eyes on any nation of the world without seeing a striking confirmation of what has been advanced. Almost universally, the actual wealth of all the states with which we are acquainted is very far short of their powers of production; and almost universally among those states, the slowest progress in wealth is made where the stimulus arising from population alone is the greatest, that is, where the population presses the hardest against the limits of subsistence. It is quite evident that the only fair way, indeed the only way, by which we can judge of the practical effect of population alone as a stimulus to wealth, is to refer to those countries where, from the excess of population above the funds applied to the maintenance of labour, the stimulus of want is the greatest. And if in these countries, which still have great powers of production, the progress of wealth is very slow, we have certainly all the evidence which experience can possibly give us, that population alone cannot create an effective demand for wealth.

To suppose an actual and permanent increase of population is to beg the question. We may as well suppose at once an increase of wealth; because an actual and permanent increase of population cannot take place without a proportionate or nearly proportionate increase of wealth. The question really is, whether encouragements to population, or even the natural tendency of population to increase beyond the funds for its maintenance, so as to press hard against the limits of subsistence, will, or will not, alone furnish an adequate stimulus to the increase of wealth. And this question, Spain, Portugal, Poland, Hungary, Turkey, and many other countries in Europe, together with nearly the whole of Asia and Africa, and the greatest part of America, distinctly answer in the negative.

SECTION III.

Of Accumulation, or the Saving from Revenue to add to Capital, considered as a Stimulus to the Increase of Wealth.

Those who reject mere population as an adequate stimulus to the increase of wealth, are generally disposed to make every thing depend upon accumulation. It is certainly true that no permanent and continued increase of wealth can take place without a continued increase of capital; and I cannot agree with Lord Lauderdale in thinking that this increase can be effected in any other way than by saving from the stock which might have been destined for immediate consumption, and adding it to that which is to yield a profit; or in other words, by the conversion of revenue into capital.[1]

But we have yet to inquire what is the state of things which generally disposes a nation to accumulate; and further, what

[1] See Lord Lauderdale's Chapter on Parsimony, in his *Inquiry into the Nature and Origin of Public Wealth*, ch. iv. p. 198. 2d. edit. Lord Lauderdale appears to have gone as much too far in deprecating accumulation, as some other writers in recommending it. This tendency to extremes is exactly what I consider as the great source of error in political economy.

is the state of things which tends to make that accumulation the most effective, and lead to a further and continued increase of capital and wealth.

It is undoubtedly possible by parsimony to devote at once a much larger share than usual of the produce of any country to the maintenance of productive labour; and it is quite true that the labourers so employed are consumers as well as unproductive labourers; and as far as the labourers are concerned, there would be no diminution of consumption or demand. But it has already been shewn that the consumption and demand occasioned by the persons employed in productive labour can never alone furnish a motive to the accumulation and employment of capital; and with regard to the capitalists themselves, together with the landlords and other rich persons, they have, by the supposition, agreed to be parsimonious, and by depriving themselves of their usual conveniences and luxuries to save from their revenue and add to their capital. Under these circumstances, I would ask, how it is possible to suppose that the increased number of commodities, obtained by the increased number of productive labourers, should find purchasers, without such a fall of price as would probably sink their value below the costs of production, or, at least, very greatly diminish both the power and the will to save.

It has been thought by some very able writers, that although there may easily be a glut of particular commodities, there cannot possibly be a glut of commodities in general; because, according to their view of the subject, commodities being always exchanged for commodities, one half will furnish a market for the other half, and production being thus the sole source of demand, an excess in the supply of one article merely proves a deficiency in the supply of some other, and a general excess is impossible. M. Say, in his distinguished work on political economy, has indeed gone so far as to state that the consumption of a commodity by taking it out of the market diminishes demand, and the production of a commodity proportionably increases it.

This doctrine, however, to the extent in which it has been applied, appears to me to be utterly unfounded, and completely to contradict the great principles which regulate supply and demand.

It is by no means true, as a matter of fact, that commodities are always exchanged for commodities. The great mass of commodities is exchanged directly for labour, either productive or unproductive; and it is quite obvious that this mass of commodities, compared with the labour with which it is to be exchanged, may fall in value from a glut just as any one commodity falls in value from an excess of supply, compared either with labour or money.

In the case supposed there would evidently be an unusual quantity of commodities of all kinds in the market, owing to the unproductive labourers of the country having been converted, by the accumulation of capital, into productive labourers; while the number of labourers altogether being the same, and the power and will to purchase for consumption among landlords and capitalists being by supposition diminished, commodities would necessarily fall in value, compared with labour, so as to lower profits almost to nothing, and to check for a time further production. But this is precisely what is meant by the term glut, which, in this case, is evidently general not partial.

M. Say, Mr. Mill,[1] and Mr. Ricardo, the principal authors of the new doctrines on profits, appear to me to have fallen into some fundamental errors in the view which they have taken of this subject.

In the first place, they have considered commodities as if they were so many mathematical figures, or arithmetical characters, the relations of which were to be compared, instead

---

[1] Mr. Mill, in a reply to Mr. Spence, published in 1808, has laid down very broadly the doctrine that commodities are only purchased by commodities, and that one half of them must always furnish a market for the other half. The same doctrine appears to be adopted in its fullest extent by the author of an able and useful article on the Corn Laws, in the Supplement to the *Encyclopædia Britannica*, which has been referred to in a previous chapter.

of articles of consumption, which must of course be referred
to the numbers and wants of the consumers.

If commodities were only to be compared and exchanged
with each other, then indeed it would be true that, if they
were all increased in their proper proportions to any extent,
they would continue to bear among themselves the same relative value; but, if we compare them, as we certainly ought
to do, with the numbers and wants of the consumers, then a
great increase of produce with comparatively stationary numbers and with wants diminished by parsimony, must necessarily
occasion a great fall of values estimated in labour, so that the
same produce, though it might have *cost* the same quantity of
labour as before, would no longer *command* the same quantity;
and both the power of accumulation and the motive to accumulate would be strongly checked.

It is asserted that effectual demand is nothing more than the
offering of one commodity in exchange for another. But is this
all that is necessary to effectual demand? Though each commodity may have cost the same quantity of labour and capital
in its production, and they may be exactly equivalent to each
other in exchange, yet why may not both be so plentiful as
not to command more labour, or but very little more than
they have cost; and in this case, would the demand for them
be effectual? Would it be such as to encourage their continued
production? Unquestionably not. Their relation to each other
may not have changed; but their relation to the wants of the
society, their relation to bullion, and their relation to domestic
and foreign labour, may have experienced a most important
change.

It will be readily allowed that a new commodity thrown into
the market, which, in proportion to the labour employed upon
it, is of higher exchangeable value than usual, is precisely
calculated to increase demand; because it implies, not a mere
increase of quantity, but a better adaptation of the produce to
the tastes, wants and consumption of the society. But to fabri-
cate or procure commodities of this kind is the grand difficulty;

and they certainly do not naturally and necessarily follow an accumulation of capital and increase of commodities, most particularly when such accumulation and increase have been occasioned by economy of consumption, or a discouragement to the indulgence of those tastes and wants, which are the very elements of demand.

Mr. Ricardo, though he maintains as a general position that capital cannot be redundant, is obliged to make the following concession. He says, "There is only one case, and that will be temporary, in which the accumulation of capital with a low price of food may be attended with a fall of profits; and that is, when the funds for the maintenance of labour increase much more rapidly than population;—wages will then be high and profits low. If every man were to forego the use of luxuries and be intent only on accumulation, a quantity of necessaries might be produced for which there could not be any immediate consumption. Of commodities so limited in number, there might undoubtedly be an universal glut; and consequently there might neither be demand for an additional quantity of such commodities, nor profits on the employment of more capital. If men ceased to consume, they would cease to produce." Mr. Ricardo then adds, "This admission does not impugn the general principle."[1] In this remark I cannot quite agree with him. As, from the nature of population, an increase of labourers cannot be brought into the market, in consequence of a particular demand, till after the lapse of sixteen or eighteen years, and the conversion of revenue into capital may take place much more rapidly; a country is always liable to an increase of the funds for the maintenance of labour faster than the increase of population. But if, whenever this occurs, there may be a universal glut of commodities, how can it be maintained, as a general position, that capital is never redundant; and that because commodities may retain the same relative values, a glut can only be partial, not general?

Another fundamental error into which the writers above-

[1] *Princ. of Polit. Econ.* ch. xxi. p. 364. 2d edit.

mentioned and their followers appear to have fallen is, the not taking into consideration the influence of so general and important a principle in human nature, as indolence or the love of ease.

It has been supposed[1] that, if a certain number of farmers and a certain number of manufacturers had been exchanging their surplus food and clothing with each other, and their powers of production were suddenly so increased that both parties could, with the same labour, produce luxuries in addition to what they had before obtained, there could be no sort of difficulty with regard to demand, as part of the luxuries which the farmer produced would be exchanged against part of the luxuries produced by the manufacturer; and the only result would be, the happy one of both parties being better supplied and having more enjoyments.

But in this intercourse of mutual gratifications, two things are taken for granted, which are the very points in dispute. It is taken for granted that luxuries are always preferred to indolence, and that the profits of each party are consumed as revenue. What would be the effect of a desire to save under such circumstances, shall be considered presently. The effect of a preference of indolence to luxuries would evidently be to occasion a want of demand for the returns of the increased powers of production supposed, and to throw labourers out of employment. The cultivator, being now enabled to obtain the necessaries and conveniences to which he had been accustomed, with less toil and trouble, and his tastes for ribands, lace and velvet not being fully formed, might be very likely to indulge himself in indolence, and employ less labour on the land; while the manufacturer, finding his velvets rather heavy of sale, would be led to discontinue their manufacture, and to fall almost necessarily into the same indolent system as the farmer. That an efficient taste for luxuries, that is, such a taste as will properly stimulate industry, instead of being ready to appear at the moment it is required, is a plant of slow growth, the

[1] *Edinburgh Review*, No. LXIV. p. 471.

history of human society sufficiently shews; and that it is a most important error to take for granted, that mankind will produce and consume all that they have the power to produce and consume, and will never prefer indolence to the rewards of industry, will sufficiently appear from a slight review of some of the nations with which we are acquainted. But I shall have occasion for a review of this kind in the next section; and to this I refer the reader.

A third very serious error of the writers above referred to, and practically the most important of the three, consists in supposing that accumulation ensures demand; or that the consumption of the labourers employed by those whose object is to save, will create such an effectual demand for commodities as to encourage a continued increase of produce.

Mr. Ricardo observes, that "If 10,000*l.* were given to a man having 100,000*l.* per annum, he would not lock it up in a chest, but would either increase his expenses by 10,000*l.*, employ it himself productively, or lend it to some other person for that purpose; in either case demand would be increased, although it would be for different objects. If he increased his expenses, his effectual demand might probably be for buildings, furniture, or some such enjoyment. If he employed his 10,000*l.* productively, his effectual demand would be for food, clothing, and raw materials, which might set new labourers to work. But still it would be *demand.*"[1]

Upon this principle it is supposed that if the richer portion of society were to forego their accustomed conveniences and luxuries with a view to accumulation, the only effect would be a direction of nearly the whole capital of the country to the production of necessaries, which would lead to a great increase of cultivation and population. But, without supposing an entire change in the usual motives to accumulation, this could not possibly happen. The usual motives for accumulation are, I conceive, either the future wealth and enjoyment of the individual who accumulates, or of those to whom he means to

---

[1] *Princ. of Polit. Econ.* chap. xxi. p. 361. 2d edit.

leave his property. And with these motives it could never answer to the possessor of land to employ nearly all the labour which the soil could support in cultivation; as by so doing he would necessarily destroy his neat rent, and render it impossible for him, without subsequently dismissing the greatest part of his workmen and occasioning the most dreadful distress, either to give himself the means of greater enjoyment at a future distant period, or to transmit such means to his posterity.

The very definition of fertile is, land land that will support a much greater number of persons than are necessary to cultivate it; and if the landlord, instead of spending this surplus in conveniences, luxuries and unproductive consumers, were to employ it in setting to work on the land as many labourers as his savings could support, it is quite obvious that, instead of being enriched, he would be impoverished by such a proceeding, both at first and in future. Nothing could justify such a conduct but a different motive for accumulation; that is, a desire to increase the population—not the love of wealth and enjoyment; and till such a change takes place in the passions and propensities of mankind, we may be quite sure that the landlords and cultivators will not go on employing labourers in this way.

What then would happen? As soon as the landlords and cultivators found that they could not realize their increasing produce in some way which would give them a command of wealth in future, they would cease to employ more labour upon the land;[1] and if the business of that part of the society which

---

[1] Theoretical writers in Political Economy, from the fear of appearing to attach too much importance to money, have perhaps been too apt to throw it out of their consideration in their reasonings. It is an abstract truth that we want commodities, not money. But, in reality, no commodity for which it is possible to sell our goods at once, can be an adequate substitute for a circulating medium, and enable us in the same manner to provide for children, to purchase an estate, or to command labour and provisions a year or two hence. A circulating medium is absolutely necessary to any considerable saving; and even the manufacturer would get on but slowly, if he were obliged to accumulate in kind all the wages of his workmen. We cannot therefore be surprized at his wanting money rather than other

was not engaged in raising raw produce, consisted merely in preparing the other simple necessaries of life, the number required for this purpose being inconsiderable, the rest of those whom the soil could support would be thrown out of work. Having no means of legally demanding a portion of the raw produce, however plentiful it might be at first, they would gradually decrease in numbers; and the failure of effective demand for the produce of the soil would necessarily diminish cultivation, and throw a still greater number of persons out of employment. This action and reaction would thus go on till the balance of produce and consumption was restored in reference to the new tastes and habits which were established; and it is obvious that without an expenditure which will en-encourage commerce, manufactures, and unproductive consumers, or an agrarian law calculated to change the usual motives for accumulation, the possessors of land would have no sufficient stimulus to cultivate well; and a country such as our own, which had been rich and populous, would, with such parsimonious habits, infallibly become poor, and comparatively unpeopled.

The same kind of reasoning will obviously apply to the case noticed before. While the farmers were disposed to consume the luxuries produced by the manufacturers, and the manufacturers those produced by the farmers, all would go on smoothly; but if either one or both of the parties were disposed to save with a view of bettering their condition, and providing for their families in future, the state of things would be very different. The farmer, instead of indulging himself in ribands, lace, and velvets,[1] would be disposed to be satisfied with more simple clothing, but by this economy he would disable the

goods; and, in civilized countries, we may be quite sure that if the farmer or manufacturer cannot sell his products so as to give him a profit estimated in money, his industry will immediately slacken. The circulating medium bears so important a part in the distribution of wealth, and the encouragement of industry, that to set it aside in our reasonings may often lead us wrong.

[1] *Edinburgh Review,* No. LXIV. p. 471.

manufacturer from purchasing the same amount of his produce; and for the returns of so much labour employed upon the
land, and all greatly increased in productive power, there
would evidently be no market. The manufacturer, in like
manner, instead of indulging himself in sugar, grapes and
tobacco, might be disposed to save with a view to the
future, but would be totally unable to do so, owing to the
parsimony of the farmers and the want of demand for manufactures.[1]

An accumulation, to a certain extent, of common food and
common clothing might take place on both sides; but the
amount must necessarily be extremely confined. It would be
of no sort of use to the farmer to go on cultivating his land with
a view merely to give food and clothing to his labourers. He
would be doing nothing either for himself or family, if he
neither consumed the surplus of what they produced himself,
nor could realize it in a shape that might be transmitted to his
descendants. If he were a tenant, such additional care and
labour would be entirely thrown away; and if he were a landlord, and were determined, without reference to markets, to
cultivate his estate in such a way as to make it yield the greatest
neat surplus with a view to the future, it is quite certain that
the large portion of this surplus which was not required either
for his own consumption, or to purchase clothing for himself
and his labourers, would be absolutely wasted. If he did not
choose to use it in the purchase of luxuries or the maintenance
of unproductive labourers, it might as well be thrown into the
sea. To save it, that is to use it in employing more labourers

---

[1] Of all the opinions advanced by able and ingenious men, which I have
ever met with, the opinion of M. Say, which states that *un produit consommé
ou détruit est un débouché fermé* (l. i. ch. 15.) appears to me to be the most
directly opposed to just theory, and the most uniformly contradicted by
experience. Yet it directly follows from the new doctrine, that commodities
are to be considered only in their relation to each other,—not to the
consumers. What, I would ask, would become of the demand for commodities, if all consumption except bread and water were suspended for the
next half year? What an accumulation of commodities! Quels *débouchés!*
What a prodigious market would this event occasion!

upon the land would, as I said before, be to impoverish both himself and his family.

It would be still more useless to the manufacturers to go on producing clothing beyond what was wanted by the agriculturists and themselves. Their numbers indeed would entirely depend upon the demands of the agriculturists, as they would have no means of purchasing subsistence, but in proportion as there was a reciprocal want of their manufactures. The population required to provide simple clothing for such a society with the assistance of good machinery would be inconsiderable, and would absorb but a small portion of the proper surplus of rich and well cultivated land. There would evidently therefore be a general want of demand, both for produce and population; while it is quite certain that an adequate passion for consumption may fully keep up the proper proportion between supply and demand, whatever may be the powers of production, it appears to be quite as certain that a passion for accumulation must inevitably lead to a supply of commodities beyond what the structure and habits of such a society will permit to be consumed.[1]

But if this be so, surely it is a most important error to couple the passion for expenditure and the passion for accumulation together, as if they were of the same nature; and to consider the demand for the food and clothing of the labourer, who is to be employed productively, as securing such a general demand for commodities and such a rate of profits for the capital employed in producing them, as will adequately call forth the powers of the soil, and the ingenuity of man in procuring the greatest quantity both of raw and manufactured produce.

Perhaps it may be asked by those who have adopted Mr. Ricardo's view of profits,—what becomes of the division of that which is produced, when population is checked merely by want

---

[1] The reader must already know, that I do not share in the apprehensions of Mr. Owen about the permanent effects of machinery. But I am decidedly of opinion, that on this point he has the best of the argument with those who think that accumulation ensures effective demand.

of demand? It is acknowledged that the powers of production have not begun to fail; yet, if labour produces largely and yet is ill paid, it will be said that profits must be high.

I have already stated in a former chapter, that the value of the materials of capital very frequently do not fall in proportion to the fall in the value of the produce of capital, and this alone will often account for low profits. But independently of this consideration, it is obvious that in the production of any other commodities than necessaries, the theory is perfectly simple. From want of demand, such commodities may be very low in price, and a large portion of the whole value produced may go to the labourer, although in necessaries he may be ill paid, and his wages, both with regard to the quantity of food which he receives and the labour required to produce it, may be decidedly low.

If it be said, that on account of the large portion of the value of manufactured produce which on this supposition is absorbed by wages, it may be affirmed that the cause of the fall of profits is high wages, I should certainly protest against so manifest an abuse of words. The only justifiable ground for adopting a new term, or using an old one in a new sense, is, to convey more precise information to the reader; but to refer to high wages in this case, instead of to a fall of commodities, would be to proceed as if the specific intention of the writer were to keep his reader as much as possible in the dark as to the real state of things.

In the production of necessaries however, it will be allowed, that the answer to the question is not quite so simple, yet still it may be made sufficiently clear. Mr. Ricardo acknowledges that there may be a limit to the employment of capital upon the land from the limited wants of society, independently of the exhaustion of the soil. In the case supposed, this limit must necessarily be very narrow, because there would be comparatively no population besides the agriculturists to make an effective demand for produce. Under such circumstances corn might be produced, which would lose the character and quality of wealth; and, as I before observed in a note, all the parts of the same produce would not be of the same value. The actual labourers employed might be tolerably well fed, as is frequently the case, practically, in those countries where the labourers are fed by the farmers,[1] but there would be little work or food for their grown up sons; and from varying markets and varying crops, the profits of the farmer might be the lowest at the very time when, according to the division of the produce, it ought to be the highest, that is, when there was the greatest proportionate excess of produce above what was paid to the labourer. The wages of the labourer cannot sink below a certain point, but a part of the produce, from excess of supply, may for a time be absolutely useless, and permanently it may so fall from competition as to yield only the lowest profits.

I would observe further, that if in consequence of a diminished demand for corn, the cultivators were to withdraw their capitals so as better to proportion their supplies to the quantity that could be properly paid for; yet if they could not employ the capital they had withdrawn in any other way, which, according to the preceding supposition, they could not, it is certain that, though they might for a time make fair profits of the small stock which they still continued to employ in agriculture, the consequences to them as cultivators would be, to all intents and purposes, the same as if a general fall had taken place on all their capital.

If, in the process of saving, all that was lost by the capitalist was gained by the labourer, the check to the progress of wealth would be but temporary, as stated by Mr. Ricardo; and the

---

[1] In Norway and Sweden, particularly the former, where the agricultural labourer either lives in the farmer's family or has a portion of land assigned to him in lieu of wages, he is in general pretty well fed, although there is but little demand for labour, and considerable competition for such employment. In countries so circumstanced, (and there are many such all over the world,) it is perfectly futile to attempt to estimate profits by the excess of the produce above what is consumed in obtaining it, when for this excess there may be often little or no market. All evidently depends upon the exchangeable value of the disposable produce.

consequences need not be apprehended. But if the conversion of revenue into capital pushed beyond a certain point must, by diminishing the effectual demand for produce, throw the labouring classes out of employment, it is obvious that the adoption of parsimonious habits in too great a degree may be accompanied by the most distressing effects at first, and by a marked depression of wealth and population permanently.

It is not, of course, meant to be stated that parsimony, or even a temporary diminution of consumption,[1] is not often in the highest degree useful, and sometimes absolutely necessary to the progress of wealth. A state may certainly be ruined by extravagance; and a diminution of the actual expenditure may not only be necessary on this account, but when the capital of a country is deficient, compared with the demand for its products, a temporary economy of consumption is required, in order to provide that supply of capital which can alone furnish the means of an increased consumption in future. All that I mean to say is, that no nation can *possibly* grow rich by an accumulation of capital, arising from a permanent diminution of consumption; because, such accumulation being greatly beyond what is wanted, in order to supply the effective demand for produce, a part of it would very soon lose both its use and its value, and cease to possess the character of wealth.

On the supposition indeed of a *given* consumption, the accumulation of capital beyond a certain point must appear at once to be perfectly futile. But, even taking into consideration the increased consumption likely to arise among the labouring classes from the abundance and cheapness of commodities, yet as this cheapness must be at the expense of profits, it is obvious that the limits to such an increase of capital from parsimony, as shall not be attended by a very rapid diminution of the motive to accumulate, are very narrow, and may very easily be passed.

The laws which regulate the rate of profits and the progress

---

[1] Parsimony, or the conversion of revenue into capital, may take place without any diminution of consumption, if the revenue increases first.

of capital, bear a very striking and singular resemblance to the laws which regulate the rate of wages and the progress of population.

Mr. Ricardo has very clearly shewn that the rate of profits must diminish, and the progress of accumulation be finally stopped, under the most favourable circumstances, by the increasing difficulty of procuring the food of the labourer. I, in like manner, endeavoured to shew in my Essay on the Principle of Population that, under circumstances the most favourable to cultivation which could possibly be supposed to operate in the actual state of the earth, the wages of the labourer would become more scanty, and the progress of population be finally stopped by the increasing difficulty of procuring the means of subsistence.

But Mr. Ricardo has not been satisfied with proving the position just stated. He has not been satisfied with shewing that the difficulty of procuring the food of the labourer is the only *absolutely necessary* cause of the fall of profits, in which I am ready fully and entirely to agree with him: but he has gone on to say, that there is *no other cause* of the fall of profits in the actual state of things that has any degree of permanence. In this latter statement he appears to me to have fallen into precisely the same kind of error as I should have fallen into, if, after having shewn that the unrestricted power of population was beyond comparison greater than the power of the earth to produce food under the most favourable circumstances possible, I had allowed that population could not be redundant unless the powers of the earth to keep up with the progress of population had been tried to the uttermost. But I all along said, that population might be redundant, and greatly redundant, compared with the demand for it and the actual means of supporting it, although it might most properly be considered as deficient, and greatly deficient, compared with the extent of territory, and the powers of such territory to produce additional means of subsistence; that, in such cases, notwithstanding the acknowledged deficiency of population, and the obvious desirableness of having it greatly increased, it was useless and foolish directly to encourage the birth of more children, as the effect of such encouragement, without a demand for labour and the means of paying it properly, could only be increased misery and mortality with little or no final increase of population.

Though Mr. Ricardo has taken a very different course, I think that the same kind of reasoning ought to be applied to the rate of profits and the progress of capital. Fully acknowledging that there is hardly a country in the four quarters of the globe where capital is not deficient, and in most of them very greatly deficient, compared with the territory and even the number of people; and fully allowing at the same time the extreme desirableness of an increase of capital, I should say that, where the demand for commodities was not such as to afford fair profits to the producer, and the capitalists were at a loss where and how to employ their capitals to advantage, the saving from revenue to add still more to these capitals would only tend prematurely to diminish the motive to accumulation, and still further to distress the capitalists, with little increase of a wholesome and effective capital.

The first thing wanted in both these cases of deficient capital and deficient population, is an effective demand for commodities, that is, a demand by those who are able and willing to pay an adequate price for them; and though high profits are not followed by an increase of capital, so certainly as high wages are by an increase of population, yet I believe that they are so followed more generally than they appear to be, because, in many countries, as I have before intimated, profits are often thought to be high, owing to the high interest of money, when they are really low; and because, universally, risk in employing capital has precisely the same effect in diminishing the motive to accumulate and the reward of accumulation, as low profits. At the same time it will be allowed that determined extravagance, and a determined indisposition to save, may keep profits permanently high. The most powerful stimulants may, under peculiar circumstances, be resisted; yet still it will not cease to be true that the natural and legitimate encouragement to the increase of capital is that increase of the power and will to save which is held out by high profits; and under circumstances in any degree similar, such increase of power and will to save must always be accompanied by a proportionate increase of capital.

One of the most striking instances of the truth of this remark, and a further proof of a singular resemblance in the laws that regulate the increase of capital and of population, is to be found in the rapidity with which the loss of capital is recovered during a war which does not interrupt commerce. The loans to government convert capital into revenue, and increase demand at the same time that they at first diminish the means of supply.[1]

The necessary consequence must be an increase of profits. This naturally increases both the power and the reward of accumulation; and if only the same habits of saving prevail among the capitalists as before, the recovery of the lost stock must be rapid, just for the same kind of reason that the recovery of population is so rapid when, by some cause or other, it has been suddenly destroyed.

It is now fully acknowledged that it would be a gross error in the latter case, to imagine that, without the previous diminution of the population, the same rate of increase would still have taken place; because it is precisely the high wages occasioned by the demand for labour, which produce the effect of so rapid an increase of population. On the same principle it appears to me as gross an error to suppose that, without the

---

[1] Capital is withdrawn only from those employments where it can best be spared. It is hardly ever withdrawn from agriculture. Nothing is more common, as I have stated in the Chapter on Rent, than increased profits, not only without any capital being withdrawn from the land, but under a continual addition to it. Mr. Ricardo's assumption of constant prices would make it absolutely impossible to account theoretically for things as they are. If capital were considered as not within the pale of demand and supply, the very familiar event of the rapid recovery of capital during a war would be quite inexplicable.

previous loss of capital occasioned by the expenditure in question, capital should be as rapidly accumulated; because it is precisely the high profits of stock occasioned by the demand for commodities, and the consequent demand for the means of producing them, which at once give the power and the will to accumulate.

Though it may be allowed therefore that the laws which regulate the increase of capital are not quite so distinct as those which regulate the increase of population, yet they are certainly just of the same kind; and it is equally vain, with a view to the permanent increase of wealth, to continue converting revenue into capital, when there is no adequate demand for the products of such capital, as to continue encouraging marriage and the birth of children without a demand for labour and an increase of the funds for its maintenance.

SECTION IX.

Of the Distribution occasioned by unproductive Consumers, considered as the Means of increasing the exchangeable Value of the whole Produce.

The third main cause which tends to keep up and increase the value of produce by favouring its distribution is the employment of unproductive labour, or the maintenance of an adequate proportion of unproductive consumers.

It has been already shewn that, under a rapid accumulation of capital, or, more properly speaking, a rapid conversion of unproductive into productive labour, the demand, compared with the supply of material products, would prematurely fail, and the motive to further accumulation be checked, before it was checked by the exhaustion of the land. It follows that, without supposing the productive classes to consume much more than they are found to do by experience, particularly when they are rapidly saving from revenue to add to their capitals, it is absolutely necessary that a country with great powers of production should possess a body of unproductive consumers.

In the fertility of the soil, in the powers of man to apply machinery as a substitute for labour, and in the motives to exertion under a system of private property, the great laws of nature have provided for the leisure of a certain portion of society; and if this beneficent offer be not accepted by an adequate number of individuals, not only will a positive good, which might have been so attained, be lost, but the rest of the society, so far from being benefited by such self-denial, will be decidedly injured by it.

What the proportion is between the productive and unproductive classes of a society, which affords the greatest encouragement to the continued increase of wealth, it has before been said that the resources of political economy are unequal to determine. It must depend upon a great variety of circumstances, particularly upon fertility of soil and the progress of invention in machinery. A fertile soil and an ingenious people can not only support a considerable proportion of unproductive consumers without injury, but may absolutely require such a body of demanders, in order to give effect to their powers of production. While, with a poor soil and a people of little ingenuity, an attempt to support such a body would throw land out of cultivation, and lead infallibly to impoverishment and ruin.

Another cause, which makes it impossible to say what proportion of the unproductive to the productive classes is most favourable to the increase of wealth, is the difference in the degrees of consumption which may prevail among the producers themselves.

Perhaps it will be said that there can be no occasion for unproductive consumers, if a consumption sufficient to keep up the value of the produce takes place among those who are engaged in production.

With regard to the capitalists who are so engaged, they have certainly the power of consuming their profits, or the revenue which they make by the employment of their capitals; and if they were to consume it, with the exception of what could be beneficially added to their capitals, so as to provide in the best way both for an increased production and increased consumption, there might be little occasion for unproductive consumers. But such consumption is not consistent with the actual habits of the generality of capitalists. The great object of their lives is to save a fortune, both because it is their duty to make a provision for their families, and because they cannot spend an income with so much comfort to themselves, while they are obliged perhaps to attend a counting-house for seven or eight hours a day.

It has been laid down as a sort of axiom among some writers that the wants of mankind may be considered as at all times commensurate with their powers; but this position is not always true, even in those cases where a fortune comes without trouble; and in reference to the great mass of capitalists, it is completely contradicted by experience. Almost all merchants and manufacturers save, in prosperous times, much more rapidly than it would be possible for the national capital to increase, so as to keep up the value of the produce. But if this be true of them as a body, taken one with another, it is quite obvious that, with their actual habits, they could not afford an adequate market to each other by exchanging their several products.

There must therefore be a considerable class of other consumers, or the mercantile classes could not continue extending their concerns, and realizing their profits. In this class the landlords no doubt stand pre-eminent; but if the powers of production among capitalists are considerable, the consumption of the landlords, in addition to that of the capitalists themselves and of their workmen, may still be insufficient to keep up and increase the exchangeable value of the whole produce, that is, to make the increase of quantity more than counterbalance the fall of price. And if this be so, the capitalists cannot continue the same habits of saving. They must either consume more, or produce less; and when the mere pleasure of present expenditure, without the accompaniments of an improved local situation and an advance in rank, is put in opposition to the continued labour of attending to business during the greatest part of the day, the probability is that a considerable body of them will be induced to prefer the latter alternative, and produce less. But if, in order to balance the demand and supply, a permanent diminution of production takes place, rather than an increase of consumption, the whole of the national wealth, which consists of what is produced and consumed, and not of the excess of produce above consumption, will be decidedly diminished.

Mr. Ricardo frequently speaks, as if saving were an end instead of a means. Yet even with regard to individuals, where this view of the subject is nearest the truth, it must be allowed that the final object in saving is expenditure and enjoyment. But, in reference to national wealth, it can never be considered either immediately or permanently in any other light than as a means. It may be true that, by the cheapness of commodities, and the consequent saving of expenditure in consumption, the same surplus of produce above consumption may be obtained as by a great rise of profits with an undiminished consumption; and, if saving were an end, the same end would be accomplished. But saving is the means of furnishing an increasing supply for the increasing national wants. If however commodities are already so plentiful that an adequate portion of them is not consumed, the capital so saved, the office of which is still further to increase the plenty of commodities, and still further to lower already low profits, can be comparatively of little use. On the other hand, if profits are high, it is a sure sign that commodities are scarce, compared with the demand for them, that the wants of the society are clamorous for a supply, and that an increase in the means of production, by saving a considerable part of the new revenue created by the high profits, and adding it to capital, will be specifically and permanently beneficial.

National saving, therefore, considered as the means of increased production, is confined within much narrower limits

P

than individual saving. While some individuals continue to spend, other individuals may continue to save to a very great extent; but the national saving, or the balance of produce above consumption, in reference to the whole mass of producers and consumers, must necessarily be limited by the amount which can be advantageously employed in supplying the demand for produce; and to create this demand, there must be an adequate consumption either among the producers themselves, or other classes of consumers.

Adam Smith has observed "that the desire of food is limited in every man by the narrow capacity of the human stomach; but the desire of the conveniences and ornaments of building, dress, equipage, and household furniture, seems to have no limit or certain boundary." That it has no *certain* boundary is unquestionably true; that it has no limit must be allowed to be too strong an expression, when we consider how it will be practically limited by the countervailing luxury of indolence, or by the general desire of mankind to better their condition, and make a provision for a family; a principle which, as Adam Smith himself states, is on the whole stronger than the principle which prompts to expense.[1] But surely it is a glaring misapplication of this statement in any sense in which it can be reasonably understood, to say, that there is no limit to the saving and employment of capital except the difficulty of procuring food. It is to found a doctrine upon the unlimited desire of mankind to consume; then to suppose this desire limited in order to save capital, and thus completely alter the premises; and yet still to maintain that the doctrine is true. Let a sufficient consumption always take place, whether by the producers or others, to keep up and increase most effectually the exchangeable value of the whole produce; and I am perfectly ready to allow that, to the employment of a national capital, increasing only at such a rate, there is no other limit than that which bounds the power of maintaining population. But it appears to me perfectly clear in theory, and universally confirmed by ex-

[1] *Wealth of Nations*, Vol. ii. B. ii. ch. ii. p. 19. 6th edit.

perience, that the employment of a capital, too rapidly increased by parsimonious habits, may find a limit, and does, in
fact, often find a limit, long before there is any real difficulty
in procuring the means of subsistence; and that both capital
and population may be at the same time, and for a period of
great length, redundant, compared with the effective demand
for produce.

Of the wants of mankind in general, it may be further
observed, that it is a partial and narrow view of the subject, to
consider only the propensity to spend what is actually possessed.
It forms but a very small part of the question to determine that
if a man has a hundred thousand a year, he will not decline
the offer of ten thousand more; or to lay down generally that
mankind are never disposed to refuse the means of increased
power and enjoyment. The main part of the question respecting
the wants of mankind, relates to their power of calling forth
the exertions necessary to acquire the means of expenditure. It
is unquestionably true that wealth produces wants; but it is a
still more important truth, that wants produce wealth. Each
cause acts and re-acts upon the other, but the order both of
precedence and of importance, is with the wants which stimulate
to industry; and with regard to these, it appears that, instead
of being always ready to second the physical powers of man,
they require for their development, "all appliances and means
to boot." The greatest of all difficulties in converting un-
civilized and thinly peopled countries into civilized and populous ones, is to inspire them with the wants best calculated to
excite their exertions in the production of wealth. One of the
greatest benefits which foreign commerce confers, and the
reason why it has always appeared an almost necessary in-
gredient in the progress of wealth, is, its tendency to inspire
new wants, to form new tastes, and to furnish fresh motives for
industry. Even civilized and improved countries cannot afford
to lose any of these motives. It is not the most pleasant employment to spend eight hours a day in a counting-house. Nor will it
be submitted to after the common necessaries and conveniences

of life are attained, unless adequate motives are presented to
the mind of the man of business. Among these motives is undoubtedly the desire of advancing his rank, and contending
with the landlords in the enjoyment of leisure, as well as of
foreign and domestic luxuries.

But the desire to realize a fortune as a permanent provision
for a family is perhaps the most general motive for the continued
exertions of those whose incomes depend upon their own personal skill and efforts. Whatever may be said of the virtue of
parsimony or saving, as a *public* duty, there cannot be a doubt
that it is, in numberless cases, a most sacred and binding *private*
duty; and were this legitimate and praiseworthy motive to
persevering industry in any degree weakened, it is impossible
that the wealth and prosperity of the country should not most
materially suffer. But if, from the want of other consumers,
the capitalists were obliged to consume all that could not be
advantageously added to the national capital, the motives
which support them in their daily tasks must essentially be
weakened, and the same powers of production would not be
called forth.

It has appeared then that, in the ordinary state of society,
the master producers and capitalists, though they may have
the power, have not the will, to consume to the necessary
extent. And with regard to their workmen, it must be allowed
that, if they possessed the will, they have not the power. It is
indeed most important to observe that no power of consumption on the part of the labouring classes can ever, according to
the common motives which influence mankind, alone furnish
an encouragement to the employment of capital. As I have
before said, nobody will ever employ capital merely for the
sake of the demand occasioned by those who work for him.
Unless they produce an excess of value above what they consume, which he either wants himself in kind, or which he can
advantageously exchange for something which he desires,
either for present or future use, it is quite obvious that his
capital will not be employed in maintaining them. When in-

deed this further value is created and affords a sufficient excite-
ment to the saving and employment of stock, then certainly
the power of consumption possessed by the workmen will
greatly add to the whole national demand, and make room for
the employment of a much greater capital.

It is most desirable that the labouring classes should be well
paid, for a much more important reason than any that can
relate to wealth; namely, the happiness of the great mass of
society. But to those who are inclined to say that unproductive
consumers cannot be necessary as a stimulus to the increase
of wealth, if the productive classes do but consume a fair
proportion of what they produce, I would observe that as a
great increase of consumption among the working classes must
greatly increase the cost of production, it must lower profits, and
diminish or destroy the motive to accumulate, before agriculture, manufactures, and commerce have reached any considerable degree of prosperity. If each labourer were actually
to consume double the quantity of corn which he does at
present, such a demand, instead of giving a stimulus to wealth,
would probably throw a great quantity of land out of cultivation, and greatly diminish both internal and external commerce.

There is certainly however very little danger of a diminution
of wealth from this cause. Owing to the principle of population,
all the tendencies are the other way; and there is much more
reason to fear that the working classes will consume too little
for their own happiness, than that they will consume too much
to allow of an adequate increase of wealth. I only adverted to
the circumstance to shew that, supposing so impossible a case
as a very great consumption among the working producers,
such consumption would not be of the kind to push the wealth
of a country to its greatest extent.

It may be said, perhaps, that though, owing to the laws
which regulate the increase of population, it is in no respect
probable that the corn wages of labour should continue permanently very high, yet the same consumption would take
place if the labouring classes did not work so many hours in

the day, and it was necessary to employ a greater number in each occupation. I have always thought and felt that many among the labouring classes in this country work too hard for their health, happiness, and intellectual improvement; and, if a greater degree of relaxation from severe toil could be given to them with a tolerably fair prospect of its being employed in innocent amusements and useful instruction, I should consider it as very cheaply purchased, by the sacrifice of a portion of the national wealth and populousness. But I see no probability, or even possibility, of accomplishing this object. To interfere generally with persons who are arrived at years of discretion in the command of the main property which they possess, namely their labour, would be an act of gross injustice; and the attempt to legislate directly in the teeth of one of the most general principles by which the business of society is carried on, namely, the principle of competition, must inevitably and necessarily fail. It is quite obvious that nothing could be done in this way, but by the labouring classes themselves; and even in this quarter we may perhaps much more reasonably expect that such a degree of prudence will prevail among them as to keep their wages permanently high, than that they should not enter into a competition with each other in working. A man who is prudent before marriage, and saves something for a family, reaps the benefit of his conduct, although others do not follow his example; but, without a simultaneous resolution on the part of all the labouring classes to work fewer hours in the day, the individual who should venture so to limit his exertions would necessarily reduce himself to comparative want and wretchedness. If the supposition here made were accomplished, not by a simultaneous resolution, which is scarcely possible, but by those general habits of indolence and ignorance, which so frequently prevail in the less improved stages of society, it is well known that such leisure would be of little value; and that while these habits would prematurely check the rate of profits and the progress of population, they would bring with them nothing to compensate the loss.

It is clear therefore that, with the single exception of the increased degree of prudence to be expected among the labouring classes of society from the progress of education and general improvement, which may occasion a greater consumption among the working producers, all the other tendencies are precisely in an opposite direction; and that, generally, all such increased consumption, whether desirable or not on other grounds, must always have the specific effect of preventing the wealth and population of a country under a system of private property, from being pushed so far, as it might have been, if the costs of production had not been so increased.

It may be thought perhaps that the landlords could not fail to supply any deficiency of demand and consumption among the producers, and that between them there would be little chance of any approach towards redundancy of capital. What might be the result of the most favourable distribution of landed property it is not easy to say from experience; but experience certainly tells us that, under the distribution of land which actually takes place in most of the countries in Europe, the demands of the landlords, added to those of the producers, have not always been found sufficient to prevent any difficulty in the employment of capital. In the instance alluded to in a former chapter, which occurred in this country in the middle of last century, there must have been a considerable difficulty in finding employment for capital, or the national creditors would rather have been paid off than have submitted to a reduction of interest from 4 per cent. to $3\frac{1}{2}$, and afterwards to 3. And that this fall in the rate of interest and profits arose from a redundancy of capital and a want of demand for produce, rather than from the difficulty of production on the land, is fully evinced by the low price of corn at the time, and the very different state of interest and profits which has occurred since.

A similar instance took place in Italy in 1685, when, upon the Pope's reducing the interest of his debts from 4 to 3 per cent., the value of the principal rose afterwards to 112; and yet the Pope's territories have at no time been so cultivated as to occasion such a low rate of interest and profits from the difficulty of procuring the food of the labourer. Under a more favourable distribution of property, there cannot be a doubt that such a demand for produce, agricultural, manufacturing, and mercantile, might have been created, as to have prevented for many many years the interest of money from falling below 3 per cent. In both these cases, the demands of the landlords were added to those of the productive classes.

But if the master-producers, from the laudable desire they feel of bettering their condition, and providing for a family, do not consume sufficiently to give an adequate stimulus to the increase of wealth; if the working producers, by increasing their consumption, supposing them to have the means of so doing, would impede the growth of wealth more by diminishing the power of production, than they could encourage it by increasing the demand for produce; and if the expenditure of the landlords, in addition to the expenditure of the two preceding classes, be found insufficient to keep up and increase the value of that which is produced, where are we to look for the consumption required but among the unproductive labourers of Adam Smith?

Every society must have a body of unproductive labourers; as every society, besides the menial servants that are required, must have statesmen to govern it, soldiers to defend it, judges and lawyers to administer justice and protect the rights of individuals, physicians and surgeons to cure diseases and heal wounds, and a body of clergy to instruct the ignorant, and administer the consolations of religion. No civilized state has ever been known to exist without a certain portion of all these classes of society in addition to those who are directly employed in production. To a certain extent therefore they appear to be absolutely necessary. But it is perhaps one of the most important practical questions that can possibly be brought under our view, whether, however necessary and desirable they may be, they must be considered as detracting so much from the material products of a country, and its power of supporting an extended population; or whether they furnish fresh motives to production, and tend to push the wealth of a country farther than it would go without them.

The solution of this question evidently depends, first, upon the solution of the main practical question, whether the capital of a country can or cannot be redundant; that is, whether the motive to accumulate may be checked or destroyed by the want of effective demand long before it is checked by the difficulty of procuring the subsistence of the labourer. And secondly, whether, allowing the *possibility* of such a redundance, there is sufficient reason to believe that, under the actual habits of mankind, it is a probable occurrence.

In the Chapter on Profits, but more particularly in the Third Section of the present Chapter, where I have considered the effect of accumulation as a stimulus to the increase of wealth, I trust that the first of these questions has been satisfactorily answered. And in the present Section it has been shewn that the actual habits and practice of the productive classes, in the most improved societies, do not lead them to consume so large a proportion of what they produce, even though assisted by the landlords, as to prevent their finding frequent difficulties in the employment of their capitals. We may conclude therefore, with little danger of error, that such a body of persons as I have described is not only necessary to the government, protection, health, and instruction of a country, but is also necessary to call forth those exertions which are required to give full play to its physical resources.

With respect to the persons constituting the unproductive classes, and the modes by which they should be supported, it is probable that those which are paid voluntarily by individuals, will be allowed by all to be the most likely to be useful in exciting industry, and the least likely to be prejudicial by interfering with the costs of production. It may be presumed that a person will not take a menial servant, unless he can afford to pay him; and that he is as likely to be excited to industry by the prospect of this indulgence, as by the prospect of buying ribands and laces. Yet to shew how much the wealth of nations depends upon the proportion of parts, rather than on any positive rules respecting the advantages of productive or unproductive labour generally, it may be worth while to remind the reader that, though the employment of a certain number of persons in menial service is in every respect desirable, there could hardly be a taste more unfavourable to the progress of wealth than a strong preference of menial service to material products. We may however, for the most part, trust to the inclinations of individuals in this respect; and it will be allowed generally, that there is little difficulty in reference to those classes which are supported voluntarily, though there may be much with regard to those which must be supported by taxation.

With regard to these latter classes, such as statesmen, soldiers, sailors, and those who live upon the interest of a national debt, it cannot be denied that they contribute powerfully to distribution and demand; they frequently occasion a division of property more favourable to the progress of wealth than would otherwise have taken place; they ensure that consumption which is necessary to give the proper stimulus to production; and the desire to pay a tax, and yet enjoy the same means of gratification, must often operate to excite the exertions of industry quite as effectually as the desire to pay a lawyer or physician. Yet to counterbalance these advantages, which so far are unquestionable, it must be acknowledged that injudicious taxation might stop the increase of wealth at almost any period of its progress, early or late;[1] and that the most judicious taxation might ultimately be so heavy as to clog all the channels of foreign and

---

[1] The effect of obliging a cultivator of a certain portion of rich land to maintain two men and two horses for the state, might in some cases only induce him to cultivate more, and create more wealth than he otherwise would have done, while it might leave him personally as rich as before, and the nation richer; but if the same obligation were to be imposed on the cultivator of an equal quantity of poor land, the property might be rendered at once not worth working, and the desertion of it would be the natural consequence. An indiscriminate and heavy tax on gross produce might immediately scatter desolation over a country, capable, under a better system, of producing considerable wealth.

domestic trade, and almost prevent the possibility of accumulation.

The effect therefore on national wealth of those classes of unproductive labourers which are supported by taxation, must be very various in different countries, and must depend entirely upon the powers of production, and upon the manner in which the taxes are raised in each country. As great powers of production are neither likely to be called into action, or, when once in action, kept in activity without great consumption, I feel very little doubt that instances have practically occurred of national wealth being greatly stimulated by the consumption of those who have been supported by taxes. Yet taxation is a stimulus so liable in every way to abuse, and it is so absolutely necessary for the general interests of society to consider private property as sacred, that one should be extremely cautious of trusting to any government the means of making a different distribution of wealth, with a view to the general good. But when, either from necessity or error, a different distribution has taken place, and the evil, as far as it regards private property, has actually been committed, it would surely be most unwise to attempt, at the expense of a great temporary sacrifice, a return to the former distribution, without very fully considering whether, if it were effected, it would be really advantageous; that is, whether, in the actual circumstances of the country, with reference to its powers of production, more would not be lost by the want of consumption than gained by the diminution of taxation.

If there could be no sort of difficulty in finding employment for capital, provided the price of labour were sufficiently low, the way to national wealth, though it might not always be easy, would be quite straight, and our only object need be to save from revenue, and repress unproductive consumers. But, if it has appeared that the greatest powers of production are rendered comparatively useless without adequate consumption, and that a proper distribution of the produce is as necessary to the continued increase of wealth as the means of producing it, it follows that, in cases of this kind, the question depends upon proportions; and it would be the height of rashness to determine, under all circumstances, that the diminution of a national debt and the removal of taxation must necessarily tend to increase the national wealth, and provide employment for the labouring classes.

If we were to suppose the powers of production in a rich and well peopled country to be so increased that the whole of what it produced could be obtained by one third of the labour before applied, can there be a reasonable doubt that the principal difficulty would be to effect such a distribution of the produce, as to call forth these great powers of production? To consider the gift of such powers as an evil would indeed be most strange; but they would be an evil, and practically a great and grievous one, if the effect were to be an increase of the neat produce at the expense of the gross produce, and of the population. But if, on the other hand, a more favourable distribution of the abundant produce were to take place; if the more intelligent among the working classes were raised into overseers of works, clerks of various kinds, and retail dealers, while many who had been in these situations before, together with numerous others who had received a tolerable education, were entitled to an income from the general produce, and could live nearly at leisure upon their mortgages; what an improved structure of society would this state of things present; while the value of the gross produce, and the numbers of the people would be increasing with rapidity! As I have before said, it would not be possible, under the principle of competition, (which can never be got rid of,) to secure much more leisure to those actually engaged in manual labour; but the very great increase in the number of prizes which would then be attainable by industrious and intelligent exertion, would most essentially improve their condition; and, on the whole, the society would have gained a great accession of comfort and happiness. It is not meant to be stated that such a distribution of the produce could be easily effected; but merely that, *with* such a distribution, the powers supposed would confer a prodigious benefit on the society, and *without* such a distribution, or such a change of tastes as would secure an equivalent consumption, the powers supposed might be worse than thrown away.

Now the question is, whether this country, in its actual state, with the great powers of production which it unquestionably possesses, does not bear some slight resemblance to the case here imagined; and whether, without such a body of unproductive consumers as these who live upon the interest of the national debt, the same stimulus would have been given to production, and the same powers would have been called forth. Under the actual division of landed property which now takes place in this country, I feel no sort of doubt that the incomes which are received and spent by the national creditors are more favourable to the demand for the great mass of manufactured products, and tend much more to increase the happiness and intelligence of the whole society, than if they were returned to the landlords.

I am far, however, from being insensible to the evils of a great national debt. Though, in many respects, it may be a useful instrument of distribution, it must be allowed to be a very cumbersome and very dangerous instrument. In the first place, the revenue necessary to pay the interest of such a debt can only be raised by taxation; and, as this taxation, if pushed to any considerable extent, can hardly fail of interfering with the powers of production, there is always danger of impairing one element of wealth, while we are improving another. A second important objection to a large national debt, is the feeling which prevails so very generally among all those not immediately concerned in it, and consequently among the great mass of the population, that they would be immediately and greatly relieved by its extinction; and, whether this impression be well founded or not, it cannot exist without rendering such revenue in some degree insecure, and exposing a country to the risk of a great convulsion of property. A third objection to such a debt is, that it greatly aggravates the evils arising from changes in the value of money. When the currency falls in value, the annuitants, as owners of fixed incomes, are most unjustly deprived of their proper share of the national produce; when the currency rises in value, the pressure of the taxation necessary to pay the interest of the debt, may become suddenly so heavy as greatly to distress the productive classes;[1] and this kind of sudden pressure must very much enhance the insecurity of property vested in public funds.

On these and other accounts it might be desirable slowly to diminish the debt, and to discourage the growth of it in future, even though it were allowed that its past effects had been favourable to wealth, and that the advantageous distribution of produce which it had occasioned, had, under the actual circumstances, more than counterbalanced the obstructions which it might have given to commerce. Security with moderate wealth is a wiser choice, and better calculated for peace and happiness than insecurity with greater wealth. But, unfortunately, a country accustomed to a distribution of produce which has at once excited and given full play to great powers of production, cannot withdraw into a less ambitious path without passing through a period of very great distress.

It is, I know, generally thought that all would be well, if we could but be relieved from the heavy burden of our debt. And yet I feel perfectly convinced that, if a spunge could be applied to it to-morrow, and we could put out of our consideration the poverty and misery of the public creditors, by supposing them to be supported comfortably in some other country, the rest of the society, as a nation, instead of being enriched,

---

[1] In a country with a large public debt, there is no duty which ought to be held more sacred on the part of the administrators of the government than to prevent any variations of the currency beyond those which necessarily belong to the varying value of the precious metals. I am fully aware of the temporary advantages which may be derived from a fall in the value of money; and perhaps it may be true that a part of the distress during the last year, though I believe but a small part, was occasioned by the measure lately adopted, for the restoration of the currency to its just value. But some such measure was indispensably necessary; and Mr. Ricardo deserves the thanks of his country for having suggested one which has rendered the transition more easy than could reasonably have been expected.

would be impoverished. It is the greatest mistake to suppose that the landlords and capitalists would either at once, or in a short time, be prepared for so great an additional consumption as such a change would require; and if they adopted the alternative suggested by Mr. Ricardo in a former instance, of saving, and lending their increased incomes, the evil would be aggravated tenfold. The new distribution of produce would diminish the demand for the results of productive labour; and if, in addition to this, more revenue were converted into capital, profits would fall to nothing, and a much greater quantity of capital would emigrate, or be destroyed at home, and a much greater number of persons would be starving for want of employment, than before the extinction of the debt. It would signify little to be able to export cheap goods. If the distribution of property at home were not such as to occasion an adequate power and will to purchase and consume the returns for these goods, the quantity of capital which could be employed in the foreign trade of consumption would be diminished instead of increased. Of this we may be convinced if we look to India, where low wages appear to be of little use in commerce, while there are no middle classes of society to afford a market for any considerable quantity of foreign goods.

The landlords, in the event supposed, not being inclined to an adequate consumption of the results of productive labour, would probably employ a greater number of menial servants; and perhaps, in the actual circumstances, this would be the best thing that could be done, and indeed the only way of preventing great numbers of the labouring classes from being starved for want of work. It is by no means likely, however, that it should soon take place to a sufficient extent; but if it were done completely, and the landlords paid as much in wages to menial servants as they had before paid to the national creditors, could we for a moment compare the state of society which would ensue to that which had been destroyed?

With regard to the capitalists, though they would be relieved from a great portion of their taxes, yet there is every

probability that their habits of saving, combined with the
diminution in the number of effective demanders, would occasion such a fall in the prices of commodities as greatly to
diminish that part of the national income which depends upon
profits; and I feel very little doubt that, in five years from the
date of such an event, not only would the exchangeable value
of the whole produce, estimated in domestic and foreign labour,
be decidedly diminished, but a smaller absolute quantity of
corn would be grown, and fewer manufactured and foreign
commodities would be brought to market than before.

It is not of course meant to be said that a country with a
large quantity of land, labour, and capital, has not the means
of gradually recovering itself from any shock, however great,
which it may experience; and after such an event, it might
certainly place itself in a situation in which its property would
be more secure than with a large national debt. All that I
mean to say is, that it would pass through a period, probably
of considerable duration, in which the diminution of effective
demand from an unfavourable distribution of the produce
would more than counterbalance the increased power of production occasioned by the relief from taxation; and it may fairly
be doubted whether finally it would attain a great degree of
wealth, or call forth, as it ought, a great degree of skill in agriculture, manufactures, and commerce, without possessing, in
some way or other, a large body of unproductive consumers,
or supplying this deficiency by a much greater tendency to
consume the results of productive labour than is generally
observed to prevail in society.

It has been repeatedly conceded, that the productive classes
have the power of consuming all that they produce; and, if
this power were adequately exercised, there might be no
occasion, with a view of wealth, for unproductive consumers.
But it is found by experience that, though there may be the
power, there is not the will; and it is to supply this will that a
body of unproductive consumers is necessary. Their specific
use in encouraging wealth is, to maintain such a balance be-

tween produce and consumption as to give the greatest exchangeable value to the results of the national industry. If unproductive labour were to predominate, the comparatively small quantity of material products brought to market would keep down the value of the whole produce, from the deficiency of quantity. If the productive classes were in excess, the value of the whole produce would fall from excess of supply. It is obviously a certain proportion between the two which will yield the greatest value, and command the greatest quantity of domestic and foreign labour; and we may safely conclude that, among the causes necessary to that distribution, which will keep up and increase the exchangeable value of the whole produce, we must place the maintenance of a certain body of unproductive consumers. This body, to make it effectual as a stimulus to wealth, and to prevent it from being prejudicial, as a clog to it, should vary in different countries, and at different times, according to the powers of production; and the most favourable result evidently depends upon the proportion between productive and unproductive consumers, being best suited to the natural resources of the soil, and the acquired tastes and habits of the people.

MOUNTIFORT LONGFIELD

Lectures on Political Economy 1834

Mountifort Longfield differs from the other authors whose writings are reprinted in this volume, all of whom established considerable reputations as economists within their own times. As an economist, Longfield was virtually unknown to his contemporaries, but has since been recognised as perhaps the most outstanding of a group of 'dissenters' who in the 1820s and 1830s diverged from the tradition established by Smith and Ricardo of explaining value on the basis of labour or cost of production, and sought an alternative treatment in terms of utility and scarcity.

Most of Longfield's working life was not devoted to the study and teaching of political economy, but of law. Born in County Cork in 1802, he gained high honours in science at Trinity College, Dublin, but was elected to Fellowship there in 1825 as a jurist and called to the Irish Bar in 1828.

In 1831 Richard Whately came to Dublin as its Archbishop, and determined to establish a chair of political economy at Trinity College along the lines of the Drummond Professorship at Oxford which he had himself occupied. Whately held an examination to discover the best qualified candidate for this new chair, and had no hesitation in selecting Longfield. So from 1832 to 1836 Longfield was the first occupant of a Professorship of Political Economy in Ireland, but already in 1834 he had been elected to the Regius Chair of Feudal and English Law, which he held until his death in 1884. In 1849 he became one of the three Commissioners under the Encumbered Estates Act (Ireland), in 1858 a Judge of the Landed Estates Court, and in 1867 an Irish Privy Councillor.

In this long and active career the years as Professor of Political Economy were only a brief interlude; yet during them Longfield 'overhauled the whole of economic theory and produced a system which would have stood up well in 1890' (J. A. Schumpeter. *History of Economic Analysis* [1954], 465).

In his *Lectures on Political Economy*, published in 1834 but delivered in the Trinity and Michaelmas terms of 1833, Longfield presented a theory of income distribution which includes a marginal productivity theory of capital, a productivity theory of wages and is based on a theory of value in which the concept of diminishing utility is presented and elaborated. This remarkable early example of consumer behaviour analysis is the section of the *Lectures* reproduced here.

BIBLIOGRAPHY

Longfield's *Lectures on Political Economy* (Dublin 1834) and his *Three Lectures on Commerce and One on Absenteeism* (Dublin 1835) were included in the series of *London School of Economics Reprints of Scarce Works on Political Economy* (in 1931 and 1937 respectively). A reprint of Longfield's economic writings, with an introduction and notes by R. D. Collison Black, has been published by Augustus M. Kelley, New York. This contains a full listing of works by and about Longfield.

The rediscovery of Longfield's economic work dates from E. R. A. Seligman's articles, 'On Some Neglected British Economists', *Economic Journal*, XIII (1903), 335–63 and 511–35. Marian Bowley. *Nassau Senior and Classical Economics* (London 1937) refers to Longfield in relation not only to Senior but also to other British and Continental utility theorists.

LECTURE VI.

Gentlemen,—Before I enter upon the subject to which I intend to call your attention this Term, I wish to recall to your minds, or to recapitulate a few of the principles which I have already attempted to establish. I defined, then, the utility of any article to be its power of satisfying the wants or wishes of mankind, either directly or indirectly; and by its value I wished you to understand its power of being exchanged for other articles. Of course therefore any thing that may be made the subject of an exchange, may be made use of as a measure of value. However, although a commodity may be a real measure, it may not be a convenient one; there may not exist ready means of comparing its value with that of other commodities. "In ruder ages, when men's wishes were confined to men's wants, the exchange of one commodity for another may have been sufficient to serve their purpose. It mattered not to them that one had cost double the time and labour of the other. Time and labour were to them no further valuable than as they served to obtain what satisfied their simple desires. Like children, their wishes did not extend beyond the present moment. As civilization, and with it, foresight, advanced, men having more wishes to indulge, became more chary of their time and labour. Each commodity then acquired a value which required some measure independent of the passing desire of the moment. Money was then resorted to." And as in the ordinary transactions of life, exchanges are generally effected through the intervention of money, it is therefore in general made use of as a measure of value: and for most purposes it is a most convenient measure, although at different times the value of money may sustain very considerable variations. There is no more ready mode of conveying a definite idea of the value of any article, than by mentioning its value as measured in money; that is, by saying how much money it will cost to obtain it in exchange.

But as most of the commodities in which the wealth of a

country consists are produced by labour, political-economists make use of it as a measure of value. It is not however, more than money, to be considered a peculiarly real measure of value, either as being of itself always of the same value, or as always demanding from the labourer the same sacrifice of ease and time. Still labour is the most convenient measure of value, because of its share in producing goods, or as it were purchasing them at the great mart of nature. It may be considered as the price which nature exacts from man for all the commodities of value which she furnishes for his use, and therefore the value of labour can be readily compared with that of other commodities; and it is a convenient measure to compare the values of those commodities with each other. For this purpose, however, that labour only must be regarded, which is expended in the most judicious and economical manner that the times and circumstances admit of.

In relation to value I also observed, that the value of every article depends upon the demand and the supply, and that indirectly the cost of production of any commodity, as well as its utility, has an effect upon its price. The cost of production, by its influence upon the supply, since men will not produce commodities unless with the reasonable expectation of selling them for more than the cost of producing them. And the utility has some effect, although not so easily calculated, since it is to its utility, in the more extended sense of the word, that the demand is to be entirely attributed.

The price is regulated by the demand and the supply, and will be such a sum as is sufficient to produce an equality between the supply and the effectual demand. I mean by effectual demand, such a demand as actually leads to the purchase or consumption of the article.

I shall this Term attempt to investigate the laws which distribute wealth among the different orders of society; but before I enter upon the subject, I think it expedient to make a few remarks upon the nature of demand, and its influence upon price and value. The measure of the intensity of any person's demand for any commodity is the amount which he would be willing and able to give for it, rather than remain without it, or forego the gratification which it is calculated to afford him. On this we may observe, in the first place, that there may exist a demand not sufficiently intense to exercise any influence upon price. Thus the demand or desire of very indigent persons for rich and costly articles of dress or furniture, equipages, jewellery, &c. does not affect their price, since such demanders cannot possibly effect a purchase, even if the prices experienced a considerable reduction. Still a demand may affect prices, although it be not sufficiently intense to lead to an actual purchase. Of this an example is, the demand of those who will not purchase at the existing prices, but who would come into the market and purchase, if a slight reduction should take place. Such a demand always does exist, and has an effect in keeping up prices, exactly similar to the bidding at an auction of the person whose bidding is next in amount to that of the actual purchaser. Ordinary sales are similar to sales by auction in this, that the seller tries to sell as dearly, and the buyer to buy as cheaply as possible; the difference only consists in the form and mode of ascertaining the greatest prices which the seller can require, without injudiciously diminishing the extent of his sales.

But it is to be remarked, that there may be, and that in fact there generally is, an excess of intensity of demand, which exercises no perceptible influence upon the prices of commodities. This is the demand of those who, if necessary, would pay more than the existing prices, but who do not, because the state of the market enables them to procure the same commodities, or more desirable substitutes, more cheaply. Thus the high prices to which provisions rise in times of scarcity, prove the existence of a latent intensity of demand, which is only called into action by the scarcity which renders it impossible to purchase provisions at the usual cheap rate: the intense demand always exists, though it may not be apparent. But in some cases the demand itself is created by a scarcity, or other peculiar circumstances; as, when we read of a besieged city being reduced to such distress for want of provisions, that a dead rat was sold for a considerable sum. Such a case might happen again, and yet such a possibility would scarcely justify us in saying that in ordinary times there existed even a latent demand for such food.

For provisions and other articles of greater or less necessity, the intensity of demand among different persons varies according to the sacrifices of other objects which they can conveniently afford to make; and yet all will effect their purchases at the same rate, viz. at the market prices, and this rate is determined by the sum which will create an equality between the effectual demand and the supply. Now if the price is attempted to be raised one degree beyond this sum, the demanders, who by the change will cease to be purchasers, must be those the intensity of whose demand was precisely measured by the former price. Before the change was made, the demand, which was less intense, did not lead to a purchase, and after the change is made, the demand, which is more intense, will lead to a purchase still. Thus the market price is measured by that demand, which being of the least intensity, yet leads to actual purchases. If the existing supply is more than sufficient to satisfy all the demand equal or superior to a certain degree of intensity, prices will fall, to accommodate themselves to a less intense demand.

But the intensity of demand varies not only in different places, and among different individuals, but in many cases the same person may be said to have in himself several demands of different degrees of intensity. Of this there is a very palpable example, when provisions, owing to their scarcity or abundance, sustain a change of price. When they rise, a diminution of consumption is the effect. But the manner in which this diminution of consumption takes place usually, is not by the total abstinence of some from food, while the rest consume their accustomed portions. On the contrary, all continue to eat, as they must, or else cease to exist; but none except those whose wealth renders them indifferent to the price of their food, consume as much as usual. With every decrease of the total supply within the country, a corresponding diminution in the consumption of the great mass of individuals must take place. But the proximate cause of this diminution in the consumption of each individual, is the rise of prices which the scarcity produces. Now that portion which any person ceases to consume in consequence of a rise of prices, or that additional portion which he would consume if prices should fall, is that for which the intensity of his demand is less than the high price which prevents him from purchasing it, and is exactly equal to the low price which would induce him to consume it. On the other hand, for that portion which, notwithstanding the high prices, he continues to consume, he must have had a demand, the intensity of which was at least equal to those high prices which did not prevent him from purchasing it. Carry on this train of reasoning in your minds through successive degrees of scarcity and consequent high prices, and you will come to the conclusion, that each individual contains as it were within himself, a series of demands of successively increasing degrees of intensity; that the lowest degree of this series which at any time leads to a purchase, is exactly the same for both rich and poor, and is that which regulates the market price; and that in the case of the rich man, the series increases more rapidly, that is to say, the intensity of his demand increases more rapidly in proportion to the diminution of his consumption, than in the case of the poor man. I have chosen the example of provisions as being the most obvious and palpable, and as most frequently affording a practical instance of the principle which it illustrated; but the same observation is equally true, although not so strikingly, in every case in which a diminution of supply would occasion a diminution in any individual's consumption, without leading him to give up the use of the article altogether.

JOHN STUART MILL

Principles of Political Economy with some of their Applications to Social Philosophy 1848

John Stuart Mill was born in 1806, the eldest son of James Mill, the disciple of Bentham and friend of Ricardo. The extraordinarily comprehensive and intensive education which the young Mill received from his father is well known and it is not surprising that it should have included a firm grounding in Ricardian political economy, begun at the age of eleven.

Mill followed his father into the service of the East India Company in 1823, and served at India House in London until 1858, when the government of India was transferred from the Company to the Crown. Mill was Member of Parliament for Westminster from 1865 to 1868, but apart from this brief interlude the remainder of his life from 1858 until his death in 1873 was devoted to study and writing, mainly in the fields of social and political philosophy. In these he came to occupy a position of commanding authority through such works as *On Liberty* (1859), *Considerations on Representative Government* (1865) and *Utilitarianism* (1867).

As a young man Mill accepted the teaching of his father and

Bentham and became the leader of the younger philosophical radicals. In 1826, however, a realisation of the limitations of utilitarian doctrine led him to a mental crisis and the exploration of such alternative philosophies as the romanticism of Coleridge and Carlyle. By the early 1840s Mill had developed a mature and independent attitude towards moral and social questions, and his *System of Logic*, published in 1843, established him as a philosopher of major importance in his own right.

The Principles of Political Economy, which appeared in 1848, was Mill's next major work. In the Preface he explained his purpose in writing it: 'It appears to the present writer that a work similar in its object and general conception to that of Adam Smith, but adapted to the more extended knowledge and improved ideas of the present age, is the kind of contribution which Political Economy at present requires. . . . No attempt . . . has yet been made to combine his practical mode of treating his subject with the increased knowledge since acquired of its theory, or to exhibit the economical phenomena of society in the relation in which they stand to the best social ideas of the present time, as he did, with such admirable success, in reference to the philosophy of his century'.

Pursuing this purpose Mill combined with his exposition of the principles of political economy a wealth of institutional detail, and developed 'some of their applications to social philosophy' in a manner at once more optimistic and more favourable to some aspects of socialism than the accepted Ricardian orthodoxy.

Nevertheless the theoretical core of the work remained the principles of Ricardo, which Mill had learned so well from his father. For this reason Mill's *Principles* has often been regarded as a mere restatement of Ricardo in a form acceptable to a wider public, with the abstractions clothed in reality and the harsh conclusions softened; but this is to neglect the considerable originality which Mill displayed. Since no brief extract can convey the special qualities of the whole work, one of the most original chapters is reprinted here—that on International

Values, wherein Mill developed the theory of reciprocal demand, which came to be recognised as an essential complement to Ricardo's theory of comparative costs.

BIBLIOGRAPHY

A new edition of the *Collected Works of John Stuart Mill* is in course of publication by the University of Toronto Press, and already includes the *Principles of Political Economy* in two volumes, with an introduction by V. W. Bladen.

One of the best short surveys of Mill's economic thought is given by Donald Winch in his introduction to the Pelican Classics edition of Mill's *Principles* (1970); the edition itself includes only Books IV and V of the original text. J. M. Robson. *The Improvement of Mankind* (Toronto 1968) is a valuable and thorough study of Mill's social and political thought, and has a useful bibliography.

For more detailed treatment of particular aspects of Mill's economic ideas, see J. Viner. 'Bentham and J. S. Mill: the Utilitarian Background', *American Economic Review*, 39 (March 1949), 360–82 (reprinted in *The Long View and the Short* [1958], 306–31); G. J. Stigler. 'The Nature and Role of Originality in Scientific Progress', *Economica*, XXII (November 1955), 293–302 (reprinted in *Essays in the History of Economics* [1965], 1–15)—this article deals particularly with the question of Mill's originality as an economist; and L. C. Robbins. *The Theory of Economic Policy in English Classical Political Economy* (1953), which deals with Mill's views on economic policy and socialism.

Mill published his *Autobiography* shortly before his death in 1873—a very personal document revealing as much about the man by its method of telling as by what it tells. The standard biography is now M. St J. Packe. *Life of John Stuart Mill* (1954).

BOOK III

CHAPTER XVIII

OF INTERNATIONAL VALUES

§ 1. THE values of commodities produced at the same place, or in places sufficiently adjacent for capital to move freely between them—let us say, for simplicity, of commodities produced in the same country—depend (temporary fluctuations apart) upon their cost of production. But the value of a commodity brought from a distant place, especially from a foreign country, does not depend on its cost of production in the place from whence it comes. On what, then, does it depend? The value of a thing in any place depends on the cost of its acquisition in that place; which, in the case of an imported article, means the cost of production of the thing which is exported to pay for it.

Since all trade is in reality barter, money being a mere instrument for exchanging things against one another, we will, for simplicity, begin by supposing the international trade to be in form, what it always is in reality, an actual trucking of one commodity against another. As far as we have hitherto proceeded, we have found all the laws of interchange to be essentially the same, whether money is used or not; money never governing, but always obeying, those general laws.

If, then, England imports wine from Spain, giving for every pipe of wine a bale of cloth, the exchange value of a pipe of wine in England will not depend upon what the production of the wine may have cost in Spain, but upon what the production of the cloth has cost in England. Though the wine may have cost in Spain the equivalent of only ten days' labour, yet, if the cloth costs in England twenty days' labour, the wine, when brought to England, will exchange for the produce of twenty days' English labour, *plus* the cost of carriage; including the usual profit on the importer's capital, during the time it is locked up, and withheld from other employment.

The value, then, in any country, of a foreign commodity, depends on the quantity of home produce which must be given to the foreign country in exchange for it. In other words, the values of foreign commodities depend on the terms of international exchange. What, then, do these depend upon? What is it which, in the case supposed, causes a pipe of wine from Spain to be exchanged with England for exactly that quantity of cloth? We have seen that it is not their cost of production. If the cloth and the wine were both made in Spain, they would exchange at their cost of production in Spain; if they were both made in England, they would exchange at their cost of production in England: but all the cloth being made in England, and all the wine in Spain, they are in circumstances to which we have already determined that the law of cost of production is not applicable. We must accordingly, as we have done before in a similar embarrassment, fall back upon an antecedent law, that of supply and demand: and in this we shall again find the solution of our difficulty.

I have discussed this question in a separate Essay, already once referred to; and a quotation of part of the exposition then given will be the best introduction to my present view of the subject. I must give notice that we are now in the region of the most complicated questions which political economy affords; that the subject is one which cannot possibly be made elementary; and that a more continuous effort of attention than has yet been required will be necessary to follow the series of deductions. The thread, however, which we are about to take in hand, is in itself very simple and manageable; the only difficulty is in following it through the windings and entanglements of complex international transactions.

§ 2. "When the trade is established between the two countries, the two commodities will exchange for each other at the same rate of interchange in both countries—bating the cost of carriage, of which, for the present, it will be more convenient to omit the consideration. Supposing, therefore, for the sake of argument, that the carriage of the commodities from one country to the other could be effected without labour and without cost, no sooner would the trade be opened than the value of the two commodities, estimated in each other, would come to a level in both countries.

"Suppose that 10 yards of broadcloth cost in England as much labour as 15 yards of linen, and in Germany as much as 20." In common with most of my predecessors, I find it advisable, in these intricate investigations, to give distinctness and fixity to the conception by numerical examples. These examples must sometimes, as in the present case, be purely suppositious. I should have preferred real ones; but all that is essential is, that the numbers should be such as admit of being easily followed through the subsequent combinations into which they enter.

This supposition then being made, it would be the interest of England to import linen from Germany, and of Germany to import cloth from England. "When each country produced both commodities for itself, 10 yards of cloth exchanged for 15 yards of linen in England, and for 20 in Germany. They will now exchange for the same number of yards of linen in both. For what number? If for 15 yards, England will be just as she was, and Germany will gain all. If for 20 yards, Germany will be as before, and England will derive the whole of the benefit. If for any number intermediate between 15 and 20, the advantage will be shared between the two countries. If, for example, 10 yards of cloth exchange for 18 of linen, England will gain an advantage of 3 yards on every 15, Germany will save 2 out of every 20. The problem is, what are the causes which determine the proportion in which the cloth of England and the linen of Germany will exchange for each other.

"As exchange value, in this case as in every other, is proverbially fluctuating, it does not matter what we suppose it to be when we begin: we shall soon see whether there be any fixed point above which it oscillates, which it has a tendency always to approach to, and to remain at. Let us suppose, then, that by the effect of what Adam Smith calls the higgling of the market, 10 yards of cloth in both countries exchange for 17 yards of linen.

"The demand for a commodity, that is, the quantity of it which can find a purchaser, varies, as we have before remarked, according to the price. In Germany the price of 10 yards of cloth is now 17 yards of linen, or whatever quantity of money is equivalent in Germany to 17 yards of linen. Now, that being the price, there is some particular number of yards of cloth, which will be in demand, or will find purchasers, at that price. There is some given quantity of cloth, more than which could not be disposed of at that price; less than which, at what price, would not fully satisfy the demand. Let us suppose this quantity to be 1000 times 10 yards.

"Let us now turn our attention to England. There, the price of 17 yards of linen is 10 yards of cloth, or whatever quantity of money is equivalent in England to 10 yards of cloth. There is some particular number of yards of linen which, at that price, will exactly satisfy the demand, and no more. Let us suppose that this number is 1000 times 17 yards.

"As 17 yards of linen are to 10 yards of cloth, so are 1000 times 17 yards to 1000 times 10 yards. At the existing exchange value, the linen which England requires will exactly pay for the quantity of cloth which, on the same terms of interchange, Germany requires. The demand on each side is precisely sufficient to carry off the supply on the other. The conditions required by the principle of demand and supply are fulfilled, and the two commodities will continue to be interchanged, as we supposed them to be, in the ratio of 17 yards of linen for 10 yards of cloth.

"But our suppositions might have been different. Suppose that, at the assumed rate of interchange, England has been disposed to consume no greater quantity of linen than 800 times 17 yards: it is evident that, at the rate supposed, this would not have sufficed to pay for the 1000 times 10 yards of cloth which we have supposed Germany to require at the assumed value. Germany would be able to procure no more than 800 times 10 yards at that price. To procure the remaining 200, which she would have no means of doing but by bidding higher for them, she would offer more than 17 yards of linen in exchange for 10 yards of cloth: let us suppose her to offer 18. At this price, perhaps, England would be inclined to purchase a greater quantity of linen. She would consume, possibly, at that price, 900 times 18 yards. On the other hand, cloth having risen in price, the demand of Germany for it would probably have diminished. If, instead of 1000 times 10 yards, she is now contented with 900 times 10 yards, these will exactly pay for the 900 times 18 yards of linen which England is willing to take at the altered price: the demand on each side will again exactly suffice to take off the corresponding supply; and 10 yards for 18 will be the rate at which, in both countries, cloth will exchange for linen.

"The converse of all this would have happened, if, instead of 800 times 17 yards, we had supposed that England, at the rate of 10 for 17, would have taken 1200 times 17 yards of linen. In this case, it is England whose demand is not fully supplied; it is England who, by bidding for more linen, will alter the rate of interchange to her own disadvantage; and 10 yards of cloth will fall, in both countries, below the value of 17 yards of linen. By this fall of cloth, or, what is the same thing, this rise of linen, the demand of Germany for cloth will increase, and the demand of England for linen will diminish, till the rate of interchange has so adjusted itself that the cloth and the linen will exactly pay for one another; and when once this point is attained, values will remain without further alteration.

"It may be considered, therefore, as established, that when two countries trade together in two commodities, the exchange value of these commodities relatively to each other will adjust itself to the inclinations and circumstances of the consumers on both sides, in such manner that the quantities required by each country, of the articles which it imports from its neighbour, shall be exactly sufficient to pay for one another. As the inclinations and circumstances of consumers cannot be reduced to any rule, so neither can the proportions in which the two commodities will be interchanged. We know that the limits, within which the variation is confined, are the ratio between their costs of production in the one country, and the ratio between their costs of production in the other. Ten yards of cloth cannot exchange for more than 20 yards of linen, nor for less than 15. But they may exchange for any intermediate number. The ratios, therefore, in which the advantage of the trade may be divided between the two nations are various. The circumstances on which the proportionate share of each country more remotely depends, admit only of a very general indication.

"It is even possible to conceive an extreme case, in which the whole of the advantage resulting from the interchange would be reaped by one party, the other country gaining nothing at all. There is no absurdity in the hypothesis that, of some given commodity, a certain quantity is all that is wanted at any price; and that, when that quantity is obtained, no fall in the exchange value would induce other consumers to come forward, or those who are already supplied to take more. Let us suppose that this is the case in Germany with cloth. Before her trade with England commenced, when 10 yards of cloth cost her as much labour as 20 yards of linen, she nevertheless consumed as much cloth as she wanted under any circumstances, and, if she could obtain it at the rate of 10 yards of cloth for 15 of linen, she would not consume more. Let this fixed quantity be 1000 times 10 yards. At the rate, however, of 10 for 20, England would want more linen than would be equivalent to this quantity of cloth. She would, consequently, offer a higher value for linen; or, what is the same thing, she would offer her cloth at a cheaper rate. But, as by no lowering of the value could she prevail on Germany to take a greater quantity of cloth, there would be no limit to the rise of linen or fall of

R

cloth, until the demand of England for linen was reduced by the rise of its value, to the quantity which 1000 times 10 yards of cloth would purchase. It might be, that to produce this diminution of the demand a less fall would not suffice than that which would make 10 yards of cloth exchange for 15 of linen. Germany would then gain the whole of the advantage, and England would be exactly as she was before the trade commenced. It would be for the interest, however, of Germany herself to keep her linen a little below the value at which it could be produced in England, in order to keep herself from being supplanted by the home producer. England, therefore, would always benefit in some degree by the existence of the trade, though it might be a very trifling one."

In this statement, I conceive, is contained the first elementary principle of International Values. I have, as is indispensable in such abstract and hypothetical cases, supposed the circumstances to be much less complex than they really are: in the first place, by suppressing the cost of carriage; next, by supposing that there are only two countries trading together; and lastly, that they trade only in two commodities. To render the exposition of the principle complete it is necessary to restore the various circumstances thus temporarily left out to simplify the argument. Those who are accustomed to any kind of scientific investigation will probably see, without formal proof, that the introduction of these circumstances cannot alter the theory of the subject. Trade among any number of countries, and in any number of commodities, must take place on the same essential principles as trade between two countries and in two commodities. Introducing a greater number of agents precisely similar cannot change the law of their action, no more than putting additional weights into the two scales of a balance alters the law of gravitation. It alters nothing but the numerical results. For more complete satisfaction, however, we will enter into the complex cases with the same particularity with which we have stated the simpler one.

§ 3. First, let us introduce the element of cost of carriage. The chief difference will then be, that the cloth and the linen will no longer exchange for each other at precisely the same rate in both countries. Linen, having to be carried to England, will be dearer there by its cost of carriage; and cloth will be dearer in Germany by the cost of carrying it from England. Linen, estimated in cloth, will be dearer in England than in Germany, by the cost of carriage of both articles: and so will cloth in Germany, estimated in linen. Suppose that the cost of carriage of each is equivalent to one yard of linen; and suppose that, if they could have been carried without cost, the terms of interchange would have been 10 yards of cloth for 17 of linen. It may seem at first that each country will pay its own cost of carriage; that is, the carriage of the article it imports; that in Germany 10 yards of cloth will exchange for 18 of linen, namely, the original 17, and 1 to cover the cost of carriage of the cloth; while in England, 10 yards of cloth will only purchase 16 of linen, 1 yard being deducted for the cost of carriage of the linen. This, however, cannot be affirmed with certainty; it will only be true, if the linen which the English consumers would take at the price of 10 for 16, exactly pays for the cloth which the German consumers would take at 10 for 18. The values, whatever they are, must establish this equilibrium. No absolute rule, therefore, can be laid down for the division of the cost, no more than for the division of the advantage: and it does not follow that in whatever ratio the one is divided, the other will be divided in the same. It is impossible to say, if the cost of carriage could be annihilated, whether the producing or the importing country would be most benefited. This would depend on the play of international demand.

Cost of carriage has one effect more. But for it, every commodity would (if trade be supposed free) be either regularly imported or regularly exported. A country would make nothing for itself which it did not also make for other countries. But in consequence of cost of carriage there are many things, especially bulky articles, which every, or almost every, country produces within itself. After exporting the things in which it can employ itself most advantageously, and importing those in which it is under the greatest disadvantage, there are many lying between, of which the relative cost of production in that and in other countries differs so little, that the cost of carriage would absorb more than the whole saving in cost of production which would be obtained by importing one and exporting another. This is the case with numerous commodities of common consumption; including the coarser qualities of many articles of food and manufacture, of which the finer kinds are the subject of extensive international traffic.

§ 4. Let us now introduce a greater number of commodities than the two we have hitherto supposed. Let cloth and linen, however, be still the articles of which the comparative cost of production in England and in Germany differs the most; so that, if they were confined to two commodities, these would be the two which it would be most their interest to exchange. We will now again omit cost of carriage, which, having been shown not to affect the essentials of the question, does but embarrass unnecessarily the statement of it. Let us suppose, then, that the demand of England for linen is either so much greater than that of Germany for cloth, or so much more extensible by cheapness, that if England had no commodity but cloth which Germany would take, the demand of England would force up the terms of interchange to 10 yards of cloth for only 16 of linen, so that England would gain only the difference between 15 and 16, Germany the difference between 16 and 20. But let us now suppose that England has also another commodity, say iron, which is in demand in Germany, and that the quantity of iron which is of equal value in England with 10 yards of cloth, (let us call this quantity a hundredweight) will, if produced in Germany, cost as much labour as 18 yards of linen, so that if offered by England for 17 it will undersell the German producer. In these circumstances, linen will not be forced up to the rate of 16 yards for 10 of cloth, but will stop, suppose at 17; for although, at that rate of interchange, Germany will not take enough cloth to pay for all the linen required by England, she will take iron for the remainder, and it is the same thing to England whether she gives a hundredweight of iron or 10 yards of cloth, both being made at the same cost. If we now superadd coals or cottons on the side of England, and wine, or corn, or timber, on the side of Germany, it will make no difference in the principle. The exports of each country must exactly pay for the imports; meaning now the aggregate exports and imports, not those of particular commodities taken singly. The produce of fifty days' English labour, whether in cloth, coals, iron, or any other exports, will exchange for the produce of forty, or fifty, or sixty days' German labour, in linen, wine, corn, or timber, according to the international demand. There is some proportion at which the demand of the two countries for each other's products will exactly correspond: so that the things supplied by England to Germany will be completely paid for, and no more, by those supplied by Germany to England. This accordingly will be the ratio in which the produce of English and the produce of German labour will exchange for one another.

If, therefore, it be asked what country draws to itself the greatest share of the advantage of any trade it carries on, the answer is, the country for whose productions there is in other countries the greatest demand, and a demand the most susceptible of increase from additional cheapness. In so far as the productions of any country possess this property, the country obtains all foreign commodities at less cost. It gets its imports cheaper, the greater the intensity of the demand in foreign countries for its exports. It also gets its imports cheaper, the less the extent and intensity of its own demand for them. The market is cheapest to those whose demand is small. A country which desires few foreign productions, and only a limited quantity of them, while its own commodities are in great request in foreign countries, will obtain its limited imports at extremely small cost, that is, in exchange for the produce of a very small quantity of its labour and capital.

Lastly, having introduced more than the original two commodities into the hypothesis, let us also introduce more than the original two countries. After the demand of England for the linen of Germany has raised the rate of interchange to 10 yards of cloth for 16 of linen, suppose a trade opened between England and some other country which also exports linen. And let us suppose that, if England had no trade but with the third country, the play of international demand would enable her to obtain from it, for 10 yards of cloth or its equivalent, 17 yards of linen. She evidently would not go on buying linen from Germany at the former rate: Germany would be undersold, and must consent to give 17 yards, like the other country. In this case, the circumstances of production and of demand in the third country are supposed to be in themselves more advantageous to England than the circumstances of Germany; but this supposition is not necessary: we might suppose that if the trade with Germany did not exist, England would be obliged to give to the other country the same advantageous terms which she gives to Germany; 10 yards of cloth for 16, or even less than 16, of linen. Even so, the opening of the third country makes a great difference in favour of England. There is now a double market for English export, while the demand of England for linen is only what it was before. This necessarily obtains for England more advantageous terms of interchange. The two countries, requiring much more of her produce than was required by either alone, must, in order to obtain it, force an increased demand for their exports, by offering them at a lower value.

It deserves notice, that this effect in favour of England from the opening of another market for her exports, will equally be produced even though the country from which the demand comes should have nothing to sell which England is willing to take. Suppose that the third country, though requiring cloth or iron from England, produces no linen, nor any other article which is in demand there. She however produces exportable articles, or she would have no means of paying for imports: her exports, though not suitable to the English consumer, can find a market somewhere. As we are only supposing three countries, we must assume her to find this market in Germany, and to pay for what she imports from England by orders on her German customers. Germany, therefore, besides having to pay for her own imports, now owes a debt to England on account of the third country, and the means for both purposes must be derived from her exportable produce. She must therefore tender that produce to England on terms sufficiently favourable to force a demand equivalent to this double debt. Everything will take place precisely as if the third country had bought German produce with her own goods, and offered that produce to England in exchange for hers. There is an increased demand for English goods, for which German goods have to furnish the payment; and this can only be done by forcing an increased demand for them in England, that is, by lowering their value. Thus an increase of demand for a country's exports in any foreign country enables her to obtain more cheaply even those imports which she procures from other quarters. And conversely, an increase of her own demand for any foreign commodity compels her, *cæteris paribus*, to pay dearer for all foreign commodities.

The law which we have now illustrated, may be appropriately named, the Equation of International Demand. It may be concisely stated as follows. The produce of a country exchanges for the produce of other countries, at such values as are required in order that the whole of her exports may exactly pay for the whole of her imports. This law of International Values is but an extension of the more general law of Value, which we called the Equation of Supply and Demand. We have seen that the value of a commodity always so adjusts itself as to bring the demand to the exact level of the supply. But all trade, either between nations or individuals, is an interchange of commodities, in which the things that they respectively have to sell constitute also their means of purchase: the supply brought by the one constitutes his demand for what is brought by the other. So that supply and demand are but another expression for reciprocal demand: and to say that value will adjust itself so as to equalize demand with supply, is in fact to say that it will adjust itself so as to equalize the demand on one side with the demand on the other.

§ 5. To trace the consequences of this law of International Values through their wide ramifications, would occupy more space than can be here devoted to such a purpose. But there is one of its applications which I will notice, as being in itself not unimportant as bearing on the question which will occupy us in the next chapter, and especially as conducing to the more full and clear understanding of the law itself.

We have seen that the value at which a country purchases a foreign commodity does not conform to the cost of production in the country from which the commodity comes. Suppose now a change in that cost of production; an improvement, for example, in the process of manufacture. Will the benefit of the improvement be fully participated in by other countries? Will the commodity be sold as much cheaper to foreigners, as it is produced cheaper at home? This question, and the considerations which must be entered into in order to resolve it, are well adapted to try the worth of the theory.

Let us first suppose, that the improvement is of a nature to create a new branch of export: to make foreigners resort to the country for a commodity which they had previously produced at home. On this supposition, the foreign demand for the productions of the country is increased; which necessarily alters the international values to its advantage, and to the disadvantage of foreign countries, who, therefore, though they participate in the benefit of the new product, must purchase that benefit by paying for all the other productions of the country at a dearer rate than before. How much dearer, will depend on the degree necessary for re-establishing, under these new conditions, the Equation of International Demand. These consequences follow in a very obvious manner from the law of international values, and I shall not occupy space in illustrating them, but shall pass to the more frequent case, of an improvement which does not create a new article of export, but lowers the cost of production of something which the country already exported.

It being advantageous, in discussions of this complicated nature, to employ definite numerical amounts, we shall return to our original example. Ten yards of cloth, if produced in Germany, would require the same amount of labour and capital as twenty yards of linen; but by the play of international demand, they can be obtained from England for seventeen. Suppose now, that by a mechanical improvement made in Germany, and not capable of being transferred to England, the same quantity of labour and capital which produced twenty yards of linen, is enabled to produce thirty. Linen falls one-third in value in the German market, as compared with other commodities produced in Germany. Will it also fall one-third as compared with English cloth, thus giving to England, in common with Germany, the full benefit of the improvement? Or (ought we not rather to say), since the cost to England of obtaining linen was not regulated by the cost to Germany of producing it, and since England, accordingly, did not get the entire benefit even of the twenty yards which Germany could have given for ten yards of cloth, but only obtained seventeen— why should she now obtain more, merely because this theoretical limit is removed ten degrees further off?

It is evident that, in the outset, the improvement will lower the value of linen in Germany, in relation to all other commodities in the German market, including, among the rest, even the imported commodity, cloth. If 10 yards of cloth previously exchanged for 17 yards of linen, they will now exchange for half as much more, or 25½ yards. But whether they will continue to do so will depend on the effect which this increased cheapness of linen produces on the international demand. The demand for linen in England could scarcely fail to be increased. But it might be increased either in proportion to the cheapness, or in a greater proportion than the cheapness, or in a less proportion.

If the demand was increased in the same proportion with the cheapness, England would take as many times $25\frac{1}{2}$ yards of linen, as the number of times 17 yards which she took previously. She would expend in linen exactly as much of cloth, or of the equivalents of cloth, as much in short of the collective income of her people, as she did before. Germany, on her part, would probably require, at that rate of interchange, the same quantity of cloth as before, because it would in reality cost her exactly as much; $25\frac{1}{2}$ yards of linen being now of the same value in her market as 17 yards were before. In this case, therefore, 10 yards of cloth for $25\frac{1}{2}$ of linen is the rate of interchange which under these new conditions would restore the equation of international demand; and England would obtain linen one-third cheaper than before, being the same advantage as was obtained by Germany.

It might happen, however, that this great cheapening of linen would increase the demand for it in England in a greater ratio than the increase of cheapness; and that, if she before wanted 1000 times 17 yards, she would now require more than 1000 times $25\frac{1}{2}$ yards to satisfy her demand. If so, the equation of international demand cannot establish itself at that rate of interchange; to pay for the linen England must offer cloth on more advantageous terms; say, for example, 10 yards for 21 of linen; so that England will not have the full benefit of the improvement in the production of linen, while Germany, in addition to that benefit, will also pay less for cloth. But again, it is possible that England might not desire to increase her consumption of linen in even so great a proportion as that of the increased cheapness; she might not desire so great a quantity as 1000 times $25\frac{1}{2}$ yards: and in that case Germany must force a demand by offering more than $25\frac{1}{2}$ yards of linen for 10 of cloth; linen will be cheapened in England in a still greater degree than in Germany; while Germany will obtain cloth on more unfavourable terms; and at a higher exchange value than before.

After what has already been said, it is not necessary to particularize the manner in which these results might be modified by introducing into the hypothesis other countries and other commodities. There is a further circumstance by which they may also be modified. In the case supposed the consumers of Germany have had a part of their incomes set at liberty by the increased cheapness of linen, which they may indeed expend in increasing their consumption of that article, but which they may likewise expend in other articles, and among others, in cloth or other imported commodities. This would be an additional element in the international demand, and would modify more or less the terms of interchange.

Of the three possible varieties in the influence of cheapness on demand, which is the more probable—that the demand would be increased more than the cheapness, as much as the cheapness, or less than the cheapness? This depends on the nature of the particular commodity, and on the tastes of purchasers. When the commodity is one in general request, and the fall of its price brings it within reach of a much larger class of incomes than before, the demand is often increased in a greater ratio than the fall of price, and a larger sum of money is on the whole expended in the article. Such was the case with coffee, when its price was lowered by successive reductions of taxation; and such would probably be the case with sugar, wine, and a large class of commodities which, though not necessaries, are largely consumed, and in which many consumers indulge when the articles are cheap and economize when they are dear. But it more frequently happens that when a commodity falls in price, less money is spent in it than before: a greater quantity is consumed, but not so great a value. The consumer who saves money by the cheapness of the article, will be likely to expend part of the saving in increasing his consumption of other things: and unless the low price attracts a large class of new purchasers who were either not customers of the article at all, or only in small quantity and occasionally, a less aggregate sum will be expended on it. Speaking generally, therefore, the third of our three cases is the most probable: and an improvement in an exportable article is likely to be as beneficial (if not more beneficial) to foreign countries, as to the country where the article is produced.

§ 6. Thus far had the theory of international values been carried in the first and second editions of this work.[1] But intelligent criticisms (chiefly those of my friend Mr. William Thornton,) and subsequent further investigation, have shown that the doctrine stated in the preceding pages, though correct as far as it goes, is not yet the complete theory of the subject matter.

It has been shown that the exports and imports between the two countries (or, if we suppose more than two, between each country and the world) must in the aggregate pay for each other, and must therefore be exchanged for one another at such values as will be compatible with the equation of international demand. That this, however, does not furnish the complete law of the phenomenon, appears from the following consideration: that several different rates of international value may all equally fulfil the conditions of this law.

The supposition was, that England could produce 10 yards of cloth with the same labour as 15 of linen, and Germany with the same labour as 20 of linen; that a trade was opened between the two countries; that England thenceforth confined her production to cloth, and Germany to linen; and, that if 10 yards of cloth should thenceforth exchange for 17 of linen, England and Germany would exactly supply each other's demand: that, for instance, if England wanted at that price 17,000 yards of linen, Germany would want exactly the 10,000 yards of cloth, which, at that price, England would be required to give for the linen. Under these suppositions it appeared, that 10 cloth

---

[1] [§§ 6–8 were inserted in the 3rd ed. (1852).]

for 17 linen would be, in point of fact, the international values.

But it is quite possible that some other rate, such as 10 cloth for 18 linen, might also fulfil the conditions of the equation of international demand. Suppose that, at this last rate, England would want more linen than at the rate of 10 for 17, but not in the ratio of the cheapness; that she would not want the 18,000 which she could now buy with 10,000 yards of cloth, but would be content with 17,500, for which she would pay (at the new rate of 10 for 18) 9722 yards of cloth. Germany, again, having to pay dearer for cloth than when it could be bought at 10 for 17, would probably reduce her consumption to an amount below 10,000 yards, perhaps to the very same number, 9722. Under these conditions the Equation of International Demand would still exist. Thus, the rate of 10 for 17, and that of 10 for 18, would equally satisfy the Equation of Demand: and many other rates of interchange might satisfy it in like manner. It is conceivable that the conditions might be equally satisfied by every numerical rate which could be supposed. There is still therefore a portion of indeterminateness in the rate at which the international values would adjust themselves; showing that the whole of the influencing circumstances cannot yet have been taken into account.

§ 7. It will be found that, to supply this deficiency, we must take into consideration not only, as we have already done, the quantities demanded in each country of the imported commodities; but also the extent of the means of supplying that demand which are set at liberty in each country by the change in the direction of its industry.

To illustrate this point it will be necessary to choose more convenient numbers than those which we have hitherto employed. Let it be supposed that in England 100 yards of cloth, previously to the trade, exchanged for 100 of linen, but that in Germany 100 of cloth exchanged for 200 of linen. When the trade was opened, England would supply cloth to Germany,

Germany linen to England, at an exchange value which would depend partly on the element already discussed, viz. the comparative degree in which, in the two countries, increased cheapness operates in increasing the demand; and partly on some other element not yet taken into account. In order to isolate this unknown element, it will be necessary to make some definite and invariable supposition in regard to the known element. Let us therefore assume, that the influence of cheapness on demand conforms to some simple law, common to both countries and to both commodities. As the simplest and most convenient, let us suppose that in both countries any given increase of cheapness produces an exactly proportional increase of consumption; or, in other words, that the value expended in the commodity, the cost incurred for the sake of obtaining it, is always the same, whether that cost affords a greater or a smaller quantity of the commodity.

Let us now suppose that England, previously to the trade, required a million of yards of linen, which were worth, at the English cost of production, a million yards of cloth. By turning all the labour and capital with which that linen was produced to the production of cloth, she would produce for exportation a million yards of cloth. Suppose that this is the exact quantity which Germany is accustomed to consume. England can dispose of all this cloth in Germany at the German price; she must consent indeed to take a little less until she has driven the German producer from the market, but as soon as this is effected, she can sell her million of cloth for two millions of linen; being the quantity that the German clothiers are enabled to make by transferring their whole labour and capital from cloth to linen. Thus England would gain the whole benefit of the trade, and Germany nothing. This would be perfectly consistent with the equation of international demand: since England (according to the hypothesis in the preceding paragraph) now requires two millions of linen (being able to get them at the same cost at which she previously obtained only one), while, the prices in Germany not being altered, Germany requires as before exactly a million of cloth, and can obtain it by employing the labour and capital set at liberty from the production of cloth, in producing the two millions of linen required by England.

Thus far we have supposed that the additional cloth which England could make, by transferring to cloth the whole of the capital previously employed in making linen, was exactly sufficient to supply the whole of Germany's existing demand. But suppose next that it is more than sufficient. Suppose that while England could make with her liberated capital a million yards of cloth for exportation, the cloth which Germany had heretofore required was 800,000 yards only, equivalent at the German cost of production to 1,600,000 yards of linen. England therefore could not dispose of a whole million of cloth in Germany at the German prices. Yet she wants, whether cheap or dear (by our supposition), as much linen as can be bought for a million of cloth: and since this can only be obtained from Germany, or by the more expensive process of production at home, the holders of the million of cloth will be forced by each other's competition to offer it to Germany on any terms (short of the English cost of production) which will induce Germany to take the whole. What these terms would be, the supposition we have made enables us exactly to define. The 800,000 yards of cloth which Germany consumed, cost her the equivalent of 1,600,000 linen, and that invariable cost is what she is willing to expend in cloth, whether the quantity it obtains for her be more or less. England therefore, to induce Germany to take a million of cloth, must offer it for 1,600,000 of linen. The international values will thus be 100 cloth for 160 linen, intermediate between the ratio of the costs of production in England, and that of the costs of production in Germany: and the two countries will divide the benefit of the trade, England gaining in the aggregate 600,000 yards of linen, and Germany being richer by 200,000 additional yards of cloth.

Let us now stretch the last supposition still farther, and suppose that the cloth previously consumed by Germany, was

not only less than the million yards which England is enabled
to furnish by discontinuing her production of linen, but less in
the full proportion of England's advantage in the production,
that is, that Germany only required half a million. In this case,
by ceasing altogether to produce cloth, Germany can add a
million, but a million only, to her production of linen; and this
million, being the equivalent of what the half million previously cost her, is all that she can be induced by any degree
of cheapness to expend in cloth. England will be forced by her
own competition to give a whole million of cloth for this million
of linen, just as she was forced in the preceding case to give it
for 1,600,000. But England could have produced at the same
cost a million yards of linen for herself. England therefore
derives, in this case, no advantage from the international trade.
Germany gains the whole; obtaining a million of cloth instead
of half a million, at what the half million previously cost her.
Germany, in short, is in this third case, exactly in the same
situation as England was in the first case; which may easily be
verified by reversing the figures.

As the general result of the three cases, it may be laid down
as a theorem, that under the supposition we have made of a
demand exactly in proportion to the cheapness, the law of
international values will be as follows:—

The whole of the cloth which England can make with the
capital previously devoted to linen, will exchange for the whole
of the linen which Germany can make with the capital previously devoted to cloth.

Or, still more generally,

The whole of the commodities which the two countries can
respectively make for exportation, with the labour and capital
thrown out of employment by importation, will exchange
against one another.

This law, and the three different possibilities arising from it
in respect to the division of the advantage, may be conveniently
generalized by means of algebraical symbols, as follows:—

Let the quantity of cloth which England can make with the

labour and capital withdrawn from the production of linen, be $= n$.

Let the cloth previously required by Germany (at the German cost of production) be $= m$.

Then n of cloth will always exchange for exactly $2m$ of linen.

Consequently if $n = m$, the whole advantage will be on the side of England.

If $n = 2m$, the whole advantage will be on the side of Germany.

If n be greater than m, but less than $2m$, the two countries will share the advantage; England getting $2m$ of linen where she before got only n; Germany getting n of cloth where she before got only m.

It is almost superfluous to observe that the figure 2 stands where it does only because it is the figure which expresses the advantage of Germany over England in linen as estimated in cloth, and (what is the same thing) of England over Germany in cloth as estimated in linen. If we had supposed that in Germany, before the trade, 100 of cloth exchanged for 1000 instead of 200 of linen, then n (after the trade commenced) would have exchanged for $10m$ instead of $2m$. If instead of 1000 or 200 we had supposed only 150, n would have exchanged for only $\frac{3}{2}m$. If (in fine) the cost value of cloth (as estimated in linen) in Germany exceeds the cost value similarly estimated in England, in the ratio of p to q, then will n, after the opening

of the trade, exchange for $\frac{p}{q}m$.[1]

---

[1] It may be asked, why we have supposed the number n to have as its extreme limits, m and $2m$ (or $\frac{p}{q}m$)? why may not n be less than m, or greater than $2m$; and if so, what will be the result?

This we shall now examine; and, when we do so, it will appear that n is always, practically speaking, confined within these limits.

Suppose, for example, that n is less than m; or, reverting to our former figures, that the million yards of cloth, which England can make, will not satisfy the whole of Germany's pre-existing demand; that demand being (let us suppose) for 1,200,000 yards. It would then, at first sight, appear that England would supply Germany with cloth up to the extent of a

s

§ 8. We have now arrived at what seems a law of International Values of great simplicity and generality. But we have done so by setting out from a purely arbitrary hypothesis respecting the relation between demand and cheapness. We have assumed their relation to be fixed, though it is essentially variable. We have supposed that every increase of cheapness produces an exactly proportional extension of demand; in other words, that the same invariable value is laid out in a commodity whether it be cheap or dear; and the law which we have investigated holds good only on this hypothesis, or some other practically equivalent to it. Let us now, therefore, combine the two variable elements of the question, the variations of each of which we have considered separately. Let us suppose the relation between demand and cheapness to vary, and to become such as would prevent the rule of interchange laid down in the last theorem from satisfying the conditions of

million; that Germany would continue to supply herself with the remaining 200,000 by home production: that this portion of the supply would regulate the price of the whole; that England therefore would be able permanently to sell her million of cloth at the German cost of production (viz. for two millions of linen) and would gain the whole advantage of the trade, Germany being no better off than before.

That such, however, would not be the practical result, will soon be evident. The residuary demand of Germany for 200,000 yards of cloth furnishes a resource to England for purposes of foreign trade of which it is still her interest to avail herself; and though she has no more labour and capital which she can withdraw from linen for the production of this extra quantity of cloth, there must be some other commodities in which Germany has a relative advantage over her (though perhaps not so great as in linen): these she will now import, instead of producing, and the labour and capital formerly employed in producing them will be transferred to cloth, until the required amount is made up. If this transfer just makes up the 200,000, and no more, this augmented n will now be equal to m; England will sell the whole 1,200,000 at the German values: and will still gain the whole advantage of the trade. But if the transfer makes up more than the 200,000, England will have more cloth than 1,200,000 yards to offer; n will become greater than m, and England must part with enough of the advantage to induce Germany to take the surplus. Thus the case, which seemed at first sight to be beyond the limits, is transformed practically into a case either coinciding with one of the limits or between them. And so with every other case which can be supposed.

the Equation of International Demand. Let it be supposed, for instance, that the demand of England for linen is exactly proportional to the cheapness, but that of Germany for cloth, not proportional. To revert to the second of our three cases, the case in which England by discontinuing the production of linen could produce for exportation a million yards of cloth, and Germany by ceasing to produce cloth could produce an additional 1,600,000 yards of linen. If the one of these quantities exactly exchanged for the other, the demand of England would on our present supposition be exactly satisfied, for she requires all the linen which can be got for a million yards of cloth: but Germany perhaps, though she required 800,000 cloth at a cost equivalent to 1,600,000 linen, yet when she can get a million of cloth at the same cost, may not require the whole million; or may require more than a million. First, let her not require so much; but only as much as she can now buy for 1,500,000 linen. England will still offer a million for these 1,500,000; but even this may not induce Germany to take so much as a million; and if England continues to expend exactly the same aggregate cost on linen whatever be the price, she will have to submit to take for her million of cloth any quantity of linen (not less than a million) which may be requisite to induce Germany to take a million of cloth. Suppose this to be 1,400,000 yards. England has now reaped from the trade a gain not of 600,000 but only of 400,000 yards; while Germany, besides having obtained an extra 200,000 yards of cloth, has obtained it with only seven-eighths of the labour and capital which she previously expended in supplying herself with cloth, and may expend the remainder in increasing her own consumption of linen, or of any other commodity.

Suppose on the contrary that Germany, at the rate of a million cloth for 1,600,000 linen, requires more than a million yards of cloth. England having only a million which she can give without trenching upon the quantity she previously reserved for herself, Germany must bid for the extra cloth at a higher rate than 160 for 100, until she reaches a rate (say 170 for 100) which will either bring down her own demand for cloth to the limit of a million, or else tempt England to part with some of the cloth she previously consumed at home.

Let us next suppose that the proportionality of demand to cheapness, instead of holding good in one country but not in the other, does not hold good in either country, and that the deviation is of the same kind in both; that, for instance, neither of the two increases its demand in a degree equivalent to the increase of cheapness. On this supposition, at the rate of one million cloth for 1,600,000 linen, England will not want so much as 1,600,000 linen, nor Germany so much as a million cloth: and if they fall short of that amount in exactly the same degree: if England only wants linen to the amount of nine-tenths of 1,600,000 (1,440,000), and Germany only nine hundred thousand of cloth, the interchange will continue to take place at the same rate. And so if England wants a tenth more than 1,600,000, and Germany a tenth more than a million. This coincidence (which, it is to be observed, supposes demand to extend cheapness in a corresponding, but not in an equal degree[1]) evidently could not exist unless by mere accident: and, in any other case, the equation of international demand would require a different adjustment of international values.

The only general law, then, which can be laid down, is this. The values at which a country exchanges its produce with foreign countries depend on two things: first, on the amount and extensibility of their demand for its commodities, compared with its demand for theirs; and secondly, on the capital which it has to spare from the production of domestic commodities for its own consumption. The more the foreign demand for its commodities exceeds its demand for foreign commodities, and the less capital it can spare to produce for foreign markets,

---

[1] The increase of demand from 800,000 to 900,000, and that from a million to 1,440,000, are neither equal in themselves, nor bear an equal proportion to the increase of cheapness. Germany's demand for cloth has increased one-eighth, while the cheapness is increased one-fourth. England's demand for linen is increased 44 per cent, while the cheapness is increased 60 per cent.

compared with what foreigners spare to produce for its markets, the more favourable to it will be the terms of interchange: that is, the more it will obtain of foreign commodities in return for a given quantity of its own.

But these two influencing circumstances are in reality reducible to one: for the capital which a country has to spare from the production of domestic commodities for its own use is in proportion to its own demand for foreign commodities: whatever proportion of its collective income it expends in purchases from abroad, that same proportion of its capital is left without a home market for its productions. The new element, therefore, which for the sake of scientific correctness we have introduced into the theory of international values, does not seem to make any very material difference in the practical result. It still appears, that the countries which carry on their foreign trade on the most advantageous terms, are those whose commodities are most in demand by foreign countries, and which have themselves the least demand for foreign commodities. From which, among other consequences, it follows, that the richest countries, *cæteris paribus*, gain the least by a given amount of foreign commerce: since, having a greater demand for commodities generally, they are likely to have a greater demand for foreign commodities, and thus modify the terms of interchange to their own disadvantage. Their aggregate gains by foreign trade, doubtless, are generally greater than those of poorer countries, since they carry on a greater amount of such trade, and gain the benefit of cheapness on a larger consumption: but their gain is less on each individual article consumed.

§ 9. We now pass to another essential part of the theory of the subject. There are two senses in which a country obtains commodities cheaper by foreign trade; in the sense of Value, and in the sense of Cost. It gets them cheaper in the first sense, by their falling in value relatively to other things: the same quantity of them exchanging, in the country, for a smaller quantity than before of the other produce of the country. To revert to our original figures; in England, all consumers of linen obtained, after the trade was opened, 17 or some greater number of yards for the same quantity of all other things for which they before obtained only 15. The degree of cheapness, in this sense of the term, depends on the laws of International Demand, so copiously illustrated in the preceding sections. But in the other sense, that of Cost, a country gets a commodity cheaper when it obtains a greater quantity of the commodity with the same expenditure of labour and capital. In this sense of the term, cheapness in a great measure depends upon a cause of a different nature: a country gets its imports cheaper, in proportion to the general productiveness of its domestic industry; to the general efficiency of its labour. The labour of one country may be, as a whole, much more efficient than that of another; all or most of the commodities capable of being produced in both, may be produced in one at less absolute cost than in the other; which, as we have seen, will not necessarily prevent the two countries from exchanging commodities. The things which the more favoured country will import from others, are of course those in which it is least superior; but by importing them it acquires, even in those commodities, the same advantage which it possesses in the articles it gives in exchange for them. Thus the countries which obtain their own productions at least cost, also get their imports at least cost.

This will be made still more obvious if we suppose two competing countries. England sends cloth to Germany, and gives 10 yards of it for 17 yards of linen, or for something else which in Germany is the equivalent of those 17 yards. Another country, as for example France, does the same. The one giving 10 yards of cloth for a certain quantity of German commodities, so must the other: if, therefore, in England, these 10 yards are produced by only half as much labour as that by which they are produced in France, the linen or other commodities of Germany will cost to England only half the amount of labour which they will cost to France. England would thus obtain her imports at less cost than France, in the ratio of the greater efficiency of her labour in the production of cloth: which might be taken, in the case supposed, as an approximate estimate of the efficiency of her labour generally; since France, as well as England, by selecting cloth as her article of export, would have shown that with her also it was the commodity in which labour was relatively the most efficient. It follows, therefore, that every country gets its imports at less cost, in proportion to the general efficiency of its labour.

This proposition was first clearly seen and expounded by Mr. Senior,[1] but only as applicable to the importation of the precious metals. I think it important to point out that the proposition holds equally true of all other imported commodities; and further, that it is only a portion of the truth. For, in the case supposed, the cost to England of the linen which she pays for with ten yards of cloth, does not depend solely upon the cost to herself of ten yards of cloth, but partly also upon how many yards of linen she obtains in exchange for them. What her imports cost to her is a function of two variables; the quantity of her own commodities which she gives for them, and the cost of those commodities. Of these, the last alone depends on the efficiency of her labour: the first depends on the law of international values; that is, on the intensity and extensibility of the foreign demand for her commodities, compared with her demand for foreign commodities.

In the case just now supposed, of a competition between England and France, the state of international values affected both competitors alike, since they were supposed to trade with the same country, and to export and import the same commodities. The difference, therefore, in what their imports cost them, depended solely on the other cause, the unequal efficiency of their labour. They gave the same quantities; the difference could only be in the cost of production. But if England traded to Germany with cloth, and France with iron, the comparative demand in Germany for those two commodities would bear a share in determining the comparative cost, in labour and capital,

[1] *Three Lectures on the Cost of Obtaining Money.*

with which England and France would obtain German products. If iron were more in demand in Germany than cloth, France would recover, through that channel, part of her disadvantage; if less, her disadvantage would be increased. The efficiency, therefore, of a country's labour, is not the only thing which determines even the *cost* at which that country obtains imported commodities—while it has no share whatever in determining either their exchange *value*, or, as we shall presently see, their *price*.

Index